GW00569954

WOKING LIBRARY
GLOUCESTER WALK   11/08
WOKING   www.surreycc.gov.uk/librari
GU21 1EP

2d10'

SURREY
COUNTY COUNCIL

Overdue items may incur charge
as published in the curre
Schedule of Charges.

Volkswagen
Beetle

© Jonathan Harvey 2008

All rights reserved. No part of this publication may be reproduced, stored in
a retrieval system or transmitted, in any form or by any means, electronic,
mechanical, photocopying, recording or otherwise, without prior permission in
writing from the publisher.

First published in 2008

A catalogue record for this book is available.

ISBN 978 1 84425 434 7

Library of Congress catalog card no. 2008926356

Haynes North America Inc.,
861 Lawrence Drive, Newbury Park, California 91320, USA

Published by Haynes Publishing, Sparkford, Yeovil, Somerset BA22 7JJ, UK,
Tel: 01963 442030 Fax: 01963 440001
Int. tel: +44 1963 442030
Int. fax: +44 1963 440001
E-mail: sales@haynes.co.uk
Website: www.haynes.co.uk

Printed and bound in Britain by J. H. Haynes & Co. Ltd,
Sparkford, Yeovil, Somerset BA22 7JJ

ACKNOWLEDGEMENTS

Various enthusiasts deserve my unending thanks for the help they have given
me in bringing this project to a successful conclusion.

Owners of Beetles went out of their way not only to allow me to
photograph their vehicles, but also to accede to my demands for the Beetle in
question to be turned at various intervals after first travelling to an appropriate
location.

A special word of thanks must go to a nucleus of members of the Historic
Volkswagen Club, the Volkswagen Owners Club of Great Britain, and the
Mexican and Brazilian Beetle Register. Likewise, to the organisers of some
of the traditionally Beetle orientated shows who allowed me to disrupt their
proceedings, or on occasion afforded special entry to an event, a big thank you.

I am indebted to Richard Hulin of Richard Hulin Motor Engineers,
Gloucester, for his invaluable help, particularly pertaining to matters technical
and of a non-standard nature.

Last but by no means least, thanks to the family for their patience and
understanding while both words and photography took precedence over things
that they would have liked me to be involved with.

Jonathan Harvey, August 2008

Haynes Enthusiast Guide

Volkswagen
Beetle

SURREY LIBRARIES	
Askews	17-Nov-2008
629.2222 MOT	£19.99

Jonathan Harvey

VOLKSWAGEN BEETLE
CONTENTS

INTRODUCTION
THE LEGENDARY BEETLE

With origins dating back to the period before the Second World War, and with serious production numbers gathering momentum as long ago as the 1950s, not that many will vividly recall the days before the Beetle was a part of everyday life. While German manufacture ceased in early 1978, it is only a few years ago that the last bastion of Beetle production, namely the Puebla plant in Mexico, finally decided to call it a day. The result is that the world's most produced single model of any kind, with in excess of 21½ million examples to its name, will be with us for many years to come. After all, even a less than complimentary journalist reporting in *Autocar* in September 1978, felt duty bound to note that 'the awkward looking things refuse to wear out'.

Although perhaps no longer on the pinnacle of popularity it once occupied, the love-it-or-loathe-it Beetle remains a collectible item of automobile history. The aim here is to start by relating the full story of its history; from its unsavoury Nazi-associated origins; through its rescue from obscurity by people from the country renowned for its grasp on small car production; its unprecedented and never-to-be-equalled rise from domestic rags to worldwide riches by the singular determination of Heinz Nordhoff, its guardian Director General of 20-years standing; its survival against the odds as a German-built entity for a further ten years after his death; its long production run in Brazilian and Mexican exile; and finally, perhaps most interesting of all, its demise after a continuous production run of 58 years.

Next, there follows descriptive analysis of all the distinctive ages of the Beetle, from so-called 'Split' – the original and unmistakably Teutonic incarnation of the car – to the somehow softer and altogether more welcoming 'Oval'. From that high point, it's the turn of the revolutionarily big-windowed Beetles of the late 1950s and much of the 1960s, defined by a continued reliance on aesthetically attractive sloping headlamps and domed hubcaps, but benefiting from an updated dashboard throughout, an upgraded engine from the summer of 1960, and the universal adoption of modern flashing indicators at the same time. Next come the vertical headlamp cars, with their chunky box-section bumpers, including the often decried 1302 and 1303 models featuring un-Beetle-like humped bonnets and, in the latter instance, heretical curved windscreens. The final German-built Beetles saw a return to the basic shape, and this pattern followed through the years when Mexican-built cars were imported for sale in various European countries. Post 1985, Brazil and, more importantly, the once carefully restrained Mexico plants were on their own, and slowly but surely a new Beetle evolved; a car desperately trying to incorporate the advances in comfort, and to a lesser extent in engine technology, into a by now cramped design of six decades ago. Last, but by no means least, space is allocated to the top of the range, hand-finished, Karmann-built cabriolet and other soft-top derivatives.

The remainder of the book puts theory into practice, with a comprehensive buyer's guide covering all the above models, where to look on each and, more particularly, what to look for, including the pitfalls to avoid that many years of ownership have instilled. A summary workshop manual for the armchair mechanic links well with the previous chapter, while thoughts on tuning the car, and the intricacies of the custom scene – both as it was in the Beetle's heyday and as it is now – ensure that no aspect of Beetling is overlooked.

Unquestionably, the Beetle is a motoring phenomenon, a vehicle recognised by all, but not universally known. The contention is that this book ties the full story together in a way not attempted previously: from 1935 to 2003; from stock to custom; from standard specification 25bhp and fuel-injected 1600 to much meatier beasts; and, of course, from pristine low-mileage early Cabriolets (worth many thousands of pounds) to the late-model basket case gasping its last en route to scrapyard or restoration.

← Of all Beetles, the models produced between March 1953 and July 1957 (the cars with a small oval rear window) are amongst the most sought-after today. Less Teutonic in appearance than the earlier cars, the build quality and aesthetic balance represents a zenith in Beetle production.

CHAPTER I
A BEETLE HISTORY LESSON

There is no apology to be made for the disparity in length of this chapter compared to the remaining ones. The Beetle's story is a fascinating one; logically – on so many occasions in its first 10 years as a design, prototype, and victim of war – it should not have survived. Then, if it hadn't been for one man's determination to build on its success for 20 years, without any thought of deviating from it as the cornerstone of Volkswagen's model range, the Beetle's story would have been of minor interest in the bigger picture of its numerous, and undoubtedly worthy, successors. Finally, once the decision had been taken to replace it with another type and style of car, against the odds it survived and remained in production for a further 30-plus years. This is a unique tale, worthy of considerable elaboration.

A dark beginning

Although the subject still remains sensitive to Volkswagen more than 70 years after the events began to unfurl, the inescapable truth is that the origins of the Beetle as we know it are inextricably entangled with the rise to supreme power of Adolf Hitler and his Nazi henchmen.

For Hitler, motor cars always held a fascination; so much so that in his party's early days of comparative obscurity, and consequent relative impoverishment, he squandered most of their hard sought funds on a large, and inevitably expensive, 60bhp Mercedes limousine. The year was 1923, and by November, as a consequence of his attempt to seize position and power in the now infamous abortive beer hall putsch, Hitler was incarcerated in Landsberg fortress. Although the five-year sentence ended with him serving little more than nine months, it was here that Hitler penned his notorious book, *Mein Kampf*, and where he made specific reference to 'breaking the motoring privileges of the upper classes'.

Ten years later, Hitler's thunderous rise had led to his appointment as Germany's Chancellor, and the opportunity for him to bring to fruition his party's long-planned strategy. In terms of motoring policy, Hitler was painfully aware that Germany had only a little over half-a-million cars on its roads, compared to more than double that number in both Britain and France. He was also, undoubtedly, informed that ordinary Britons benefited from such vehicles as the diminutive and relatively cheap Austin 7, as did Italy's populace with the equally pocket-sized Fiat Topolino. All that was available in Germany in this class were what Heinz Nordhoff would later describe as 'ersatz' vehicles, or 'cars of reduced size with double the faults'. Although so-called economy cars from mainstream manufacturers were nearing production, none could realistically be purchased by the average German worker, whose income of fewer than 2,000 Marks per year ensured that even a motorbike was barely affordable.

Hitler's determination to push Germany forward was exhibited at the 1933 Berlin Motor Show, one of his first engagements as Chancellor. Dressed in a dark suit, he spoke of adventurous plans for: a programme of Autobahn building; the toning down, or even the abolition of punitive car taxes; of drastic cuts in the repressive and stringent laws surrounding motorists; and of the simplification of the process whereby a person could achieve the goal of obtaining a licence. Above all, Hitler demanded that the German automobile industry build him a small car for the people. Frankly, most in the audience thought Hitler's speech little more than propaganda for forthcoming elections, but in such a supposition they were wrong. Whatever his motives – defined variously as: a means of bribing working class Germans to bestow upon him their unending allegiance by meeting their demands for an affordable automobile; the creation of a modern, effective, and strategic road system suited to any future military aspirations; or simply indulging his personal passion

← **The engine room of Beetle world domination – the famous headquarters building at Wolfsburg and Nordhoff's workplace from its construction in 1959 – with cars produced at the time of the master's supremacy.**

for the greater good of Germany – Hitler forged ahead, as recalcitrant manufacturers, battered and bruised by the after-effects of the severe depression of 1929, would find to their cost.

Ferdinand Porsche was one for whom Hitler's words must have had special interest, for he had already been involved in several abortive attempts to produce a people's car. Later in 1933, and almost as additional tinder to fire the designer, Porsche was summoned to a private meeting with Hitler at the Hotel Kaiserhof. The one topic on the agenda was a people's car, Hitler making it clear that he was not interested in cycle-cars or three-wheelers. His preference was for a four-wheel-drive, front-mounted, air-cooled, diesel-engined vehicle, to be sold at a figure totalling fewer than 1,000 Reichmarks. Shocked by the practicalities of producing anything at such a low price-point, Porsche was nevertheless keen to take up the challenge, and by January 1934 was ready to publish what has become known as his Exposé – or Memorandum, to give the document a more meaningful title.

The passing of just 12 months demonstrated just how much Germany had changed. Opening the 1934 Berlin Motor Show, Hitler, now suitably regaled with the military trappings of the burgeoning dictator, fired a duly impressive warning shot across the bows of all those in the motor trade who had thoughts of continuing in the way they had become accustomed to. 'Germany has only one automobile for every 100 inhabitants', he bemoaned. 'France has one for each 28, and the United States one for each six. That disparity must be changed. I would like to see a German car mass-produced so it can be bought by anyone who can afford a motorcycle. Simple, reliable, economical transportation is needed. We must have a real car for the German people – a volkswagen!'

Not intended to be a eulogy to Hitler's role in the birth of the Beetle, his efforts can be summarised as those of a playground bully; the individual who would use his power to break all opposition to Porsche's plans. Four years to the day after he made his first accommodating speech at the Berlin Motor Show he was back once more. This time the menace in his message was abundantly clear. 'It is my irrevocable decision to make the German motor-car industry one of our greatest industries, independent of the insecurity of international imports, and place it on a solid and sure basis. Let there be no doubt: so-called private business is either capable of solving

this problem or it is not capable of continuing as private business. The National Socialist State will under no circumstances capitulate before either the convenience, the limitations, or the ill-will of individual Germans.' As if to further reinforce this message, when presented with Opel's own version of a people's car, the P-4, Hitler stormed away from the stand, refused to countenance a reduction in the car's price to bring it closer to the amount the volkswagen might sell for, and ensured that henceforth it would be difficult for the manufacturer to obtain the necessary materials to build the car in the first place.

Ferdinand Porsche and his Volksauto

Ferdinand Porsche was born in Maffersdorf, Austria, on 3 September 1875. The son of a tinsmith, his working life started at the age of 15 as an apprentice in his father's business. Three years later he moved to Vienna, where he took a post with Bela Egger, the owner of the United Electrical Company. Once based in the city he was able to attend Vienna Technical University on a part-time basis, and within four years he had been promoted to the position of head of the experimental department.

Porsche's next move was to join Ludwig Lohner as chief designer in the automobile department, producing the Lohner Porsche Chaise – an electrically-powered automobile – capable of travelling 50 miles without recharging. This vehicle was exhibited at the Paris Exposition of 1900 to great acclaim, establishing Porsche once and for all as an innovative designer. Five years later, just as Lohner was quibbling about spending yet more money on even more advanced designs, Porsche was approached by Austro-Daimler with the most tempting of offers.

In 1906, Porsche took over as technical director and a board member of Austria's largest motor manufacturer. Over the years he worked on a varied itinerary of projects, ranging from sports cars to aero-engines. It was while he was at Austro-Daimler that Porsche first thought of a small car for the people – his volksauto. Meeting considerable resistance from his fellow directors, nevertheless Porsche persevered until the day came when his activities relating to sports cars was cut to a minimum following the death of the works driver at the Italian Grand Prix. The volatile Porsche stormed out, only to appear shortly afterwards in April 1923 as the technical director at Daimler-Motoren AG in Germany.

Although his successes were plentiful, Porsche still hankered after building a small car, but once more was thwarted, thanks to a combination of recession and the reluctance of management to take such a step. Eventually, feeling sidelined, he resigned and returned to Austria, where he took up an appointment as technical director and chief designer at the Steyr works. His main achievement here was to modify one large car design and introduce another, the Austria, a five-seater luxury car, which proved a great success at the 1929 Paris Auto Show. Sadly, at this point Steyr's finances collapsed and the company transferred into the hands of the self-same financiers who controlled Austro-Daimler. To Porsche's disgust, small car projects were abandoned at the insistence of the financiers, who argued that Austro-Daimler already did the job more than adequately. 18-months after he joined Steyr, Porsche left, a disillusioned man.

Already 55 years old in 1931, the only logical course open to Porsche was to establish his own design office; a move which, unbeknown to all at the time, hastened the appearance of the Beetle. After developing a radically new form of suspension, the torsion bar, as part of a project for the Wanderer

Auto Company, he set about work on his long-thwarted aim of building a small car for the masses, but not a scaled-down version of what already existed. Labelling his intention as Project 12, what emerged looked less like a conventional automobile and more like an insect, or Beetle. Planned to incorporate four-wheel independent suspension, and to be sufficiently light in weight for a low-horsepower engine to be sufficient, the backbone of the car was a tunnel along the front-to-rear centreline.

Fritz Neumeyer of the Zündapp Works, having already expressed more than a passing interest in developing a small car to supplement his motorcycle activities, heard of Porsche's project and his lack of available funding to develop it further. The Zündapp Volksauto was duly born, with only one fundamental change to Porsche's initial ideas. Neumeyer insisted Porsche developed a water-cooled, five-cylinder, radial engine, instead of the noisy air cooled unit already planned and used to power his motorcycles. Disaster followed disaster as the prototype aluminium over a wooden frame bodied cars were put to test. Engines boiled, torsion bars shattered, and when he realised just how costly the stamping presses required to make the final shaped steel body parts would be, Neumeyer decided to call a halt and paid Porsche off accordingly.

Later in 1931 Porsche was approached by Fritz von Falkenhayn, head of the NSU motorwerks.

← The V3 series of just three cars which date from 1936/37. Their primary role was to participate in long-journey tests. V3/2, the car depicted, had a part wooden body and is shown in Porsche's garden.

whereby NSU had agreed to cease car production both then, and in the future, at the point Fiat in reality bought the operation.

The Beetle's Birth Certificate

Bereft once more of a tangible project that would produce his longed-for people's car, Porsche concentrated on presenting his Hitler-inspired proposal, or memorandum, to the Transport Ministry, where it duly arrived on 17 January 1934.

Porsche's document was an undoubted blueprint for the future Beetle. 'The volkswagen', he understood, 'should not be a small car that perpetuates the tradition of previous products in this range by merely and precisely copying their pattern of reduced dimensions, power, weight, and more. While such a vehicle as this might be cheap in terms of purchase price, from the point of view of a healthy national economy it would be of little value due to its reduced passenger comforts and lifespan....' Porsche's definition of a volksauto was, as a result, one of a 'complete and entirely practical car that can compete on equal terms with any other similarly functional vehicle'. Consequently, 'a fundamental change of thinking' was necessary to convert any car so far in use to a volksauto. Porsche then proceeded to summarise his definition of a people's car.

↑ **Pictured at the Bad Camberg gathering of Volkswagen enthusiasts in 2007, this replica represents the V3 prototype dating from 1936 to 1937, and is normally resident in the Autostadt museum at Wolfsburg.**

He, too, wanted a small car, and by 1933 Porsche had tweaked his original Project 12 designs to offer something even closer to the form the Beetle would take a few years later. Amongst this vehicle's key attributes was a 1.5-litre air-cooled flat-four engine capable of 72mph, and the body was shapelier than that of the Zündapp project car. Sadly, Porsche was to be thwarted once more when von Falkenhayn received a letter from the managing director of Fiat, reminding him of an agreement signed in 1930,

→ **A second picture of the car above demonstrates how the prototypes suffered from the lack of a rear window, although there was a flat glass panel between the engine and passenger area, and the driver could just about see between the air-cooling vents.**

1. A volkswagen should not be a small car whose dimensions are reduced at the expense of both handling and life expectancy, while it remains relatively heavy. Instead, it should be a functional car of standard dimensions but comparatively low weight, an objective that can be achieved by fundamentally new processes.
2. A volkswagen should not be a small car with limited power at the expense of maximum speed and good climbing ability, but rather a practical vehicle with the necessary power to achieve normal maximum speeds and climbing capabilities.
3. A volkswagen should not be a small car with reduced passenger space at the expense of comfort, but instead it should be a fully functional vehicle with normal, or rather comfortable, space within the bodywork.
4. A volkswagen should not be a vehicle with limited uses, but instead should be capable of fulfilling all conceivable purposes by simply exchanging the bodywork, for use not only as a passenger car but also as a commercial vehicle and for certain military purposes.
5. A volkswagen should not be fitted with unnecessarily complicated equipment requiring increased servicing, but should rather be a vehicle with as far as possible simple and foolproof equipment, reducing servicing to an absolute minimum.

Porsche concluded as a result that the following attributes and specifications would be required to create the perfect people's car: the best possible suspension and handling; a maximum speed of around 100kph; a climbing ability of around 30 per cent; a closed four-seater body for the passengers; and the lowest possible purchase price coupled to the most economical running costs. The design would therefore demand a track of 1,200mm, a wheelbase of 2,500mm, an engine offering 26PS achieved at a maximum speed of 3,500rpm, a kerb weight of 650kg, an average fuel consumption of 8-litres/100km, and a full swing axle. The result would be a volkswagen with a selling price of 1,550 Reichmarks.

Progression to production

Shortly after presenting his Exposé, Porsche was informed that the RDA, the Reich Association of the German Automobile Industry, or the car manufacturers' trade association, would be working with him to produce the people's car. Their brief from Hitler was 'to further the motorisation of the German people on the basis of co-operative action and by enlisting the best talents of German car manufacture'. The subsequent contract duly issued on 22 June 1934 contained two clauses of concern

← The W30 series, dating from 1936 to 1938, more or less followed the V3 cars and were produced under sufferance by Daimler Benz. As their collective title implies, 30 such vehicles were built, and the total cost was 140,918.05 Reichmarks. Note the knuckle-scraping bonnet and the near vertical headlamp pods.

A W30 replica prototype on loan from Wolfsburg, pictured at the Bad Camberg meeting of enthusiasts in 2007.

to Porsche. The first, relating to rushed timescales, had little bearing on the Beetle we know today; the second, committing Porsche to a selling price of just 990 Reichmarks, had much more significance, for this influenced the way in which the successful design known the world over emerged, both in terms of the weight of the chassis and body, and in the type and style of engine developed. The Nazi government recognised that by 1934 the average German worker's savings had fallen below the 1,000-

Reichmark point and as such a selling price below this point had a distinct advantage. Nor did Hitler or his aides deem this to be an unrealistic goal for Porsche. Opel's new car for the people, the P-4, had a selling price of 1,450 Reichmarks, but this included a 20 to 25 per cent dealer commission, making the vehicle including margin for the manufacturer worth only a little more than what was requested of Porsche, particularly as the volkswagen would be supplied direct to purchasers.

→ Like the V3, the W30 lacked a proper rear window, while the rear side-windows were smaller than those of the V3 because of the decision to increase the door size.

Through an extensive catalogue of prototypes from the V1, V2, and V3, to the W30, V303, and finally the VW38 and VW39, the always distinctive shape of the Beetle progressively developed. Initially the cars lacked a rear window, had 'suicide' doors, and featured a very small opening boot lid disguised to look larger by a similarly contoured adjoining fixed metal section, to which the vehicle's headlights were attached. Most notably, and as a result of the enforced enlistment of 120 SS troops, the W30 cars were tested way beyond the norm for any private manufacturer, amassing an astonishing total of 2.4 million kilometres between them, while of all the prototypes, be they single cars or a series of vehicles, the earliest to include all the features recognised today, epitomised by the split-pane rear window, was the VW38.

The combined consequence of price pressure on the one hand, and such extensive testing on the other, was a radically different vehicle way in front of potential competitors and distinctly ahead of its time. The car offered unparalleled efficiency, durability, and serviceability. The RDA, however, soon took the collective point of view that the Beetle was both extremely ugly and unacceptably unconventional. The truth of the matter was that, for reasons of personal interest, RDA members didn't want the project to succeed. Initially, some members had thought that to pay lip-service was all that was necessary with a project that would prove little more than a whimsical propaganda move by Hitler's Nazi regime. Speaking many years later, Heinz Nordhoff, who had represented Opel at many of the meetings, put a further spin on the situation. 'It soon became apparent that the jealousy between the automobile companies was far too deep-rooted to make a concerted effort possible.... How and where such a car would be manufactured, after a satisfactory design had been achieved, remained completely open, and there might have been a hidden hope that the whole very unwelcome plan would go on the rocks when this decision had to be faced.'

The combination, at a relatively early stage, of progress slower than the Nazi regime deemed appropriate, and the RDA's controversial proposal that all German car manufacturers should be invited to design a volkswagen to sit alongside Hitler's preferred option, led relatively rapidly to a decision that would assist considerably in the Beetle's chances of survival after the war when its

mentors both civilian and military had been swept away forever. The RDA as an organisation was swiftly relieved of its responsibilities and ordered to hand over all the relevant paperwork to the Transport Ministry. Working swiftly, in 1937 the Volkswagen Development Company (Gesellschaft zur Vorbereitung des Volkswagens) was formed. Owned by the Nazi party, and with Porsche, ex-car salesman and Hitler's confidante Jakob Werlin, plus Bodo Lafferentz, aide to the chief of the German Labour Front, Robert Ley, as its board of management, the company had 480,000 Reichmarks allocated to it initially with the specific purpose of facilitating a considerable acceleration in the Beetle's development.

Lafferentz was the individual charged with the task of finding an appropriate site on which to build a factory solely for the purpose of manufacturing Beetles. Suitability came in the form of proximity to both transportation facilities and raw materials. A 20-square mile site, part of the estate surrounding Schloss Wolfsburg, was deemed ideal, and despite opposition from the family owning it, Hitler laid the foundation stone in May 1938 at the centre of a well-orchestrated propaganda rally. The RDA's self-centred, uncooperative manner had thus led directly to the building of a factory that would result in each surviving post-war member's long-term harm. Without a dedicated, purpose-built factory at its beck and call, it is unlikely that the Beetle would have survived the Nazi era.

↑ **This archive photograph depicts a column of VW38 prototypes, the first incarnation of the Volkswagen that was instantly recognisable as the Beetle. These cars were driven over thousands of miles, stopping off at cities, towns, and villages in a well coordinated propaganda exercise.**

↑ As early as 1938, plans were emerging to develop versions of the Beetle for military usage. The most produced and best known was the Kübelwagen, a rugged, reliable off-road vehicle with exceptional ground clearance. Extremely simple in its construction, its lightweight nature made it an ideal machine in the sands of the North African desert. Officially designated the Type 82, the Kübel was only produced as a two-wheel drive vehicle.

↓ The Schwimmwagen, or Type 166, was undoubtedly the most versatile of German vehicles built during the war. Shorter than the Kübel by some 400mm, it was powered by the same engine, but benefited from four-wheel drive and, uniquely, a propeller driven from the end of the crankshaft, allowing rivers and lakes to be crossed with ease.

Production plans and savings schemes

Projected production plans of the Nazi era serve to indicate why the factory, known today as Wolfsburg, was to be the largest car assembly plant under one roof. Robert Ley, a significant lackey in the Nazi regime, reported to an astounded world that it was the Führer's will that within a few years no fewer than six million volkswagens must have been made available for travel in Germany. Warming to the theme, Ley predicted that within ten years time there would be 'no working person in Germany who does not own a Volkswagen'. To meet such an obvious demand it was predicted that monthly production would rise quickly from a modest 400 units per month at the end of 1938 to an astonishing, but inevitable, 10,000 in just one year. Necessary to meet Hitler's demands, considering the prediction was made at a time when not a sod of earth had been turned, let alone a full factory built, these forecasts were later revised, but still by the beginning of 1940 a target of 6,000 cars monthly was set. For the future, production was set to rise to 450,000 cars per year by 1944.

With such ambitions, Hitler felt justified in boasting that his factory, which would emulate the showpiece

Ford plant at River Rouge, but of course be bigger than it, would sport a 1,350-metre (1,476 yard, or three-quarter mile) front. The factory's near self-sufficiency and essential technical equipment would place it in a European-wide category of its own. The plan was that 10,000 workers on a first shift, supplemented by a second of an additional 7,500, would build 500,000 cars per year. A further development stage allowed for a workforce of some 30,000, and a consequent increase in production to a number between 800,000 and one million Beetles per year.

The foundation stone was duly laid amidst a swirling mass of Nazi pomp and propaganda in May 1938, and progress towards the now duly named KdF (Kraft durch Freude or Strength through Joy) factory's completion was rapid, albeit that Italian labourers rather than German ones completed the work.

Irrelevant to the post-war story of the Beetle's survival, but nevertheless an interesting concept on the road to creating extra KdF sales, was the infamous Saving Scheme. Within a package of rules whereby default in payments, or simple changes of mind, resulted in the harshest of penalties, workers purchased stamps at a rate of a minimum of 5 Reichmarks per week, saving to a point where they were eligible for a car, but might have to wait for a further five years to receive one. 336,688 savers joined the scheme, but, as is well known, not a single one received a Beetle. Events overtook both the savers and the Beetle. Hitler both aggressively declared war and by the spring of 1945 had lost it. Beetle production was restricted to little more than a handful of cars, all reserved for high-ranking party officials or similar dignitaries. Wartime production turned to the likes of the little Jeep-like Kübelwagen, its amphibious brother the Schwimmwagen, and an assortment of Beetle-bodied saloons with high ground clearance, such as the interestingly named Kommandeurwagen.

Into the care of the British

Although the Nazi-owned KdF factory was liberated by American troops on 11 April 1945, as it fell into the British zone of occupation, the former KdFWagen's far from certain future soon lay in the hands of the British military government.

The situation across defeated Germany was complex, and nowhere more so than at the

↑ The Type 82E was an interesting variation on the military theme as it utilised a straightforward Beetle body mounted on the higher running gear of the Kübel. Note the central exhaust pipe, seen on a number of early vehicles. This example, dating from 1943 (despite its registration), would have been one of the first to benefit from a 1131cc engine developing 25PS.

↓ The KdF-Wagen (Strength-through-Joy car) of the Nazi era. Details such as hubcaps and exhaust pipes varied from model to model. Whatever, to see a KdF-Wagen now is a rare treat. Few were built and not many have survived.

Volkswagenwerk. Under Law 52 (a decree that might best be summarised as the blocking and control of German property, and circulated during 1945 by the Supreme Headquarters Allied Forces Europe for implementation by the military government in Germany) all Nazi-associated 'offices, departments, agencies, and organisations forming part of, or attached to, or controlled by it' were to be preserved, maintained, and safeguarded, at least on an interim basis. The home of Hitler's car for the people inevitably fell into this category, and as such demolition was ruled out. If a military ancestry could have been proved, the factory would have been destroyed. Nevertheless, under the Level of Industry Plan for Germany (a scheme devised to ensure that Germany's post-war production capacity was moderate) the factory was still deemed surplus to requirements on the grounds that Beetle production hadn't started before the beginning of hostilities. As a result, it was eligible for entry on the reparation's list; thus making it open to seizure as a whole, or in lots, to any of the Allied countries.

A need for transport

The British military government officially took over the trusteeship of the factory in June 1945. In August of the same year a Senior Resident Officer, Major Ivan Hirst, was duly appointed. That for the rest of

→ **Major Ivan Hirst, a Yorkshireman, arrived at the war-torn factory with no specific orders other than to take control. It was his belief in the Volkswagen, and his ingenuity in the face of adversity that ensured the Beetle's survival to the point when it was possible to appoint a German General Director.**

his life Hirst always told the story of his arrival at the factory and its associated township, which had been renamed Wolfsburg in late May by the town council, with no specific orders other than to take control, is perhaps not surprising.

A quick survey revealed that well over two-thirds of the factory had been badly damaged by Allied bombs, but miraculously the power station had survived intact. Equally fortuitous to the Beetle's future had been the wartime decision to remove the unused car assembly line for the purpose of making more room available for aircraft industry related work, and in the process inadvertently safeguarding it from bomb damage. During May 1945, under the ad hoc managership of Rudolf Brörmann, the most senior remaining official of the old Nazi era regime, and using a scratch workforce, a precedent was set when 110 Kübelwagens were assembled from parts found around the site for American usage.

The need for transport was equally important if not more so to the British, while the inherited responsibility to the local population of providing work, housing, and the wherewithal to obtain food virtually predetermined the decision to restart production at Wolfsburg. First thoughts inevitably centred upon the versatile Kübelwagen, but the issue was not straightforward. In 1938, Ferdinand Porsche had visited the Budd Corporation in the United States, where he had acquired a licence to make the all-steel body of the KdFWagen using their techniques. In return for this privilege, he had agreed that should he produce a variation on the saloon body (assumed at the time most likely to be a cabriolet version of the people's car). Ambi-Budd of Berlin, a wholly-owned subsidiary, would build the bodies. The result of this agreement was that Kübelwagen bodies were despatched from Berlin to the KdF-factory. Increasingly regular bombing raids on the German capital took its toll on Ambi-Budd, and by the end of the war only a few Kübelwagen dies remained. More difficulties were to come, for under the division of both Germany as a whole and Berlin particularly, the factory fell within the Soviet sector, and the desire to cooperate with requests from British-controlled Wolfsburg inevitably evaporated.

Colonel Michael McEvoy, a knowledgeable automotive engineer and entrepreneur before the war, was based at the headquarters of the British Army of the Rhine and was the officer to whom Royal Electrical and Mechanical Engineers officers based at Wolfsburg reported. His knowledge of the Beetle in its pre-war KdFWagen guise was better than that of many. A visitor to the 1939 Berlin Motor Show, he'd had the good fortune to test-drive Hitler's car, and now he saw the opportunity arise to resurrect the vehicle. Fully supported by Ivan Hirst, who, as well as having read about the KdFWagen in a pre-war issue of *The Autocar*, had also had the chance to examine a captured Kübelwagen in Normandy. Suitably impressed by the vehicle's light alloy engine and its all-round independent suspension, Hirst joined with McEvoy in advocating the cause of the saloon.

Fortunately, fate played its hand once more. Hirst found a three-year-old Beetle abandoned in the factory. After organising its refurbishment – a process that included a new coat of British khaki green – Hirst directed that the car should be driven to the headquarters of the British Army of the Rhine where its qualities as a more than adequate form of much-needed transport could be powerfully advocated and demonstrated by McEvoy. Fully aware that other manufacturers, and in this instance most notably Ford, who theoretically were the designated automobile producer for the British zone, were in no position to supply vehicles, orders were duly placed for far more Beetles than realistically the factory could hope to produce. One often-quoted figure is for 20,000 cars, although by August 1946 reference was made to a firm contract on the part of the British Army of the Rhine for 40,000 Beetles.

Early day production

Recalling his earliest days at Wolfsburg for the American author Terry Shuler, Hirst wrote that 'the big presses were found to be repairable. New body assembly jigs and welding equipment had to be made. VW had to start its own production of carburettors, fuel pumps, clutches, and dampers; all items normally outsourced. It was also necessary to open a foundry for the crankcases and transmission housings. The outside supplier had been suddenly shut down, since it had mainly supplied the aircraft industry which was being eliminated.'

Writing in *The Journal of the Royal Electrical and Mechanical Engineers* in April 1962, the former Major addressed more of the issues, once again in serious style. 'In view of the strict rationing of steel, suppliers were reclaiming rejected forgings by welding and then obliterating the weld by re-striking them under the drop stamp. Another difficulty was uneven ductility of sheets, due to lack of instruments for the annealing furnaces at the mills.… Sheets large enough for the VW roof panel were not available, and therefore a butt-welder had to be designed and built at the works, to make one large sheet out of the two.'

On a more trivial note, some of Hirst's recollections undoubtedly amused the audiences of enthusiasts he was frequently asked to address throughout the years until his death in March 2000. Take as an example his story relating to the lack of a suitable adhesive to fasten cloth to the Beetle's door panels, the somewhat dubious substitution of fish glue and the consequent prevailing odours when a Beetle so doctored was driven in the rain. In similar vein, the use of nothing more substantial than cardboard to insulate the battery terminals from a pressed steel cover proved a recipe for damage to ladies' stockings if they sat on the Beetle's rear seat. As the acid fumes from the battery ate away the cardboard, the spring used to hold the cover in place could easily become hot, acting like an electric fire; a danger to nylons and a direct consequence of the battery's positive terminal coming into contact with the cover.

Hirst's ingenuity, although stretched to its limit in the instance of the vehicle's carburettor referred to above, serves to demonstrate why, against the odds the ad hoc nature of British management of the factory proved fruitful. Made by Pierburg in Berlin, under licence from Solex, inevitably carburettor supplies failed to meet demand. Hirst, whose family business was as clock and watchmakers, stripped a carburettor down, dividing the constituent parts into those that could be manufactured within the factory complex, and those that couldn't. He enlisted the services of a camera business, Voigtländer, in nearby Brunswick, a firm used to precision working, to make the smaller, more intricate parts such as the float and jets in brass.

Nevertheless, the advantages afforded the factory as a British-administered business cannot be underestimated. The military government were able to supply the necessary credit for production to resume in the first instance, and, despite the problems related in the preceding paragraphs, the factory enjoyed precedence in the supply of what materials were available over all other candidates.

The Beetle – a vehicle of dubious merit

↓ Dating from 1946, this is one of the 10,020 examples built during that year. It is probably the oldest Beetle in regular use on British roads. Although far from pristine, this unrestored example demonstrates many of the characteristics of an early post-war Beetle. These included nipple-style hubcaps, banana-shaped overriders, the horn set behind and above the front bumper, and a lack of chrome, bright-trim and VW badges. The paint colour of this car is incorrect, and the bumpers and hubcaps would most likely not have been painted black at this time. Also, later doors have been fitted, as quarter-lights were not introduced until October 1952.

Fortunate also to the Beetle's success story were the now easily recognisable misjudgements about its potential. The Society of Motor Manufacturers and Traders in Britain, albeit testing a Kübelwagen, typified the response to its attributes. 'We do not consider that the design represents any special brilliance, apart from certain of the detail points, and it is suggested that it is not to be regarded as an example of first-class design to be copied by British Industry.' As for the saloon specifically, the engine was deemed to be 'somewhat noisy and rough', and AC Cars reported that, 'As a civilian vehicle, considerable modification would be required to conform to the expected standard', and specifically that, 'No attempt has been made to reduce engine noise. In fact the design is such that the whole bodywork is acting as a diaphragm and amplifies the normal engine noise.' Ford also noted the generally excessive noise levels, and condemned the Beetle for both its high fuel consumption and indifferent performance. Most damning of all was the report produced by the commission headed by Lord Rootes. 'The vehicle does not meet the fundamental technical requirements of a motorcar. As regards performance and design it is quite unattractive to the average motorcar buyer. It is too

ugly and noisy.' The report concluded that, 'To build such a car commercially would be a completely uneconomic exercise'.

Production story

Against this verbal battering, Hirst and his team continued to work hard, gradually setting in place further aids to the Beetle's survival. In March 1946, the workforce celebrated the first occasion when they had been able to build 1,000 cars in a month, a feat they would replicate more or less throughout the year. Their modest success ensured that by September 1946 a four-year reserve was placed upon Wolfsburg, the importance of which can be appreciated when it is realised that this meant the factory could not be dismantled during this period.

Although fewer cars were produced in 1947 than had been the case in 1946 (8,987 compared with 10,020) – mainly because of an overdue sheet metal delivery, an acute coal shortage, and a sharp cold spell in the first two months of the year – two extremely important decisions were made and the attendant policies carried out. In October 1946 the British military government had approved the establishment of a sales organisation in its sector of Germany. Initially comprising two distributors and 28 dealerships, Hirst developed a service workshop as a result, providing both service manuals and repair bulletins. Additionally, a damage file was set up, affording the technical department a recognised and organised way of dealing with problems. This move, and its rigid enforcement, put Volkswagen ahead of its potential rivals.

The second decision occurred more or less out of necessity. The British Government had realised that its taxpayers were carrying the heavy costs of food imports to the British Zone, and to make matters worse payment was in US dollars. Further, still reeling from the financial costs of the war with Hitler, British currency reserves were seriously depleted. The decision was made that German industry generally, and Wolfsburg particularly, must export some of its goods to earn foreign currency, a move that would pay for essential imports. The Beetle was duly launched at the Hanover Trade Fair as a vehicle suitable for export and, although the programme was delayed by further shortages in the materials available, the principle had been established. Ben

Pon, a name forever associated with the concept of the VW Transporter, and his brother brought five Beetles into Holland in October 1947, becoming the first authorised importer for the Netherlands in the process. By the end of the year 56 cars had been exported. Hirst and his colleagues recognised two factors; first that the package offered to importers had to be better than the standard models built to date, and second that spares had to be readily available wherever the Beetle was. In the first instance, care was taken to offer a better paint finish, improved upholstery, and a modicum of chrome, while in the second it was not unknown for the export of cars to be delayed until Hirst was satisfied that a sufficient supply of parts was to accompany them.

Planning for the Beetle's future

While it might appear that the British intended to run Volkswagen indefinitely, nothing could have been further from the truth. Although the decision was not Ivan Hirst's to make, his words are sufficient to repudiate such claims. Recalling the early days of the so-called Wolfsburg Motor Works, a term which Hirst did not approve of, the Major noted that, 'some people wanted me to fly a British flag over the plant! I said, "No, it's not war booty. It doesn't belong to the British."' Elaborating, he confirmed that the British 'were trustees who felt that in some form or another VW should remain German. The ethos was that we were there to control and disarm Germany, and to plant the seeds of a new government that would be more stable than Weimar…'

Although now largely overlooked in the Volkswagen story, Herman Munch, a Berlin lawyer with little or no knowledge of the automobile industry, was duly appointed under occupation rules as the legal authority for the property, becoming both Head Trustee and General Director with effect from 1 August 1946. Hirst and his team were the operational masters, Munch's duties lay elsewhere, but it was his inadequacy as a car manufacturer that led to the search for a suitable deputy and the eventual engagement of a man that would take both Volkswagen and its Beetle to unimagined heights, creating in the process the most popular vehicle of all time. With Heinz Nordhoff's appointment in January 1948, not as deputy to Munch, but as a replacement for him, Britain's part in the Beetle story was more or less over.

September 1949 saw the official handover by the British military government of Wolfsburg to the State of Lower Saxony, in whose boundaries it lay. Under Ordinance 202, Lower Saxony was 'responsible for the control of the Volkswagenwerk, but on behalf of and under the direction of the Federal government.…' The question of ownership was left open for many years and proved irrelevant to the Beetle's success.

Heinz Nordhoff – the Beetle's champion 1948-1968

Heinz Nordhoff ruled Volkswagen for a little over 20 years until his death in April 1968 at the age of 69. After initial reservations, for in his own words 'the Volkswagen has more flaws than a dog has fleas', he became the Beetle's greatest advocate, its supreme ambassador, and increasingly, as the years went by, its most powerful defender.

Ten years into what might loosely be termed his reign, and at a time when the Beetle had already become a phenomenon worldwide, Nordhoff, his workforce, and posthumously, Ferdinand Porsche, were awarded the prestigious Elmer A. Sperry award, an honour presented from time-to-time by

↑ **Early Beetles were equipped with a starting handle. Note the mushroom design of the air filter, and the crescent-shaped bumper protectors, which were known by enthusiasts as banana overriders.**

three American engineering societies to individuals or bodies who had made significant contributions in the world of transport. Nordhoff's speech explained why the Volkswagen story had been one of success, and why, too, that success was intrinsically linked with the Beetle's progression. No excuse is proffered for reproducing a substantial section of Nordhoff's words here.

Nordhoff's message to the automobile world

'When I assumed the responsibility of putting this wrecked factory into high-volume production, the car itself was still "full of bugs". It really was what you call an "ugly duckling". As usual, I had the dubious benefit of a great many well-intentioned advisors. Not only should I not foolishly break my own neck on this hopeless undertaking, I should change name, design, everything about the car, in no time. Perhaps I was too busy to listen, and in any case I myself knew exactly what to do.

'There was so much to be done. Weak points in the design had to be ironed out, bottlenecks in production had to be broken, problems of material procurement, quality control, and personnel had to be solved. There was no sales organisation – the party was to have seen to that. And I was determined that, of all things, Volkswagen should have the best service in the world. So I brushed away all temptations to change model and design. In any sound design there are almost unlimited possibilities – and this certainly was a sound one. I see no sense in starting anew every few years with the same teething troubles, making obsolete almost all the past. I went out on a limb. I took the chance of breaking away from the beaten path, and of doing something unusual but highly constructive for transport-hungry Europe, and not Europe alone.

'Offering people an honest value, a product of highest quality, with low original cost and incomparable resale value, appealed to me more than being driven around by a bunch of hysterical stylists trying to sell people something they really do not want to have. And it still does! Improving quality and value steadily, without increasing price; improving wages and living and working conditions, without "passing the buck", in reverse, to the customer; simplifying and intensifying

service and spare parts system; building a product of which I and every other Volkswagen worker can be truly proud, and at the same time earning enough profit, under an economic system of free enterprise, to improve production facilities with the most modern equipment, to no small extent bought in this country, and thus increase production and productivity every year – these things are, in my opinion, an engineer's task. The ownerless and capital-less company has to live on its own. It is not in a position to issue new shares – it simply has to come along by itself, and, believe me, it does.

'I am firmly convinced that there will always be a market in this world, which we are far from covering now, for simple, economical and dependable transportation, and for an honest value in performance and quality. I am convinced that all over the world … there are millions of people who will gladly exchange chromium plated gadgets and excessive power for economy, long life, and inexpensive maintenance.

'So I have decided to stick to the policy that has served us so well. Based on Professor Porsche's original design, the Volkswagen of today looks almost exactly like the prototype model that was produced more than 20 years ago, but every single part of this car has been refined and improved over the years – these will continue to be our "model changes". This policy has required, of course, a great deal in the way of determination and courage, on the part of myself and members of our organisation. But it has led us to success, and there is no greater justification than success, as every engineer will agree.'

The messages contained in the Elmer A. Sperry speech were repeated on many occasions. On the occurrence of the presentation of the five-millionth Beetle to be produced to the International Red Cross, an event which occurred on 5 Dec 1961, Nordhoff perhaps summarised his philosophy more succinctly than on any other occasion. His speech centred around the development of: 'one model to its highest technical excellence'; Volkswagen's dedication 'to the attainment of the highest quality'; the destruction of the 'notion that such high quality can only be attained at high prices'; plus the importance of giving 'the car the highest value' and building it 'so that it retains that value'.

Background to a professional

Born in 1899, Nordhoff graduated as a certified mechanical engineer from the Polytechnic Academy in Berlin in 1925 and went to work for BMW as an aircraft design engineer. In 1929, Nordhoff joined Opel, by then already a subsidiary of the vast General Motors Corporation, and worked in the service organisation, initially as a department head, and later as the technical consultant to the company's sales manager. During the 1930s, Nordhoff made several trips to the United States to study GM's production methods and sales techniques. Elected to the Opel board of management in the latter part of the decade, in early 1939 Nordhoff moved to Berlin to direct the Opel office there. In 1942 he was appointed director-general of the Opel factory in Brandenburg, then the largest lorry factory in Europe.

Against this background Nordhoff joined Volkswagen, the only reason preventing his continued employment at Opel being a minor honour bestowed by the Nazis and a resultant US work veto at the company that lay in their sector of a divided Germany. Nordhoff was the professional to the gifted amateurs that comprised the British custodian team at Wolfsburg. So hard did he work in the early days, that for six-months his bed and his office were in adjacent rooms. 'I am committed with my every fibre,' was his remark. He spoke of Wolfsburg having to stand on its own two feet. 'It will be up to us to build this, the biggest car factory in Germany into a decisive factor in the German peacetime economy.'

Many years later, in an interview for *Jeme* magazine, Nordhoff recalled what faced him on his appointment. To start with there was no cost-accounting system, nobody from Hirst and Munch downwards had an accurate idea of how much it cost to build a Beetle; the reality of the situation was that the price of one car bore very little relation to the next. 'I had to start from scratch in the real sense of the word. 7,000 workers were painfully producing at the rate of a mere 6,000 cars a year, providing it did not rain too much.' Addressing the workforce, Nordhoff sounded a dire warning. 'It still takes us 400 hours to build a car. If we go on like this, we won't be going on much longer. We have to get it down to 100 hours per vehicle.' Despite the murmurs of disbelief, under Nordhoff's guidance that is exactly what happened. The American magazine *Time*, interviewing Nordhoff in the mid-1950s, found that he had advocated 'pressure-vacuum production'.

'The combination of large stocks of material on the inside,' Nordhoff explained, 'and no reserve of cars on the outside … exerts a psychological pressure on workers to produce faster.' *Time* added, 'in six months, production almost tripled to 1,800 cars a month; by mid-1949, Nordhoff had so much faith in his product that he arbitrarily ordered production doubled.'

Export drive

The British-led attempts at export were neither comprehensive nor far-reaching, and Nordhoff foresaw that it was essential to introduce a Deluxe version of the Beetle that would be widely accepted. The addition of a little chrome, improved upholstery, and slightly better paintwork, was not sufficient. As a result, Nordhoff masterminded production of a true Export model. Immediately distinguishable by a wider variety of paint options, the new Beetle also featured a reasonable amount of bright trim; most notable on the vehicle's running boards, waistline, and bonnet, and appropriately crowned by a VW roundel located just below the windscreen. The chromed bumpers were redesigned, appearing, thanks to a central groove, simultaneously more expensive and sturdy, and, inevitably, the hubcaps were now chromed. The utilitarian horn was concealed behind the left front wing. Inside the Export Beetle, basic black trim and fittings were largely replaced by more expensive-looking ivory, a new three-spoke steering wheel was fitted, and the car benefited from a full cloth headlining, improved upholstery, redesigned and easily adjustable front seats, and other additions such as protective rails in the luggage compartment associated with a Deluxe model. Launched in July

↓ **Pictured during the course of the celebrations to mark the production of the millionth Beetle, is Heinz Nordhoff, the architect of Volkswagen's post war success. Appointed to take office in January 1948, he retained the post of Director General until his death in April 1968.**

1949, the Export model proved an immediate success both abroad and at home, and sales of the more basic Beetle, now known as the Standard model, became insignificant by comparison.

Forging ahead

Nordhoff's export policy proved invaluable to Volkswagen, taking them in the shortest period of time to the top echelons of European manufacturers. Yearly production figures for the Beetle demonstrate more clearly than anything else its overwhelming success.

1950	81,979	77% increase on 1949
1951	93,709	14% increase on 1950
1952	114,438	22% increase on 1951
1953	151,323	32% increase on 1952
1954	202,174	34% increase on 1953
1955	279,986	38% increase on 1954
1956	333,190	19% increase on 1955
1957	380,561	14% increase on 1956
1958	451,526	19% increase on 1957
1959	575,407	27% increase on 1958
1960	739,455	29% increase on 1959

The 1960s proved to be more of a decade of consolidation and model range development, but nevertheless, most of the world having succumbed to the Beetle's charms, clever marketing and a growing cult status engendered more sales, culminating in the astonishing figure of in excess of one million cars of one design being built in the 12 months of 1965. A European-wide recession in the latter months of 1966 and throughout most of 1967 explains the significant drop in Beetle production figures in the latter year, while the following year's total confirms that the car had not declined in popularity.

1961	827,850
1962	877,014
1963	838,488
1964	948,370
1965	1,090,863
1966	1,080,165
1967	925,787
1968	1,186,134

Significant landmarks have been recorded frequently, the most often quoted, and rightly so, being the manufacture of the one millionth Beetle after the war, an event that occurred on 5 August 1955.

50,000th	13 May 1949
100,000th	4 March 1950
250,000th	5 October 1951
500,000th	3 July 1953
1,000,000th	5 August 1955
2,000,000th	28 December 1957
3,000,000th	25 August 1959
4,000,000th	9 November 1960
5,000,000th	5 December 1961

During 1962, the millionth Beetle to be exported to the USA was sold.

Achieving production numbers

At the unprecedented festival to celebrate the arrival of the millionth Beetle, a gold-painted, diamante-encrusted affair, Nordhoff's release to the 1,200 assembled journalists amounted to some 20 closely-typed sheets. Export was at the forefront of his mind and key to his success. 'These celebrations have

→ **This well-known picture of Nordhoff dates from the 1960s, at a point when a few were beginning to question his long-accepted policy of product improvement, rather than replacement. In 1965, once more confounding his critics, he witnessed the unparalleled feat of producing one-million Beetles in a single 12-month period.**

provided a glimpse of the world which Volkswagen has conquered and will continue to conquer,' Nordhoff told his audience. In 1948, Volkswagen's sales network had consisted of 40 distributors in Germany and one abroad. By 1955 the numbers were hardly recognisable as emanating from the same organisation, for the distributors in Germany alone amounted to 1,000, while abroad an incredible 2,800 had been recruited. Nordhoff was proud to note that 55 per cent of the year's production was allocated to export, with 35,000 Beetles destined for the USA, 28,000 to Sweden, 18,000 to Belgium, 14,000 to Holland, and 10,000 to Austria. Even then, Nordhoff planned for more, much more, reminding his workforce, and even his competitors, that 'we are far from sitting on top of the world'.

To support the notion of growth, Nordhoff was continually looking to expand. Classic amongst such ambitions was the decision to remove Transporter production from Wolfsburg to a new factory at Hanover, an event planned in 1955 and finalised a year later, not because Wolfsburg was overstretched at that point, but rather in anticipation of the day that such a thing would become the case. Additionally, Nordhoff was conscious that his Wolfsburg workforce would be difficult to increase, while at Hanover there was a new labour-pool to tap into. Wolfsburg itself was enlarged, the small Brunswick

factory grew, and in 1957 Volkswagen purchased a former aircraft engine plant at Altenbauna, near Kassel, this time for the production of reconditioned engine and transaxle units. Rebuilt and operational during 1958, this further plant could expect to work on 150,000 such units per year, while again drawing on a virgin workforce, thus avoiding labour problems for Wolfsburg.

While an early quest had been to sell sufficient cars overseas to escalate cash availability to buy more machinery, in the latter years of the 1950s the task became one of meeting demand. Such was the backlog, the marketing department were charged with the task of devising a slogan to counteract the feelings of disappointment and frustration prevalent amongst potential purchasers. The slogan 'Es lohnt sich, auf einen Volkswagen zu warten', loosely translated as 'A Volkswagen is worth waiting for', went some way to stem any ripples of dissatisfaction. However, speaking in Switzerland in March 1960, Nordhoff himself referred to the worrying disparity between the demand for cars and Volkswagen's ability to produce them. He told his audience that two years ago he had decided, 'to do something decisive to normalise the relationship. In 1959, we invested 500 million D-marks and boosted production by 1,000 Volkswagens per day to 3,000 per day. In 1960, we once again invested 500 million

While most of the world continued to struggle with antiquated semaphores, from May 1955 the American market luxuriated in modern indicators. Mounted on the front wings (fenders in US parlance), the shape of the flasher encouraged enthusiasts to nickname it the 'bullet-shaped' indicator.

D-marks and in January boosted production by 100 VWs per day. In February, by another 100 per day, and in March, once again by 100 per day. By the end of 1960 we shall produce 4,000 Volkswagens daily. Then we believe we shall have reached a balance between supply and demand, so that we can finally deliver Volkswagens to customers without a waiting period …'

Nordhoff's determination proved fortuitous. A future Director General, Carl Hahn, at that point employed to look after Volkswagen of America, and himself instrumental in the creation of the Beetle as a cult vehicle, indicated to author Walter Henry Nelson that he believed Nordhoff's decision to be a 'turning point'. 'No one thought it possible to sell so many motor cars, but when the big US market for imported small cars developed in 1959, Volkswagen was ready for it and best able to supply it.'

Although, by the early 1960s, Nordhoff had been successful in his goal of matching supply to demand, and could turn at least part of his attention to developing the Volkswagen range, it didn't mean that the Director General believed his work was over. In 1963, a fully automated Beetle assembly line

was opened at Wolfsburg, immediately cutting the number of hours taken to build a car. A year later, on 8 December, a new plant at Emden, constructed specifically to cater for export market Beetles, started production. Receiving body-shells from Wolfsburg, engines from Hanover, transmissions and frames from Kassel, plus front axles from Brunswick, while looking after the seats and wiring harness locally, Emden produced 500 Beetles per day initially. The first car bore a simple message on its bonnet: a note so simple that every non-German speaking viewer would have understood too. 'Der erste VW aus Emden für Übersee'. Within 15-months capacity had been extended, resulting in 1,100 cars being produced per day.

Playing the export game to the full

During the 1960s, one of Volkswagen's key marketing straplines posed a most impressive question: 'Why is the Volkswagen a favourite in 136 countries?' The intended answer revolved

↓ **This beautifully restored Beetle is typical of the early Export models Nordhoff was keen to establish across Europe and beyond.**

around the Beetle's many assets: an ability to go off road; its traction in ice and snow; the legendary air-cooled engine ensuring an ability 'to stay cool even when its hot outside'; the car's ability to manoeuvre 'into the smallest parking space'; even its remarkable resale value. However, another answer could well have been – because Nordhoff persevered until he had achieved his goal of successfully penetrating a country's automobile market. His tactics varied; he might have been content to set up a network of dealers through a Volkswagen-controlled local headquarters, either wholly owned by Volkswagen AG, or franchised by them to a suitable body. Another option was to establish a subsidiary capable of building its own Beetles from completely knocked down (CKD) kits supplied by Wolfsburg, or even offering full manufacturing facilities.

A simple analysis of export figures might suggest that everything Nordhoff touched turned to gold, but it wasn't that simple. By June 1952, Ben Pon, the man who had kick-started the export machine into some sort of action in October 1947 with just five cars, was collecting the 10,000th Beetle for the Netherlands, and the Swedish lorry maker Scania-Vabis, who turned Volkswagen importer with four sample vehicles in the autumn of 1948, would go on to claim the accolade of top European importer, when on 20 January 1961 it took delivery of its 200,000th Beetle. Similarly, the ever-increasing number of countries eager to welcome the Beetle on board looked rosy for Volkswagen's finances. In 1950, Nordhoff exported one third of all production to a total of 18 countries. A year later a further 11 countries had joined the Volkswagen fraternity, and by 1953 that figure had escalated to 86, with resultant earnings for Wolfsburg of 254.2 million DM in foreign currencies. Within another couple of years the numbers of dealers in Germany alone had risen to 970, and there was a total of 2,498 dealers on the export scene, covering in excess of 200 countries – and so the story goes on.

A series of case studies serves to indicate that while some markets were simple to conquer, others took time, money, and a great deal of effort. Most notable of this last category was the USA, while special circumstances were required to add the home of the small car, Great Britain, into the Volkswagen web. Brazil, and to a lesser extent Australia, proved easy game.

The Bug story

Nordhoff's first attempt to conquer the vast American market occurred as early as 1949. That production couldn't keep pace with demand was immaterial, for Nordhoff wanted US dollars to buy American machinery. He selected Ben Pon, the ebullient Dutchman, already referred to above, to act as his emissary. Pon duly arrived in New York on 17 January 1949 armed with the first Beetle to be exported to America officially. Almost before landing he faced a barrage of press criticism, for despite attempts to present the car as the 'victory wagon' the near-universal comment was that here was 'Hitler's car'. Dealers visited were equally scathing, and after three weeks, at a point when the money began to run out, Pon sold the car and its attendant parts for what he could, settled his hotel bill, and ran. Nordhoff was inevitably disappointed, particularly when Pon reported, 'It is too early to try to sell Volkswagens in the United States, as dealers selling European cars there don't know how to service them'. Nordhoff decided that he had no other option but to visit the United States himself.

Nordhoff's trip, in his own words, proved to be 'an utter failure'. He met exactly the same response as Pon had done. He was harried with the same anti-Nazi, anti-Hitler remarks, and dealers were much keener to promote the heavy, wide, and lengthy cars American owners had been deprived of during the war years, and now, after an unhappy period of deprivation, could once more contemplate. Extravagance of design and an abundance of chrome – both of which features were sadly lacking in the Spartan and intrinsically Germanic Beetle – were the order of the day.

Although Nordhoff is quoted as saying that he 'realised then that we would have to make our own way in the world without a source of American dollars', his determination led him to a further attempt in 1950. On this occasion Nordhoff contracted with a distributor of foreign cars, the extravert Max Hoffman. His core business was undoubtedly the luxury end of the market, Porsche and Jaguar being just two of the well-known names in the showrooms. Nevertheless, he was willing to add the Beetle to his expanding portfolio. A cocktail party scheduled for the afternoon of Sunday 16 July, with engraved invitations describing the Beetle as 'the famous Volkswagen popular-priced West

German car', launched Nordhoff's latest initiative. Perhaps the very nature of this ceremony is sufficient to demonstrate why the Hoffman deal, while not doomed to failure, was certainly far from a success. Put simply, Hoffman's customer base did not centre on budget cars. Although Hoffman told a reporter from the *New York Times* with confidence that he would soon be selling 1,000 Beetles per month, and that 'ultimately 3,000 would be sold monthly', his best month in three years of trying realised just 160 cars. Hoffman declared to one reporter, 'I tried, and I tried hard, but I just couldn't do it'. Allegedly, he approved of the engineering, and of the quality, but the concept and Hoffman were incompatible. Conversely, reports soon leaked out that Hoffman wasn't pushing the Beetle, in that his salesmen preferred to promote the more exciting and also more profitable models, resulting in the Beetle being pushed to the back corner of the showroom. A further concern was that he preferred to sell the Beetle to other dealers, who were then automatically responsible for what Nordhoff regarded as the dual key issues of servicing and spare parts. The figures opposite indicate the extent of Hoffman's failure, and explain why, during the course of 1953, his contract was terminated.

Once again, Nordhoff was without representation in what he deemed to be his key market. On this occasion he decreed that Volkswagen and nobody else would establish a sales organisation. Arbitrarily dividing the country into two halves, Nordhoff appointed Geoffrey Lange to look after the west, and another colourful character in the developing story, Will van de Kamp, to act as his counterpart in the East.

Lange, a German who had visited and become enamoured with the Californian lifestyle was fortunate in that a Los Angeles dealer, John von Neumann, who had already been acquiring cars from Hoffman unofficially, was more than happy to be taken under his wing. Lange set up his office in San Francisco with the intention of creating what he described as 'an enthusiastic young tree', while regarding the development on the West Coast as 'something like my godchild'.

Van de Kamp was a totally different kind of individual. Organisation was not his strong point, but persuasion was. Despite his lack of English on arrival, and throughout his time in the United States, Van de Kamp could sell Beetles. Walter Henry Nelson summarises his attributes better than any subsequent author: 'Will Van de Kamp was an evangelist, possessed of a near-fanatic missionary zeal, his catechism laid down by Wolfsburg. He believed passionately in the Volkswagen … he never doubted for a second that Volkswagen would become a tremendous success in the United States.' Within a year both Lange and Van de Kamp had successfully created more than the beginnings of a national network, as evidenced by the chart of sales that follows.

VOLKSWAGEN SALES IN AMERICA

Year	Sales
1949	2
1950	157
1951	390
1952	611
1953	1,013
1954	6,614
1955	30,928
1956	55,690
1957	79,524
1958	104,306
1959	150,601
1960	191,372

Van de Kamp's runaway enthusiasm for the product didn't necessarily mean that he had the skills required to develop an efficient and logical organisation. As the number of dealers grew, there was less need for evangelism, and much more for a thoughtful process of expansion, with good administrative back-up. Van de Kamp was persuaded to leave Volkswagen on 31 December 1958. Some time previously, Lange had been moved to Australia. With both men gone, Nordhoff could offer a single US job to his former personal assistant, and a future Director General of the Volkswagen organisation, Carl Hahn. His contribution to the worldwide success of the Beetle came in what at first must have been seen as a most unexpected way, but this is a separate story to cover under a different heading.

To conclude the story of Beetle success in the USA, the 15 distributors and 342 dealers of 1956 had increased to virtually 500 by the end of 1960, and close on 900 by 1965. 1960 had seen the 500,000th Volkswagen to be exported to the USA. When Carl Hahn was recalled to Germany in 1964, annual sales of 276,187 Beetles in America amounted to nearly 70 per cent of the US foreign-car market, while in the year of Nordhoff's death, 1968, 423,008 cars were sold. Finally, although the decision had been taken to move away from the Beetle by Nordhoff's successor, in October 1969, there were 41,811 Beetles sold in America: an all-time record!

Denting British barriers

Britain, the traditional home of small car manufacture, and the country whose citizens were most likely to object to the Beetle's presence so soon after the war, had to be a target market that was handled with care. Nordhoff's tactic was to utilise British people to promote the German car.

Perhaps the best-known name in the story of the Beetle's invasion of Britain is John Colborne-Baber, the Surrey-based car dealer who in 1948 was offered a 1947 Volkswagen by a Swedish gentleman. This car, known by enthusiasts far and wide by its registration JLT 420, inspired Colborne-Baber to specialise in Beetle sales. In a pamphlet specially produced for Colborne Garages in 1974, the tale is told of how Colborne-Baber bought Beetles primarily from Control Commission personnel returning from Germany. 'These cars were basic, utility vehicles with hopsack upholstery and rather poor paintwork. They were gutted, reupholstered in leather (then cheaper than Rexine, due to an anomaly in the hire purchase laws) and resprayed. This meant that the customer could specify his own internal and external colour scheme, in fact a custom-built Volkswagen.' Colborne-Baber advertised in both *The Autocar* and *Motor* magazines, offering to buy spare parts and packs, at that point being offered to anyone taking a Beetle out of Germany, and coincidentally forming the first Volkswagen parts service in Britain. Although Colborne-Baber visited Nordhoff at Wolfsburg in 1952, and was duly granted a franchise to sell new Beetles, his import licence restricted him to selling only to foreign visitors in the UK, namely American forces stationed at Manston in Kent.

Stephen O'Flaherty, whose Dublin-based company was assembling Willys overland jeeps and station wagons in the immediate post-war years, met Heinz Nordhoff in 1949 and was granted a franchise to import Beetles into Ireland. His company was renamed Volkswagen Distributors Limited, and soon began to assemble Beetles from CKD kits.

Curiously, Nordhoff chose the Irishman over Colborne-Baber as the ideal person to establish a

↑ **Known by enthusiasts far and wide by its registration number, JLT 420, the car pictured, dating from 1947, could well have been the first to be driven by a private individual on British soil. Its bright appearance is not original, in that the Colborne-Baber garage that acquired it from a Swedish gentleman soon came to specialise in respraying and retrimming Beetles to make them less austere. With a mileage in excess of 300,000 on the clock, as might be expected the car has been restored more than once over the years, but for some considerable length of time it has been an integral part of Colborne-Baber business.**

↓ **In years gone by, the Split pictured caused a great deal of interest at the shows it attended. For this car wasn't a straightforward product of the Wolfsburg factory. Instead, it had been assembled in the Irish Republic from a kit supplied by Germany. Ireland, under the auspices of Stephen O'Flaherty, a familiar name in the history of Beetle imports to Britain, had been assembling Beetles from as early as 1950, and would continue to do so long after this post-October 1952 car first made its way on to Irish roads. Local content was somewhat limited, but did extend to items such as the shamrock-engraved window glass. The vehicle is now resident in the Autostadt museum in Wolfsburg.**

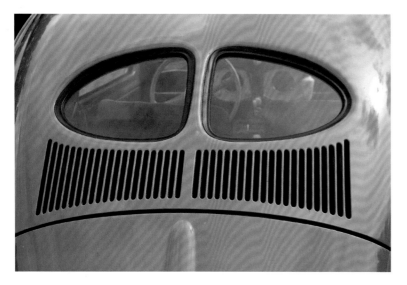

↑ **From the start of production to March 1953, Beetles were recognisable by their split rear window. Far from a design feature, this was a cost-saving expedient; curved glass was both difficult and costly to manufacture. However, once introduced, with the advent of the Oval, a quick trade in sawing out the metal between the two panes of older cars developed.**

market for the Beetle in Britain, granting him the franchise to import new Beetles. With the financial support of two Englishmen, and with O'Flaherty at the helm, Volkswagen Motors Limited came into being on 1 January 1953. There was no shortage of car dealers who wished to be involved with the Beetle, for at the time the demand for vehicles far outstripped the supply. The demise of the Bradford-based Jowett company only served to increase the desire to be involved with Volkswagen, although conversely many large and established dealers were unable to even consider taking on the Beetle for fear of losing an existing franchise. The resultant network of distributors and dealers established in 1953 tended to be something of a hotchpotch affair, which would cause problems for the British operation later, but at least by July, when pressure from Wolfsburg was exerted for the first cars to be delivered, the bones of an organisation were in place.

The first order placed by Volkswagen Motors Limited was for 200 cars. These were duly delivered in batches of 20, each one accompanied in true Nordhoff manner by £10-worth of spares. Despite the euphoria amongst the dealers and management, 1953 was not a good year for the fledgling company, with just 945 recorded sales and a year-end loss of £4,024. Additionally, it soon became apparent that there was a considerable way to go before all sections of the community would be happy to see the Beetle established on British roads. A staggering 75 per cent of cars arriving in the country were damaged between the point of entry at Harwich and Volkswagen's collection centre in High Meads. At the docks, some railway workers would pass along the

lines banging the doors and panels with hammers. Others of a similar mentality would opt to turn car batteries upside down once the Customs and Excise inspection had taken place, the result being that acid leaked over each vehicle's floor. At one stage, and after due consultation with Wolfsburg, the possibility of ceasing imports altogether was contemplated if a serious improvement didn't occur within three months.

To counteract such problems, and after consulting with Nordhoff, Volkswagen Motors Limited chartered a ship, *The Aphia*, capable of moving 80 cars at a time direct to London, where distributors were expected to collect their product. However, two further issues would emerge. The first concerned Volkswagen's success, for at one stage Volkswagen Motors Limited were advised that due to general demand it was not possible to supply any more right-hand-drive Beetles. The man who became Managing Director by the end of 1953, J. J. Graydon, resolved this problem, for he immediately went to Wolfsburg and Nordhoff to demand assistance. Although there was no firm indication that Beetle sales would take off in Britain, Nordhoff immediately instigated Saturday working to satisfy the needs of the British market. Red tape in the form of import quotas operated by the Board of Trade was the other restrictive issue. Each importer was allocated a proportion of the total amount. Some, including Volkswagen, were desperate to acquire more than their quota, while others failed to take up what they were entitled to.

Fortunately, after a slow start, Beetle sales started to increase. In 1954, 3,260 cars were sold, while over the next couple of years the figure hovered around the 5,000 mark. In 1958, the first year that Volkswagen Motors Limited benefited from extra investment capital due to its absorption into the Thomas Tilling Group of companies, sales rose to 7,436 vehicles, a figure surpassed the following year when 9,227 Beetles were sold.

Although the sales level in Britain was far from comparable to that in America, if the discrepancy in populations is ignored, Nordhoff's tactic had nevertheless paid off. In 1960 the 50,000th car was imported, four years later the 100,000th Beetle arrived on British shores, while by 1968, and a year that was later to be seen as a turning point for the Beetle, the British operation was perceived to be the largest foreign car importer in the country.

On the South American trail

Although somewhat quirky to European eyes, in that as the years went by their presentation of models (including the Beetle) appeared to be a mixture of the old and outdated with the new, the Brazilian operation was for many years not only important on its home market, but also as a supplier of whole cars, or CKD kits, to other Volkswagen outposts.

Unlike America and Britain, Brazil and its residents appeared receptive to the Beetle from the earliest days. Nordhoff's first tentative contact with the country came in 1949 when a Chrysler franchisee imported a handful of Beetles. By 1953, and after a personal visit from Nordhoff, sufficient advances had been made to establish Volkswagen do Brasil. Heading the operation was Dr F. W. Schultz-Wenck, a German who would later take Brazilian citizenship. Initially a CKD kit operation, selling a little over 2,200 cars between 1953 and 1957, the Brazilian subsidiary turned to full manufacture in purpose-built premises. The 107,600sq ft plant was located some 14 miles from São Paulo in São Bernardo do Campo, and the first of many vehicles, a Transporter, emerged from its halls on 2 September 1957. Full Beetle manufacture started in January 1959, the same month that Nordhoff officially opened the plant, and during the course of 1960 the 10,000th car left the line. By 1966, annual production of all the models the factory was involved with had risen to an amazing 95,000 vehicles, while more significantly still Volkswagen do Brasil could account for 62 per cent of all passenger cars sold in Brazil, and 42 per cent of total motor vehicle manufacture.

Brazilian Beetle manufacture continued long after Nordhoff's death, and for some years after the demise of German-built Beetles. Nordhoff's desire to make the Beetle a global model had resulted in the development of South America's largest automobile factory. On his death it was entirely understandable that the inhabitants of Wolfsburg would wish to pay their last respects, and that the town fathers would declare official mourning. That this was also regarded as a priority in São Bernardo do Campo is testament to the importance to the Brazilian economy of the Beetle and its mentor for 20 years.

The Beetle goes down-under

The Volkswagen story in Australia, although relatively straightforward in terms of Nordhoff's strategy, can be over-complicated by delving into the intricacies of ownership. Although one or two Beetles had found their way to the country in the relatively early post-war years, the first official import occurred on 11 October 1953. This car was delivered to Regent Motors (Holdings) Ltd based in Melbourne. Its

↓ At first glance the Beetle shown looks like any late model Oval, which indeed it is. However, there is a story behind every car, and this example spent many years of its long life in Australia where it was originally assembled from a CKD (Completely Knocked Down) kit supplied by Wolfsburg. Local content was restricted to items such as window glass and carpets.

primary purpose was to generate press and public interest in advance of the comparatively imminent arrival of a further 30 Deluxe Beetles, which were to be distributed throughout the country.

Despite a somewhat muted response, fortunately tempered by press recognition that Volkswagen were not prone to exaggeration or boasting about their product, CKD kits were despatched from Wolfsburg through Regent Motors to the factory of Martin and King Industries Pty Ltd based in Clayton, a Melbourne suburb. The railway rolling-stock builders were charged with the task of assembling and assessing the kits. By the summer of 1954 assembly had started, and Regent Motors had successfully appointed six other state distributors throughout Australia. A tally of the figures at the end of the year showed that Wolfsburg had shipped out 3,084 CKD cars, plus a further 1,286 complete Volkswagens, while sales totalled 1,746 Beetles and 299 Transporters. This level of sales equated to 1.2 per cent of the entire market, indicating that market resistance to the product, to its German origins, its small size compared to the average Australian vehicle, and even to its unknown reliability, was still strong, but at least a start had been made.

Regent Motors' response was apt; for they decided the best way to promote the Beetle was to subject it to Australia's demanding reliability trials. In the 1955 Redex Trials, which included 143 creek crossings in the space of just 82 miles, the Beetle took both first and second place. The following year, Beetles took first, third, fourth, and sixth place in the gruelling 8,745 miles Mobilgas Trial, and the pattern was firmly established. Perhaps thanks to the Beetle's successes, resistance to it on the part of the buying public rapidly ebbed away. In 1958, the 50,000th Volkswagen to be assembled in Australia was celebrated, and a year later in 1959, the Beetle accounted for more than 10 per cent of the Australian car market. As 1960 dawned, a total of some 73,000 Volkswagens, including the Transporter, had been sold in Australia, while during that year 24,211 Beetles, plus a further 244 sunroof models were assembled.

A combination of changing Government rules and regulations, and Wolfsburg's increasingly healthy financial situation, resulted not only in an increasing degree of local content in Beetle assembly, but also to the formation of a new company in December 1957 – Volkswagen (Australasia) Pty Ltd, of which the Volkswagenwerk in Germany owned 51 per cent of the shares. By 1964, and at a point when celebrations to mark the 200,000th Australian-made VW were looming, Volkswagen AG became the sole owner of the Australian operation, and 85 per cent of the content of each Beetle was manufactured in Australia. 31,364 Volkswagens were registered that year, the Beetle accounting for the vast majority of them. Also by this time, in recognition of the fact that Wolfsburg and its German satellites could still only meet 85 per cent of the demand for Beetles across the world, the Australian operation was exporting both parts and accessories to 20 countries. Indeed, the majority of the Beetles sold in New Zealand were of Australian origin, with in excess of 2,000 cars annually making their way from one country to the other.

Creation of a cult

So far the phenomenal rise of the Beetle has been explained by Nordhoff's resolve to increase production to meet demand, his relentless determination to improve his product and offer the finest service and parts facilities anywhere, and above all by his drive to ensure that every conceivable export market was closely scrutinised, with a way being sought to establish the Beetle as a core product on the country's roads. However, one other element played a key role in the Beetle's success story, and it had nothing to do with any of the sound, practical methodology outlined above. A revolutionary approach to marketing or, more specifically, advertising the product, originated in America, and helped to turn the humble Beetle into a car of the stars, with its own cult following.

Not unnaturally, the Detroit car manufacturers had watched the rise of Volkswagen in the United States with a degree of suspicion, which later turned to outright concern. By 1958, 37 per cent of total Beetle production was destined for the USA where eager buyers awaited. For General Motors, Ford, and others, their collective answer was to create compact cars of their own; the now long-forgotten Falcons, Corvairs, and Valiants.

In anticipation of such launches, and conscious that sales of 160,000 vehicles per year warranted more than word-of-mouth recommendation (disregarding the fact that there was a six-month waiting list for a new Beetle at the beginning of 1959), the newly-appointed head of the Volkswagen operation in America, Carl Hahn, decided he should advertise. Far from satisfied by the bland, or less than honest presentations made by leading American agencies, Hahn turned to a fledgling company of just 10-years standing, whose principal client at the time was a department store. DDB, taken from the initials of its founder Bill Bernbach and his partners Ned Doyle, and Mac Dane, had already established a reputation for creativity; individuals capable of breaking out of the mould.

Arthur Railton, who in 1965 became Vice-President of Volkswagen in America and specifically in charge of public relations, subsequently wrote a book entitled *The Beetle – a most unlikely story*. In this volume, more clearly than anywhere else, is the ingenuity of DDB, and Bill Bernbach specifically, brought to light. According to Julian Koenig, DDB's first copywriter, Hahn had apparently briefed his selected agency for the best part of 90 minutes, while an eager Bernbach took notes as fast as he could.

Hahn told DDB that, "people are waiting six months to buy this car when they can get another car right away". When the meeting ended, Bernbach handed Koenig a note with a headline written on it: "Why do people wait six months for a VW when they can get any other car immediately?" That concept became one of the first five ads.… It didn't appear just as Bernbach had originally proposed, because VW refused to allow mention of "any other car". Hahn's position was that, "we are a guest in America and we don't do ourselves any good by criticising Detroit". Schmitz [Hahn's advertising assistant brought with him from Germany] objected on another ground. He said the original was too specific – why tell people they'll have to wait six months? It could be less, so why be specific? The headline was rewritten by Bernbach to read, "Why are people buying Volkswagens faster than they can be made?"'

The combination of witty thought-provoking straplines, together with realistic artwork created both a look and style not previously known in advertising generally, and car promotion specifically. Gone were the days of stylised artist's drawings, changing the Beetle into a limousine, which it wasn't, while making its interior more spacious than reality. Out went the practice of airbrushing

Regular size. **Large economy size.**

photographs to flatter the product; banished were the images of suave and sophisticated owners, dutifully accompanied by a beautiful female. Straplines and copy were increasingly self-deprecating and unnervingly honest.

The cult of the Beetle was created through such straplines as: 'Think Small'; 'Ugly Is Only Skin-deep'; 'No point showing the '62 Volkswagen. It still looks the same' (against the background of a blank space where normally a photo would have been placed); 'Impossible' (against an image of a Beetle with its boot lid in the air and steam bellowing from an imaginary radiator); 'It makes your house look bigger' (against a tiny image of a Beetle on a blank sheet of paper); and 'Lemon', the best known advert of all, against a picture of an apparently perfect Beetle, rejected by one of the 3,389 quality inspectors at Wolfsburg, thanks to a blemish in the chrome strip on the glove compartment. Would-be purchasers

↑ **The appointment of the American advert agency, Doyle Dane Bernbach, revolutionised not just Volkswagen's advertising, but also that of the rest of the motor manufacturing world. DDB's style was one of honesty in imagery, one clear message per advert, and stunningly original text.**

Although not quite as desirable to the average Beetle collector as the Split and Oval models, early 1960s Beetles are eminently more practical. Apart from the distinct advantages of a much larger rear window, from August 1960 Beetles possessed a 34PS engine and benefited from synchromesh on all gears. Fittings and fixtures were still of the highest quality, and Beetles of this era seem less prone to rust than many a later example. The car photographed is finished in Pastel Blue.

lined up in the showrooms chanting the DDB slogans. Volkswagen recognised the selling power of the adverts, and slowly but surely DDB's influence spread across the Beetle's empire.

The cult of the Beetle engulfed the rich and famous. Owners in the 1960s included King Budouin and Queen Fabiola of the Belgians, Princess Margaret and her then husband Lord Snowdon, Charles Lindbergh, and Dr Benjamin Spock, while even Disney jumped on the bandwagon with the famous series of Herbie films. A US brochure produced in 1968 added another name to the rich and famous Beetle-owning set, while also returning to a take on the very first DDB strapline. With a front cover bearing the heading, 'Why do so many people buy Volkswagens?', a double page spread was allocated to the Beetle-buying habits of the actor Paul Newman.

The Beetle under Nordhoff had grown from an ugly-bug oddity to a phenomenon; a seemingly unstoppable machine.

The end of an era

Speaking to an assembly of distributors and dealers less than four months before his death in April 1968, Nordhoff, who was already four years past the

customary retirement age, pronounced that, 'as an engineer who knows many cars, and quite apart from the fact that I'm a Volkswagen man, I would always rate the good old Beetle as one of the happiest combinations among the automobiles of the world'. Crucially, he once more pledged his allegiance to the car declaring that, 'the star of the Beetle is still shining with undiminished brightness, and you can see for yourselves every day what vitality there is hidden in this car which has been pronounced dead more often than all those designs of which hardly a memory remains'.

Unable, or perhaps unwilling, to comprehend the reasons why sales of the Beetle should continue to escalate many years past the accepted sell-by date of any vehicle previously produced, a small band of journalists were the first to question Nordhoff's allegiance to a one-model policy.

When Nordhoff addressed a German service organisation in 1957 he told them that it was his 'firm conviction that sticking to what we have is one of the most important elements of our success, but year by year, a fresh wave of rumours appears: there is going to be a new Volkswagen. Can anybody seriously believe that we would change this car, which has scored so many successes? You can rest assured that I shall not make this mistake. We shall concentrate on eradicating gradually, and positively, all those small and large design errors inevitable in any car, and this is what we are doing.' The track record was good, with the original 25bhp engine being replaced by a new 30bhp unit at the end of 1953, less than a year after a major overhaul of the car's bodywork. At the point Nordhoff made his speech a further important re-design was imminent; this time involving both window size and interior fittings. More was to come, each revamp being covered in detail in the following chapters.

Two years after Nordhoff had been particularly clear to all about his philosophy, the German magazine *Der Spiegel* asked, or more realistically goaded, him as to why Volkswagen hadn't launched a new model, a replacement for the Beetle at the 1959 Frankfurt Motor Show. The Director General's reply was stock. 'It should not be the aim of the motor industry simply to bring out new models, but rather to produce and sell. Which is to say that it should fulfil the wishes of the public with regard to the type and quantities on offer, and then to offer something that, in our opinion, is attractive enough....' Dissatisfied, the magazine pushed further, provoking Nordhoff to declare that, 'I have faith in my judgement of the technical and economic boundaries to which a design may be pushed. We are starting on the four millionth Volkswagen in the production life you criticise so sharply.' Provokingly, *Der Spiegel* countered with the remark that Nordhoff wanted to hang on to the old design until the market trampled it underfoot, to which his abrupt reply terminated the interview. 'What car is about to trample the Volkswagen underfoot? Of course, the day will come when we have to build a new car, but I have already said that we are starting on the fourth million, and then we will continue to five.... Your question was, "Why no new Volkswagen at the 1959 motor show?" My answer in brief was, because demand for this vehicle is so great, because not a single manufacturer in Europe can point to anything like three million satisfied owners of a single type....'

As Beetle sales continued to grow during the 1960s, Nordhoff had little need to justify his policy. The launch of the larger family saloon, the VW1500, in 1961 countered any lingering doubts that Nordhoff was unable to think of any other product, while his decision in 1964 to start work on a new version of the Transporter, to replace the still incredibly popular first generation model, a programme which came to

fruition in the summer of 1967 with the arrival of the Bay window model, confirmed that no design was sacrosanct, whatever its past glories. As a footnote, even the Beetle could be similarly promoted as a new model following extensive bodywork alterations for the '68 model year, this following the successive introduction of more powerful engines in the form of first a 1300 and then a 1500 power-plant. Volkswagen's profitability likewise gave no cause for concern. In 1960 Volkswagenwerk AG returned a profit of 72.2 million DM; four years later it had risen to 120 million DM; and in 1966 to 376 million DM.

1966, however, was witness to the onset of a sharp and serious recession, which engulfed the whole of Europe, including Germany. Volkswagen had for so many years been linked with the success of the German economy, indeed had been cited as the specific cause of the country's economic miracle, that when things started to go wrong it was appropriate to cast blame in that direction. A new government had entered office in the latter months of 1966, and Nordhoff, anxious to avoid inflicting hardships on his employees by cutting jobs, demanded that action was taken to stimulate the automobile industry. Angry that his pleas not only went unheeded but that the government made it more difficult to buy cars through the raising of petrol taxes and auto-insurance rates, while cutting in half the tax deductions made to those who used their cars for work, Nordhoff openly condemned government policy. When cornered, politicians tend to be at their most dangerous, and the colourful Finance Minister, Franz-Josef Strauss, immediately went to task, launching a cascade of criticism on both Volkswagen and Nordhoff, using allies in the press to promulgate his cause. Strauss accused Volkswagen of 'hoarding up vast financial reserves over many years', while declaring that, 'two glorious initials on a car don't make up for the lack of comfort'. Nordhoff he proclaimed had produced 'too many cars and too few ideas'. The *Bild* newspaper rallied to Strauss's calls, declaring that, 'VW has been asleep', while the Finance Minister condemned Nordhoff for his persistence with the 'wrong models'. Noting a gradual decline in the Beetle's share of the home market, as Ford, Opel, and others had introduced their own much more modern designs, he taunted Nordhoff with the question of 'what happens when the Americans stop being amused by the Beetle?' The truth of the matter was that government

⬇ **The summer of 1967 and the '68 model year saw the arrival of a dramatically updated Beetle. New and visibly more robust box-shaped bumpers, accompanied by shorter boot and engine compartment lids and larger valances, played second fiddle to vertically-set headlamps and redesigned front wings, while larger rear light clusters further altered the appearance of both the 1300 and 1500 Beetle. This example of a 1968 model year car is finished in Royal Red.**

policy had exacerbated the economic slump in the automobile industry, but also that apologists were happy to use Nordhoff as a scapegoat.

Against this background Nordhoff's health was on the decline and there was pressure for him to retire. His own chosen successor, Carl Hahn, recalled to Wolfsburg after his tenure of office in America was complete, became a victim of his association with Nordhoff. Government influence had seen to it that those who chose Nordhoff's successor were hostile to him and of his policies. As such, Kurt Lotz, a man with ample business experience but no background in the automobile industry was selected. With this task accomplished, the Beetle was more or less instantaneously transferred to death row.

The Lotz years

Almost immediately upon assuming Nordhoff's mantle, Kurt Lotz set about a conscious strategy of undoing the work of the last 20 years. Interviewed in *The Autocar* of 24 April 1969 he told the magazine

that, 'we were a monolithic firm under the presidency of a sovereign. We have now diversified, and instead of offering a single range we have adopted a strategy of parallel divisions.' Later in the same interview he revealed that Nordhoff's team had been systematically removed from the board of management within less than 12 months of his death. 'On 31 December last year, the average age of our board was 62. A few months later, following a number of retirements, it was down to 47. Now only one of my direct colleagues is older than myself.... It is superfluous for me to refer to the effects of this rejuvenation on the firm as a whole.' In less guarded moments Lotz was to announce of the Beetle that 'Wolfsburg will never see the 20 million mark.... we won't repeat Ford's mistake', while making a direct criticism of Nordhoff with his snide remark that, 'it was bitter to discover that too little had been invested in the future during a period of high profits'.

Throughout his tenure of office Lotz committed many fundamental errors of judgement. One such is sufficient to explain why, after just four years, he was unceremoniously removed from the top job

XPP 479F

at Wolfsburg, despite his feeble attempts to cling to power. Desperate to prove his was a company of many models, and modern cars too, he unwisely badged the defective K70, inherited with the purchase of NSU, as a VW. Aerodynamically flawed, leading to high fuel consumption, stylistically at best questionable, the K70 was plagued with production faults, ensuring that the cost of manufacture remained high. Lotz had to accept a minimal margin of profit, equating to just 33DM per car, as he was determined to pitch it against Volkswagen's own 411 series, the last of the old-school air-cooled models prepared in the Nordhoff era, but launched after his death. So eager was Lotz to promote the K70 that he openly criticised the 411, but still a disenchanted public walked away from his protégé. Continued low production, and an engine unsuitable for use anywhere else in the Volkswagen range, only served to tighten the noose Lotz had placed round his own neck.

With the recession of Nordhoff's last years over, Volkswagen should have bounced back into a period of expansion and prosperity. Beetle sales were buoyant; 1968 had seen the all-time record of such cars exported to America, with a massive 423,008 new owners recorded. Internationally,

production had bounced back from 925,787 units in 1967, to 1,186,134 in 1968, and 1,219,314 the following year. But Lotz's misguided judgements also saw profits tumble from 339 million DM in 1968, to just 190 million DM in 1970, and in the year of his replacement, 1971, nothing more than a paltry 12 million DM. His successor, Rudolf Leiding, a former boss of both Volkswagen in Brazil and the relatively recently acquired Audi operation, had a big job in front of him.

Before leaving the Lotz era, his specific dealings with the Beetle have to be recalled, for inevitably it was Nordhoff's successor who was responsible for the biggest break with tradition in nearly 25 years of continuous production of the car after the war. Although Lotz was put in post to change Volkswagen's direction, even he had to admit in his 1969 *Autocar* interview that despite 'producing and marketing an old product', the Beetle still 'maintains its attractions', even if its 'impact' is 'tending to die down on some markets'.

In an attempt to update the Beetle's looks, Lotz sanctioned a major front-end redesign. The Super Bug in the USA, or the 1302 in Europe and Britain, benefited from a much larger boot, facilitated by MacPherson strut suspension, which took up

↑ **Volkswagen's first dabble into water-cooling, the NSU-designed K70, was an unmitigated disaster, from its uninspiring angular three-box design, and its host of minor faults, to its heavy fuel consumption, and reputation for rapid rusting.**

↑ The new introduction for the '71 model year, the 1302 Beetle was variously known as the Super Beetle, or Super Bug, and to its detractors as the 'pregnant look' Beetle. Devised in the Lotz era as a means of updating the Beetle by offering more luggage space, the incorporation of MacPherson struts allowed the spare wheel to sit flat under the boot, which itself was much larger. This example, badged as a 1302S, thanks to its 1584cc twin-port engine, is finished in the bright tones of Gentian Blue.

considerably less room than the traditional torsion bar layout, while the spare wheel lay flat under the luggage area. The 1302 (so-called because Simca had already made use of the 1301 model designation) was also available with a new larger engine; a 1600 unit which developed 50bhp, and replaced Nordhoff's highly regarded 1500 Beetle. When so endowed the car was badged as a 1302S, a development of model branding already allocated to both the other larger passenger carrying vehicles in Volkswagen's range. At the risk of delving into too much detail, both the 1300 and 1600 engines were given twin inlet port cylinder heads with the intention of improving breathing. Sadly, due to piston failures at autobahn speeds, the twin-port engines proved to be less reliable than any other that had graced the Beetle previously.

The 1600 Beetle had been specifically developed for the American market, thanks to the power-

draining emission equipment demanded by increasingly stringent legislation imposed by individual states. As now proved to be the norm, Lotz's strategy was at best confusing, or at worst fundamentally flawed. The new car ran alongside the old torsion bar models in most countries, so there were two different Beetles with a 1300 engine, both offered with Deluxe trim, but varying in front end body shape. The basic 1200 Beetle remained in the range for the European market, while the 1600 engine was offered to most only with the new front end. However, in Germany it was possible to buy a 1300S: a torsion-bar Beetle with a 1600 engine, while it wasn't totally unprecedented to offer the 1200 engine in the new body.

The 1302 range received some praise, at least initially. Apart from the new front-end suspension, which some thought gave a more comfortable ride, these cars also benefited from the double-jointed rear-axles first fitted to both the original Beetle with semi-automatic transmission and all US versions of the vehicle from the '68 model year. Unhappily, but somewhat predictably, the reshaped front wings, the new front valance, and the wider and visually humped bonnet, soon found its detractors, with one author years later summarising the criticisms thus: '[The 1302's] front end now looked uncomfortably bloated, like an ageing boxer's bulging nose.'

Aware of the potential harm to Volkswagen any loss of American business would cause, Lotz acted decisively when he discovered that a proposed US standard would require a minimum distance between the driver and the windscreen, a minimum that no Beetle with a flat screen and dashboard in close proximity to each other could meet. Lotz instructed that a redesign take place affecting the Super Beetle, the car now being marketed in the USA. The result was to introduce a completely new plastic dashboard with the kind of layout and room favoured by other car manufacturers of the time. To make this possible, a curved windscreen replaced the traditional near flat affair. Events had overtaken Lotz before the 1303 was launched in the summer of 1972 for the '73 year model. Although not the disgraced Director General's fault in this instance, the irony of the matter was that Lotz had authorised considerable expenditure for both the redesign and retooling, but the proposed US standard never went into effect!

At face value during the four years of Lotz's rule the Beetle was performing better than ever, and with it Volkswagen should have prospered. In 1969, 1,219,314 Beetles were manufactured: more cars than ever before. The following year, 1970, there was a slight drop to a total of 1,196,099, but still better than Nordhoff's finest achievement, while the Beetle bounced back to even greater heights in 1971, achieving a new production record of 1,291,612 cars. Although Lotz's programme to find a replacement for the Beetle trundled along, and inevitably was an expensive affair, his wider strategies cost Volkswagen greatly. There had to be a change at the top, but for fans of the Beetle even Lotz's replacement wasn't good news.

↓ **The pinnacle of Beetle production was undoubtedly the 1303S Cabriolet. Its curved front screen allowed the driver more space forward of the steering wheel, and with the modern MacPherson struts taking care of the front suspension, while the rear featured double-jointed drive shafts, the driving experience was more in tune with contemporary cars of the day. This American-specification example is identified by the energy-absorbing bumper mounts, large wing-mounted indicators, and protective rubber strips with plastic end-mouldings on the bumpers. The engine is equipped with a fuel-injection system, and cars so endowed can be detected by a bulbous rear valance and single tailpipe exhaust.**

The Beetle makes way for the Golf

The years covering the Beetle's demise as a car manufactured in Germany remain to this day the most sensitive period of Volkswagen's post-war history. In the Lotz era it was fashionable to blame Nordhoff for any misfortune that befell the company, and to a certain extent that position is still promulgated in official circles. Although many years later it was convenient to imply that the classic Beetle was directly linked to the New Beetle, an acknowledged saviour of Volkswagen's fortunes in the United States, where the relationship with the Rabbit/Golf had been very much love/hate, and rather more of the latter, since its launch, official histories still blame Nordhoff and his Beetle for difficult trading times in the 1970s. While subtly worded, the following extract from *Volkswagen Chronicle – Historical Notes*, written by Markus Lupa, edited by Volkswagen AG and published by them too, confirms that as recently as 2003 the official stance remained sceptical regarding the man who created Volkswagen as we know it.

Nordhoff, wrote Lupa, 'held firmly on to the Volkswagen saloon, which during his leadership was perfected into the technically mature Beetle, as well as the combination of mass-production and the global market orientation, leading the Volkswagenwerk to the pinnacle of the European automobile industry. In order to maintain this position far-reaching changes were necessary after Nordhoff's death....'

Whether or not the decision to replace the Beetle after Nordhoff's death was the correct one, Lotz singularly failed to make any significant progress. However, he did succeed in sowing doubts in the minds of his dealers, motoring journalists far and wide, and, in the longer-term, the buying public. His successor, Rudolf Leiding, was altogether a different kind of animal. His background was pure Volkswagen, having joined the fledgling team immediately after the war, and diligently working his way upwards through the service department to the top job there. In 1958, Nordhoff put Leiding in charge of the Kassel plant, while in 1965 he was transferred to Auto Union. Galvanising that newly-acquired branch of the Volkswagen Empire into action, Leiding was despatched to Brazil to reverse an alarming decline from the subsidiary's 80 per cent market stranglehold

to just 66 per cent. Task accomplished, it was back to Audi-NSU to solve a crucial unit cost issue, from where he replaced Lotz in October 1971. This man had sound and crucially relevant knowledge of the motor industry. He was ruthless and had the determination to carry out a task. He might have decided to rebuild the relationship between the Director General and the Beetle, established by Nordhoff; but he didn't. Leiding wanted a new range of cars, and as quickly as possible. Within a very short period of time he had swept away Lotz's vagaries, utilised Audi's recent technological advances and sown the seeds of a complete range of front-wheel-drive, water-cooled cars: the embryonic Golf, Passat, and Polo. Curiously, there was a role for the Beetle in the new Volkswagen, albeit a more minor one.

Writing many years after the traumatic events of his equally short four-year reign at the top, for the Volkswagen de México publication, *A Never Ending Story*, Leiding explained thus:

'In Mexico the Beetle could count on having buyers for many years to come. In Europe, however, the situation was very different. The beginning of 1972 marked the production of car number 15,000,000 across the world, the vast majority having emanated from the Wolfsburg factory. This was a laudable achievement, but at the same time, the Beetle's day had passed, and its production was becoming a liability.... In Wolfsburg we were working hard on a whole new line of models, which we hoped would be our salvation. When one has money in his pocket, such an undertaking is an easy task, but under those circumstances and with the pressure of time upon us, it was anything but easy. But we couldn't give up. Golf was the name of the model, which would take the place of the Beetle. It had to be ready by the beginning of the following year....'

Elsewhere in the same article, Leiding added: 'It is undeniable that for Mexico the Beetle was the ideal automobile. In this country, where the paved roads ended and other models failed, the Beetle kept right on going towards its goal, over rocky highways and seemingly impassable dirt roads.... In this market the Beetle had displaced its competitors....'

Leiding's decision was that while the Beetle would be retained on the German manufacturing list, guaranteeing its availability to a relatively small

number of fans who would never countenance a new water-cooled model, whatever its technical advances, or other attributes, the main thrust of Beetle production and sales would emanate from Brazil and its satellites, plus the ever-dependable operation in Mexico. Production of the Beetle duly ended at Wolfsburg on 1 July 1974 at 11.19am, the total number manufactured at the factory since 1945 coming to a staggering 11,916,519. The Emden plant, already a centre for Beetle manufacture, took up the cause, while Cabriolet production, covered in detail in Chapter 6, and never a part of the Wolfsburg story in genuine production terms, was unaffected.

Just a few months into his Director Generalship, on 17 February 1972, Leiding had overseen the celebrations relating to the Beetle finally breaking the world production record previously held by the Model-T Ford. 15,007,034 Beetles had been built worldwide. Asked if he predicted that 20 million would be produced, Leiding answered in the affirmative, but he was far less certain about a 30-millionth Beetle. Accomplished and astute as he was, it would be for his successor, Toni Schmücker to make two more decisions affecting the Beetle's future. Weighed down both physically and mentally by successive oil crises, and horrendous development costs, Leiding bowed to pressure and resigned in favour of an ex-Ford man at the top. Schmücker took up the reigns on 10 February 1975.

Leiding's track record for Beetle production is more or less irrelevant as his policy has been explained. His profit and loss account is much more relevant! One factor is pertinent to the Beetle: the enormous investments made to produce Volkswagen's new range had a direct effect on the Beetle's selling price. While the general inflationary situation was not good in Europe in the early to mid 1970s, Volkswagen required an additional 20 per cent in just a single year on the price of every Beetle to part-finance its replacement; a move which was hardly conducive to additional sales in a difficult trading period.

Year	Beetle production	Profit/loss
1972	1,220,686	86m DM profit
1973	1,206,018	109m DM profit
1974	791,053	555m DM LOSS

The final years

Changes at the top at Volkswagen became increasingly irrelevant to the Beetle's story as the years went by. At the start of Toni Schmücker's term of office as Director General, the Beetle range was drastically reduced, resulting in the disappearance of the 1303 and 1303S in saloon form, plus all torsion bar versions of the car except the basic 1200, and

↑ **When Volkswagen's hierarchy became disillusioned with the Beetle as a means of providing its profitability, the search was intensified to find a suitable successor. After a lengthy period of woolly thinking and procrastination, one-time Beetle champion Rudolf Leiding hit on the idea of the Golf – the world's first genuine hatchback. With the notable exception of the American market, the Golf proved itself a worthy successor to the Beetle, although it is worth noting that the older car outlived the first-generation Golf by some 20 years.**

a model designated as the Custom in the USA, and the 1200L in Europe. (More specific details of these models are given in Chapter 4.) Worldwide production figures dropped significantly, with 441,116 sales in 1975, 383,277 the following year, and 258,634 in 1977. Against this background, and bearing in mind a simultaneous leap in Golf numbers, from 419,620 in 1975 to 553,989 in 1977, Schmücker decreed that German production of the Beetle would come to an end on 19 January 1978. 16,255,000 such cars had been built since the war, against a backdrop of 19,300,000 worldwide.

Other Beetle strongholds, undoubtedly influenced by what was happening in Germany, fell by the wayside at a similar time. The South African operation stopped Beetle production in January 1979, the last car being a straightforward 1300. Although South Africa had been one of the first countries to assemble Beetles from CKD kits and started manufacture in its own right before many others, sales levels weren't high compared to other production centres. A total of 209,916 Beetles were either assembled or manufactured between August 1951 and the end of production. In Australia manufacture ceased in 1968, although not necessarily because the Beetle as a product was failing, as a return to CKD assembly was immediately instigated. This in turn came to an end in March 1977, at a point when 260,055 Beetles had been sold. Irish assembly finished in 1977, and Yugoslavian work on the Beetle came to a halt a little earlier in 1976.

Brazilian Beetles

The story in the Latin American stronghold of Brazil, as the 1970s unfolded, was very different. Not only was the Beetle performing well on the home market, but also the company was still busy supplying kits to other countries for assembly of their own Beetles. In March 1972, the millionth Beetle left the Sao Paulo factory, but whereas the number of German-built Beetles began to decline from this point, sales escalated in Brazil. In 1974 237,323 cars were sold, and with this pattern continuing it wasn't a surprise when the two millionth car rolled off the assembly line in 1976. Brazilian-built Beetles were exported to some 60 countries, the operation having added a new account to its name in 1975, after Volkswagen sales activities were updated in Nigeria in 1974 with the formation of Volkswagen of Nigeria Ltd, a joint enterprise between partners including the Nigerian Federal Government and Volkswagen AG. The new company was charged with building a factory for the assembly of Beetles, the first of which, produced from a Brazilian kit, left the assembly line in March

→ **Beetles produced in Brazil were always somewhat quirky in nature compared to those manufactured both at Wolfsburg and other factories within Volkswagen's empire. This brochure image dating from the 1990s indicates that the side windows of the Beetle are identical to those of a pre-1965 German model!**

Fusca.
As boas idéias são simples.

1975. Nigeria would continue to sell Beetles until the time came when Brazil, having ceased production itself a couple of years earlier, could no longer supply appropriate kits; a situation paralleled in Peru.

If, perchance, there was still a demand for the Beetle in Europe despite Schmücker's axe, it might at first glance have appeared logical that Brazil would supply cars to Germany and its neighbours. However, over the years the Sao Paulo operation had become increasingly singular in many respects. Gradually the differences between a German-built Beetle and a car of Brazilian origin became readily identifiable. When German-built cars received larger windows all round in 1965, Brazil didn't follow suit. Disc brakes only became an option in 1973; dual-circuit brakes weren't introduced until 1978. Similarly, Brazil made its own changes to the Beetle that weren't part of the German package. Between 1960 and 1973, the wheels were of a style similar to those of a Porsche 356, being ventilated, five-bolt, open-centre rims. The 1600 engine, first introduced as an option in 1976, was fitted with twin carburettors, while in 1978 the company devised its own unique steering wheel. These examples are just a few of the many that could be referred to if this was intended to be a specification guide to Brazilian built Beetles.

Gerhard Schreiber, the selected author and collator of *A Never-Ending Story*, the volume already referred to covering the history of Volkswagen in Mexico, further clarified the main reason why the Brazilian operation could never have been handed the destiny of the Beetle in a post-German manufacture world. 'Within the VW Group the rule was that all technical development and most of the technical supervision of auto-production, with the exception of VW do Brasil, was to be done under the auspices of the parent company in Wolfsburg....'

Growing affluence in Brazil, and an increasing desire to own larger and more comfortable vehicles, did eventually affect Beetle sales. Specifically, the introduction of a new Volkswagen, the Gol, in May 1980, a car similar in appearance to any other vehicle from the VW stable at the time, but one that retained an air-cooled engine, was harmful to Beetle sales, as this was a smallish family car at a reasonable price. In 1984, the year that the Gol top-of-the range model was endowed with a water-cooled engine, Beetle sales dropped to just 34,000 units. It wasn't long before the decision was made to axe the Beetle from the range. Suitably garlanded with flowers and

bearing a large placard, the last Brazilian Beetle rolled off the assembly line on 7 December 1986, at a point when a little over 3,321,251 cars had been built over a timespan of 27 years.

Amazingly, and against all the odds, production of the Fusca, the Brazilian name for the Beetle, restarted in August 1993. On 4 February, and under pressure from the Brazilian President, the government of the day signed a deal allowing the state-funded car industry, Autolatina, to facilitate the reintroduction of the Beetle, at a subsidised price. Brazil's prosperity, which had led to the car's original demise, also created a new band of would-be car owners, people who required a budget model and, as far as the government were concerned, not a harmful Japanese import. Beetles once more rolled off the assembly line, this time at a rate of 200 per day, or around 20,000 per annum. Sadly, the Fusca's rebirth was short-lived. Government tax incentives came to an end in 1996, while sales demand was not as strong as once had been expected. The last Brazilian Beetle came off the assembly line on 11 July 1996.

After the end of German manufacture

As Leiding had predicted would be the case, the end of Beetle manufacture in Germany was not necessarily witness to the demise of the Beetle elsewhere, and for that matter a select band of other European countries. Inevitably, would-be British owners lost out due to their requirement for a right-hand-drive car, while increasingly stringent legislation in the USA ensured that what happened in Europe was deemed inappropriate for America. Long before the cobwebs had started to form at the Emden factory, once the last German-built stronghold, Beetles had started to arrive from Mexico, Volkswagen's chosen satellite for the reasons outlined above. Although distinguishable from the German product by, for example, a smaller rear window, the differences were few and far between, and over the next few years a steady trickle of Beetles, marked by a distinct increase in the number of special, or limited-edition, models, made their way into the country. In 1983, Beetles were readily available in Austria, Italy, and Switzerland, plus, of course, Germany itself. A small number of Beetles

→ A sad moment for all Beetle enthusiasts, as the very last such car to be manufactured is rolled off the Mexican assembly line in July 2003. Many Última Edición models have been snapped up to be stored for posterity.

found their way into the Netherlands, via the well-known Pon dealership, but although approved, supplies were far from consistent. Sadly, by the end of the year Switzerland no longer imported Beetles; a direct result of new noise pollution legislation, the Beetle exceeding the acceptable decibel level from a cold start. Despite European sales of some 15,000 Beetles in 1984, and the record of the 100,000th car to be exported having being achieved in the same year, during 1985 it was decided to cease imports. The last batch of 3,150 cars, marketed as the 50 Jahre Käfer, arrived at Emden on 12 August 1985, many of them being snapped up by enthusiasts. Total production at Puebla during the period when Beetles were sent to Europe varied between 51,697 in 1978, to a high of 57,120 in 1982, and a low of 41,810 cars the following year.

The Mexican Beetle

Free from the restrictions of supplying Beetles to Europe from the summer of 1985, the Mexican plant at Puebla could adjust the car's specification to meet the needs of its core domestic market. Although this development took a few years to materialise, and was greatly helped by a government aid programme, including tax incentives produced to combat the worst effects of a slump in the economy – when it did occur, it paid handsome dividends. Annual production in the early 1990s hit unheard-of levels, exceeding the figures achieved when Mexico was supplying the Beetle to Europe. Extra workers had to be recruited, to the tune of 900 men, to cope with a daily production level that had risen from less than 100 to 460 Beetles very quickly. Beetle production had dropped to just 16,746 cars in 1986 and saw little improvement through the rest of the decade. In 1990 there was a massive jump to 84,716 Beetles, followed by 85,681, 86,613, and 98,236 cars respectively over the next three years. Economic problems in Mexico saw figures falter over the next few years, something that offering a variety of special-edition models failed to rectify. Nevertheless, the Beetle was sufficiently popular that it remained a part of the range for another 18 years after exports to Germany ceased. As a valid aside, it is worth noting that following the decision to axe Beetle manufacture in Germany, the Mexican plant continued to build the Beetle for a few months over a quarter-of-a-century,

Volkswagen de México
Último Sedán del Mundo
30 de Julio 2003

Tú colaboración fue la clave
para el éxito del "Auto del Siglo"

Danke   Gracias   Thanks

PRODUCCION MUNDIAL
VWM 21 '529,464
30 DE JULIO DE 2003

↑ The Última Edición
brought together many
aspects of Beetles from
days gone by, typified by
the addition of a Wolfsburg
Crest badge on the bonnet
of the car. The final Beetles
were available in just two
colours – Aquarius Blue,
as depicted, and Harvest
Moon Beige.

and five more years than the entire glory period of Heinz Nordhoff's reign.

Within less than two years of the decision to cease imports of the Mexican-built Beetle to Germany, and thanks to the demise of anarchic Brazilian Beetle production, Volkswagen de México became the last manufacturing bastion. Having already been responsible for production of the 20-millionth Beetle worldwide on 15 May 1981, (Nigeria producing the 20,000,001st), 11 years later on 23 June 1992, Mexico built the 21-millionth car, a vehicle that emerged to a further fanfare of achievement. The company sadly would also build the very last Beetle, but this was a further 11 years away.

For Volkswagen de México, one other production figure would remain particularly important, for in October 1990 they celebrated the manufacture of the one-millionth Beetle to be built at Puebla. Beetles were available on the Mexican market from 1954; first year sales amounting to just 618 cars in a country not renowned for its wealth, but whose market to that date had been dominated by luxury gas-guzzlers. The Beetle's reliability and build quality, plus its low selling-price, was sufficient to break this mould, in turn opening up car ownership to a whole new section of the community. By 1963, the last year before the formation of the wholly Volkswagenwerk AG-owned Volkswagen de México, 6,378 cars were sold. Nevertheless, 41 dealerships and a 12.5 per cent market share was deemed insufficient compared to the advances made by both General Motors and

Ford. From straightforward import, to CKD assembly, the Beetle in Mexico was now to move rapidly towards full production. Growing sales, from 8,245 in 1964, to 13,189 in 1965, and 18,519 the following year, were added justification for moving from an inherited plant at Xalostoc, to a purpose-built and spacious factory in Puebla. The first truly Mexican-built Beetle rolled off the assembly line on 3 October 1967.

In 1968, with sales of 23,709 cars, the Beetle accounted for 22 per cent of the Mexican domestic market, placing it ahead of all products from the stables of other manufacturers and importers for the first time. Since that initial high, the Beetle lost pole position on the domestic market only once, that being in 1995. The 1970s started on a high with a new record of 35,303 cars being produced in the first year of the new decade. For the next three years, production grew annually to a high of 77,391 Beetles in 1974. Production then fell back to a low of 25,917 cars in 1977, the last year before sales in Europe would demand extra capacity at Puebla.

Última Edición

That the Beetle had survived to the new millennium was undoubtedly beyond the expectations of its creator, Ferdinand Porsche, its rescuer, Ivan Hirst, and its detractor, Kurt Lotz. Whether Heinz Nordhoff's undying advocacy of the car during his lifetime and his swansong reference to its 'star ... still shining with undiminished brightness', meant that he expected it to be produced for a further 35 years after his death we will never know.

Beetle sales in 2000 amounted to a healthy 41,620 cars, dipped slightly to 38,850 in 2001, and dropped further to 24,407 in 2002. Sales declines had occurred before, but when by the middle of 2003 only a little over 7,500 cars had been produced, the writing appeared to be on the wall at last. On Thursday 10 July, Dr Jens Neumann of the management board of Volkswagen AG confirmed that production would indeed end shortly. The last Beetles, 3,000 Ultimate Edition models, were to be manufactured with effect from Neumann's announcement, as extra capacity was needed at the Puebla plant to cope with the demand for other models in the range. There was no implication that the Beetle was bowing out because it was no longer fit to be a part of the range. On the contrary, as Neumann pointed out, 'true stars, and their fans, know when its time to quit'; in other words while they are still at their best.

On Wednesday 30 July at 9.05am the very last Beetle, an Aquarius Blue Última Edición, left the production line, the 21,529,464th car of this single type so to do, and a production record that will never be equalled.

The New Beetle

No history of the Beetle would be complete without at least a passing reference to the New Beetle, the front-wheel-drive, water-cooled model that shared a platform with the fourth-generation Golf. Skilfully designed to regenerate interest in Volkswagen's products in the USA, where sales had dropped to such a level that serious consideration had been giving to withdrawing the brand altogether, the New Beetle appealed to those engulfed with in-vogue nostalgic feelings for the Fifties and those aware of the classic reliability of the old Bug, something that could not necessarily be said of later products from the Volkswagen stable.

Although the New Beetle was built in Mexico, alongside the classic model, its appeal to the market purchasing the original car was non-existent. The New Beetle could never be regarded as providing economy motoring, while its basic price would have been far beyond the means of most Mexicans, and certainly those contemplating the purchase of a classic Beetle or budget car. However, its presence in America did the trick, and Volkswagen experienced better performance figures there than they had done since the heyday of the original car.

↓ **When the New Beetle was first launched in 1998 it caused immense interest. British admirers, deprived for some time of a right-hand-drive version, queued up to import 'left-hookers', and immediately paraded their purchases at the many VW Shows across the country. However, a hard core of original Beetle enthusiasts would have nothing to do with the Golf-based water-pumper, protesting furiously that the jelly-mould should never have been associated with the Beetle name.**

CHAPTER 2
SPLITS AND OVALS
1949 TO JULY 1957

Although the Beetle had been in production to the extent of 1,745 cars in 1945; 10,020 in 1946; 8,987 in 1947; and 19,244 in 1948; it was only in July 1949, with the introduction of the Export, or Deluxe, model that the Beetle's specification was truly standardised. To satisfy the demands of those seeking the most basic transport, the Standard model, a car that in future years would account for an increasingly small percentage of Volkswagen's market, supplemented the Export Beetle. The third element of the Beetle range came in the form of two exclusive and comparatively expensive options, a four-seater Cabriolet, and a two-plus-two soft-top Coupé. The convertible models are covered separately in Chapter 6. The introduction of Beetles with a near full length fabric sunroof, a feature applicable to both the Standard and Deluxe model, occurred at the end of April 1950, and with this development replicated the line-up of options presented by Porsche and the Nazi regime at the factory foundation-laying ceremony in May 1938.

Nordhoff's policy of continual model improvement ensured that there was sufficient change between one year and the next for any enthusiast to readily identify the age of a car by its attributes. However, within the period covered in this chapter, there are two distinct phases in the Beetle's development characterised by its appearance. In the first, the Beetle's rear window comprises two small panes of glass divided from each other by a strip of metal. For many years, enthusiasts have known these cars as Split-window models. In March 1953 the two panes of glass became one elliptical-shaped window, and the era of the Oval, in enthusiasts' terminology, had arrived.

The Beetles described in this chapter, and those that follow, are of German manufacture unless specifically stated to be otherwise. Variations in specification to suit the demands of a given market, most notably the important American one, are noted. Until the summer of 1955, Volkswagen's

model year and the calendar year coincided, although significant specification changes were far from restricted to 1 January of each year. However, at the start of August 1955, the '56 model-year car was launched, as Volkswagen had adopted the system favoured by, amongst others, the American car manufacturers.

The 1949 Export Beetle

Although the Export model was primarily introduced as part of Nordhoff's plan to deliver the German car to as many markets across Europe and the world as possible, it was also available in German dealerships, where the alternative title of Deluxe Beetle was more appropriate. The initial Export specification was almost entirely one of enhanced trim and greater choice in paint colours, along with a serious campaign to improve the quality of fixtures and fittings. The key elements of engine performance and mechanical specification were the same as those of Beetles produced before the arrival of the Export model, and as the no-frills cars still being produced and marketed as the Standard model.

Externally, the Export model could be distinguished by a wider selection of bodywork colours than its Standard counterpart – shades which included Pastel Green, Bordeaux Red, and Medium Brown. Although the pattern for the Standard model took a few years to settle down, the eminently dull medium-grey shade, known as Pearl Grey, typifies the limited options available for such models in the early days. All paint colours were duly allocated with code numbers, and it's not unusual to this day to hear enthusiasts refer to the colour of a car by its 'L' number, particular examples being L11 for Pastel Green, and L21 for Pearl Grey! The latter, which soon became an exclusive preserve of the Standard Model, was deleted in March 1953, at the same time as the Split-window Beetle. Its replacement, Jupiter

← **Every four years owners and enthusiasts of Beetles built before July 1957 gather from around the world at the little rurally-located German town of Hessich Oldendorf. Together with the vintage meet at Bad Camberg, this is where Ovals and Splits are commonplace.**

↑ The car pictured dates from 1946 and the era when the British were in charge at Wolfsburg. This was the kind of Beetle Nordhoff inherited in 1948 when he was appointed Director General. Paint quality was poor, and some of the manufacturing techniques were, to say the least, haphazard. To compete in the world market, Nordhoff quickly realised that it was necessary to develop a Deluxe version of the Beetle, complete with chrome trim, glossy paint, and consistent build quality. Many very early Beetles fell into the hands of ex-servicemen, who tended to bring their bounty back to their home country.

→ Although the Standard, or base, car continued to find favour in Germany, its overall popularity waned after the introduction of the Deluxe, or Export, car in the summer of 1949. Standard Beetles can be recognised by painted bumpers and hubcaps, a lack of decorative trim, and a horn mounted on the bumper. This car dates from late 1949.

Beetle basics

Beetles produced in 1949, both before and after the introduction of the Export model, shared the same basic characteristics. Many features described are also pertinent to cars produced in earlier years.

OVERALL MEASUREMENTS

Length	4,050mm
Width	1,540mm
Height	1,500mm

CHASSIS SPECIFICATION

Construction:	Frame with tunnel-shaped centre section forked at the rear, and welded-on platforms.
Front axle;	Independent suspension through longitudinal upper and lower torsion bars, two square sets of torsion bar leaf-springs passing through beams.
Rear axle:	Independent suspension through swinging half axles with spring plates, one solid round torsion bar spring on each side.
Steering:	Special worm steering gear with divided track rod.
Turns of steering wheel:	2.4 (lock to lock)
Turning circle:	11m
Tyres:	5.00-16 – rim 3.00 x 16
Brakes:	Mechanical, foot and hand brakes operating on four wheels.
Wheelbase:	2,400mm
Track:	Front 1,290mm; rear 1,250mm
Net weight:	700kg
Total weight:	1,100kg
Fuel consumption:	38mpg (Imp), 32mpg (US), 7.5 litres per 100km
Fuel tank capacity:	8.8gall (Imp), 40 litres

ENGINE

4-cylinder, 4-stroke rear engine with horizontally opposed cylinders, air-cooled.

Bore:	75mm
Stroke:	64mm
Capacity:	1131cc
Compression ratio:	5.8:1
Maximum PS:	25 at 3,300rpm

PERFORMANCE

Maximum and cruising speed:

        65mph (source 1952 brochure);
        68mph (source 1950 brochure).

Climbing ability: First gear 32%; second gear 18%; third gear 9%; fourth gear 5%.

↑ **The 25PS engine became a standard part of the Beetle's make up in the 1940s, and was only finally eclipsed by the more powerful 30ps engine in the final days of 1953. With a bore and stroke of 75mm and 64mm respectively, and a compression ratio of 5.8:1, 25PS was achieved at 3,300rpm. Note the 'Coffee Can' air filter.**

↑ **Until October 1952 the Standard model's horn was mounted over the bumper in full view. Note the banana-shaped overrider, a characteristic of early Beetles.**

↓ **The style of hubcap pictured, with a very large VW logo, was used in 1948 and the earlier months of 1949.**

← This example of an Export model dates from the second year of such cars, having been manufactured in July 1950. While Volkswagen made the inevitable series of improvements between years, to all but the complete anorak this car epitomises early Deluxe specification. The amount of bright trim and chrome was limited in comparison to examples built after October 1952, and ventilation was yet to be conquered, the car being minus quarter-lights and even the notorious front-quarter-mounted ventilation flaps known as 'crotch-coolers'. The paintwork here went by the highly original name of Medium Brown. The metal strip between the dainty overriders was added by some owners for protective purposes.

→ Although Nordhoff and his team had gone to considerable lengths to produce the Deluxe, or Export, car, some would-be owners away from the home market were keen to acquire a cheaper Beetle. As a compromise, Volkswagen produced what was unofficially known as the Export Standard model; the basic Beetle with some additional bright work. This example, which dates from late 1949, was originally finished in the archetypal early Standard model colour of Pearl Grey, but when it underwent a full restoration a number of years ago, the then owner decided to adopt a shade normally associated with the Export model.

→ The archetypal colour for a Standard model, Jupiter Grey, was offered between March 1953 and July 1963.

← For the enthusiast with an interest in the minutiae, rear lights and trim rings in the years 1949 and 1950 would prove fascinating. After starting with a generous bright ring, later in 1949 the trim became much narrower. However, by 1950 and through to the autumn of 1952, when the housing was redesigned, the trim disappeared altogether. Throughout, the tail lights had one simple purpose – namely to illuminate the car's rear at night. The single brake light was housed in the 'nose' designed to illuminate the number plate.

Grey (L225) became synonymous with base-model Beetles and remained the key option for such cars until the end of July 1963.

Linked to an improved array of paintwork options was the introduction of more chrome and general bright work. Briefly, this consisted of re-shaped, sturdier, grooved, chromed bumpers, complemented by delicate overriders both front and rear. Other chromed items included the car's door handles, headlamp rims, and hubcaps, all of which were painted on the Standard model. Aluminium bright trim strips enhanced the appearance of the running boards, and this feature was extended to a central strip on the car's bonnet and bright-work trim on the waistline. While previously the horn had been an exposed affair, mounted behind the front bumper (where it would remain on the Standard), on the Export model it was now mounted behind the car's front left wing. The horn's audibility was improved by the insertion of a seemingly decorative grille concealing a convenient hole in the wing. For the sake of symmetry a second decorative – or, in this instance, dummy – grille balanced the first. The boot lid was adorned with a solid aluminium VW insignia positioned close to the windscreen.

Internally, the Export Beetle had similarly enhanced trim levels. Bright trim around the two open-fronted glove pockets was introduced to improve the quality image, while black handles and knobs were replaced with ivory-coloured ones. This extended to the steering wheel, the previous three-spoke black affair that remained a part of the Standard model's package, being substituted with a more elegant two-spoke affair finished in matching ivory. Even the speedometer, plus the clock or radio,

← Early semaphore indicator housings had a ribbed surface and visible rivets. Not often seen at a UK auto-jumble, a rare item like this can be picked up at some of the European vintage meets – at a price!

← The petrol tank in an early Beetle's boot was a decidedly intrusive affair, as might be deducted from the photograph. Holding 8.8 gallons and fitted with a massive 100mm filler cap, the only way to fuel up the car was to open the boot lid. The tank was redesigned in August 1955 for the '56 model year.

→ A pre-October 1952 centrally located brake and number-plate light, colloquially known as a 'Pope's nose'.

→ Pre-October 1952 Export models featured a round horn grille on each front wing. The one pictured masked a hole to enable the noise made by the horn to be heard more clearly. The other grille was merely decorative.

surrounds were now made out of ivory Bakelite. The quality of the fabric covering both the seats and door panels was greatly improved. Likewise, the design of the front seats was progressed so that not only did they become adjustable for rake, but could also be moved backwards and forwards using a spring-loaded handle. The Standard model retained the clumsy wing-nut method of seat adjustment. Additional luxury appeared in the shape of a full length cloth headlining, replacing the dubious combination of a small lining and acres of bare painted metal. Cloth grab handles for the use of rear seat passengers were mounted on the pillars immediately behind the doors, while two bolster cushions adorned the back seat. The luggage compartment behind the back seat was both carpeted and protected by metal rails. As a final thoughtful touch, great care was taken to match the carpet shade to the paintwork of the car.

Beetles built in 1950, 1951, and before October 1952

A true expert would be able to find omissions in the 1949 specification outlined above, but it is not the intention to itemise every single change made to the Beetle over the years, but rather to highlight those of greater interest. For example, in October 1949 both the Export and Standard model were offered with a larger roller pedal accelerator. The interest here is not that of the increase in size, rather that Volkswagen bucked the general trend by not discarding the roller in favour of the increasingly popular treadle style accelerator control.

April 1950 saw a significant advance for Export model buyers, in that the mechanical (or cable) brakes were replaced by modern hydraulic ones. Those responsible for brochure copy were clearly charged with selling this message for many years to come. The following extract is reproduced from an American market brochure published in 1952:

'The hydraulic brakes act swiftly and uniformly on all four wheels with very light pedal pressure, and give an unusual quick stop, thus giving you protection and safety.'

A little earlier in the same month of 1950 Volkswagen made its first effort to overcome the problems of poor air circulation. This was attempted

↓ The sunroof was introduced in April 1950 and was available on both Export and Standard models. Made by Golde, the unit was originally formed out of rubberised canvas-type fabric. Five bows supported the top when the roof was in the closed position, and opening was simplicity itself. All that was necessary was to turn a lever and slide the material back – accordion fashion – as per the picture.

by a small cut-out section at the top of both door windows, permitting the driver and front seat passenger to ease their windows down slightly, thus allowing air to circulate without causing excessive draughts.

Reference has already been made to the introduction in April 1960 of the full-length sunroof Beetle. Made by the specialist manufacturer Golde and fitted at the factory, the rubberised canvas sunroof was supported by five bows when in the closed position, while when opened it folded back in concertina style.

From January 1951, a further attempt was made to improve air circulation. This came in the form of ventilation flaps inserted in the front quarter panels. In a way too effective, this device has latterly been nicknamed the 'crotch cooler' thanks to its unfortunate effect of blowing icy blasts of air at intimate sections of both the driver's and front passenger's anatomy. After a few months of complaints, at least an operating wire was added, as was a mesh grille, thus avoiding the ingress of unwanted insects.

April 1951 saw the arrival of two items of trim that served to further distinguish the Deluxe from the lowlier Standard, while proclaiming Volkswagen's emphasis on quality to all. The first item was the inclusion of a polished aluminium trim insert to the rubber surrounding the windscreen, something that immediately improved the feel of the product. The second was the addition of an exquisite and meticulously executed bonnet badge that portrayed in full enamelled colour a modified version of the coat-of-arms of Count Schulenburg, on whose requisitioned land the Wolfsburg factory stood.

Also in April, double-acting telescopic shock absorbers replaced the rear single-lever type on all but the Standard model, thus offering owners of Export models a more comfortable ride. In November 1951, the superfluous, and often owner discarded, rear seat bolsters were discontinued.

The revised Beetle of October 1952

Most observers of the Beetle's development tend to think of the removal of the central rib between the two panes of glass at the car's rear to be truly significant, as outlined at the start of this chapter.

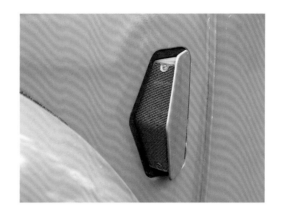

← The ventilation flap inserted in the front quarter-panel was first seen in January 1951. A fly-mesh was added in August of the same year. Known in enthusiast terms as the 'crotch-cooler', it was discontinued in October 1952 when quarter lights were brought in.

← The Wolfsburg crest bonnet badge in this early form was fitted to Export models from April 1951 to July 1959.

↓ The Beetle was revamped in October 1952 and featured a different style of bumper, additional trim, and a new dashboard. To enthusiasts, such cars are known as 'Oval dash Splits', or more charmingly as 'Zwitters'.

↑ This post-October 1952 Split highlights the most important changes made to the Beetle in the autumn of that year. Note specifically the more robust curved-section bumpers with larger overriders than was the case previously, and the somewhat fussy bright-work inserts to the rubber surrounding the split panes of the rear window. (The taillights are incorrect for the year.)

→ This close-up shot illustrates two points: the bright-work inserts added to each window surround in October 1952, and the genuine period accessory of anodised aluminium vent embellishers.

However, the reality of the situation is that the Beetle was dramatically modified for re-launch in October 1952, even though visually the changes weren't as striking as the single alteration of March 1953 vintage. For enthusiasts, cars built after 1 October became known as 'Oval dash Splits', or in more recent times, 'Zwitters'; meaning a late model split window Beetle fitted with the dashboard that came to characterise Beetles built between March 1953 and July 1957.

← Reproduced from a brochure released at the time when the split-window Beetle had been thoroughly revised. The smaller illustrations and the accompanying captions indicate why the new model was better than the old. The artwork is all from the pen of Bernd Reuters.

Changes made to the Beetle in October 1952 affected all areas of the car, ranging from the cosmetic to the mechanically beneficial. Seriously-challenged copywriters for Volkswagen's publicity material had great difficulty squeezing all the information required into the space available. Selected extracts from a post-October '52 and pre-March '53 brochure follow:

'Acceleration and flexibility have been considerably improved by the installation of a new downdraft carburettor with accelerator pump …' (Solex 28PCI, previously 26VFIS.)

'Following intense research work in the laboratory and in the experimental field a really sound synchromesh transmission has been developed, with which gear changing is a pleasure …' (Synchromesh restricted to the forward gears, except first, of the Export model.)

'New, modern, strengthened bumpers with big, sturdy overriders add to the car's protection and appearance …' (No longer grooved, the bumpers are chromed on Export models and painted on the Standard – The Standard's horn was now relocated behind the wing as per the Export.)

'Super balloon tyres with bigger volumes and lower pressure absorb the road shocks …' (Tyres: 5.60 × 15, previously 5.00 × 16; wheel rims now 4J × 15.)

'Vent-wings, which remain in any position and can be locked, safely provide a draught-less ventilation …' (Quarter-lights replace crotch-coolers; finished in chrome on the Export and painted on the Standard.)

'All the windows are framed with highly polished mouldings …' (following the bright inserts added to the windscreen surround in April 1951, the remaining windows are given the same 'modern and characteristic effect'.)

'The attractive rear end is … enhanced by two combined tail and stop lights on the fenders, adding security to fine appearance' (Previously the single brake light had been housed centrally as a part of the number-plate cover. The new light clusters incorporated two separate lenses, the stop section light appearing similar in shape to a typical drawing of a heart – hence the enthusiasts' terminology of a Beetle with heart-shaped tail lights!)

← From October 1952, throughout the years of the Oval Beetle and beyond, this sturdier style of bumper, compared to that of earlier years, was the norm. This authentically-painted example comes from a Standard model. Many such cars are shown with bumpers painted in the car's body colour, which is inaccurate.

← Known in enthusiast circles as the heart-shaped light, for obvious reasons, this style of brake light, introduced in October '52, remained in use until July '55 for most countries, but was superseded in October '54 for the US market.

← The bonnet insignia in this form was added to Export models in October '52 and replaced exactly ten years later.

← An additional, if rather obscure, way of identifying a post-October 1952 Split is to check out the grilles on the lower front wings of the car. Once circular, from this point the grilles were oval in shape, automatically making them larger than previously. This style of grille remained a part of at least one model of Beetle's make-up until the 1974 model year. The car photographed is of South African origin, as evidenced by the clear reflector, a legal requirement in that country.

→ **With effect from 10 March 1953, flat, split rear panes were a thing of the past, as the Beetle was endowed with a new curved oval-shaped rear window. 23 per cent larger than previously, the window was now made out of safety glass rather than plate glass. Deluxe models, as per this example, continued to be trimmed with anodised aluminium.**

↓ **An early model Oval, such as the example depicted here, was more or less identical to the last of the Splits (the cars produced after October 1952). A single tailpipe and heart-shaped rear lights are typical characteristics of both Beetles.**

Curiously, although the brochure contained a detailed illustration of the restyled Beetle's dashboard, no specific reference was made to its new design. This and a selection of other less significant, but nevertheless still important, amendments are itemised below:

Dashboard – totally redesigned, speedometer directly above steering wheel. Centre allocated to large grille (concealing radio speaker if fitted), with radio blanking panel below. Single large glovebox at opposite end of dashboard to speedometer, together with a small rectangular ashtray.
New speedometer design.
Interior light relocated to position above left door pillar – (between split rear panes before).
Padding added to engine bay to reduce noise levels.
Grilles on front wings, oval rather than previous circular shape.
VW bonnet badge no longer cast – now pressed with cut-outs between letters, etc.

The Oval window Beetle introduced in March 1953

The change from two separate panes of plate glass to one slightly curved single piece of safety glass, offering a 23 per cent increase in size in the process, was just about the only change made to the Beetle on 10 March 1953. However, this launched a new era in Beetle mythology, creating a softer, less Teutonic feeling to the vehicle.

Of far greater significance was Volkswagen's decision to upgrade the 25PS engine, originally introduced in the war years and as described earlier, to a new and more powerful 30PS unit. The change took place on 21 December 1953, although to all but the most knowledgeable, visually the old and new engines looked the same. The bore was increased from 75mm to 77mm, although the stroke remained at 64mm. The four inlet valves were increased in diameter from 28.6mm to 30mm to facilitate better breathing, while the distributor gained a vacuum advance mechanism. The compression ratio was increased at the same time from 5.8:1 to 6.1:1. (A further increase occurred in August 1954 to 6.6:1). As a result of these changes, capacity was increased to 1192cc from 1131cc, while power was boosted by 5ps to 30ps.

Although hardly earth shattering in today's terms, nevertheless the motoring press of the day genuinely welcomed the boost. *Wheels* magazine reported that, 'under normal conditions the Volkswagen performs briskly up to 55/60mph. After that, more speed comes on slowly. The test car had a moderate top of 62.5mph, with a one-way run of 64mph…. Initial acceleration is good for a car of this size. The test car took only 23.8 seconds for one standing start 1/4-mile. Times for 20-50mph through the gears are also good.' (0-60mph in 34 seconds). *Motor* noted that in addition to the engine changes, 'the top gear ratio has been lowered slightly, to improve acceleration'. Under a heading of 'sustained speed', *Motor* continued with a suitably favourable turn of phrase. 'The improved engine has also brought about a five per cent increase in maximum speed, the latest model recording 66.1mph compared with the 62.8mph of the 1953 type.'

Volkswagen's contemporary sales literature made little reference to the performance of the new engine, merely quoting a top speed of 68mph as previously suggested for the 25ps unit. Its thrust was on reliability and longevity. 'It will be many a year

→ The 30ps engine was introduced in December 1953.
Capacity increased from 1131cc to 1192cc, the bore from
75mm to 77mm and the compression ratio was initially
raised from 5.8:1 to 6.1:1. The engine had a top speed of
68mph, compared to its predecessor's 63mph. Note the
original corrugated sound-deadening material.

before a better engine for its size can be built.
There is not another car on the road that gives such
mileage (38 miles per Imp gallon) and yet has an
engine that can run 75,000 miles without requiring
major repairs....'

Developments in 1954 and 1955

Other than to serve as a reminder that at the
start of August 1955 Volkswagen's model year
policy changed, the development of the Beetle's
specification was far from headline-grabbing.

    Examples destined for the USA and Canada
started to develop a different specification,
particularly with regard to the indicators, brake lights,
and tail lights. In October 1954, the heart-shaped
tail light was discontinued in both Canada and the
United States. In its place came a double-filament
bulb, plus a single red plastic cover. The aim of
the new arrangement was to make the brake light
more visible. The following April, the same breed
of cars were fitted with sealed-beam headlamps,
distinguishable by a clear outer lens, resulting in the
parking/side lights being clearly visible. Optionally,
such cars could be specified with wing-mounted
indicators instead of the old semaphores, although
in the following month these became part of the
American and Canadian Beetle's make up. Not to
be confused with the indicators fitted to all Beetles
from the '61 model year, the American indicators
sat adjacent to the vehicle's headlamps rather than
on the top of the wing, were cone shaped, the
housings being painted in the body colour of the
car, while the lens that followed the general shape
of the pod was clear. Inevitably, in enthusiast circles,
this style of indicator has been nicknamed the bullet-

← The elegant lines of
a 1950s Beetle with an
Oval rear window are
shown to perfection here.
Rearward visibility was
somewhat limited, but the
car was undoubtedly more
attractive than the Split.

→ This style of dashboard was introduced in October
1952 and ran throughout the years of Oval production.
Although perhaps not quite as symmetrical as the version
that succeeded it, most Beetle admirers think it was a
particularly attractive design.

→ Bullet indicators were the exclusive preserve of the North American market, succeeding semaphores in May 1955. Unlike the later indicators, the bullet-style ones were positioned close to the outer rims of the headlamps. The body of the indicator was always painted in the same colour as the car, and the flat-fronted lenses were finished in clear rather than coloured plastic. The units were manufactured for Volkswagen by Hella.

→ From August 1955 until May 1961 all tail lights looked like the one pictured.

→ Bumpers such as the ones pictured were fitted to American-specification Beetles as a matter of course with effect from April 1955. Soon nicknamed the 'towel rail' for obvious reasons, the purpose of the additional metalwork was to help line up the Beetle's bumpers with those of bigger American-built cars, and thereby protect it against parking knocks. However, such was the appeal of the 'towel rails' that they became an official option for all Deluxe Beetles right through to the demise of the curved bumper in the summer of 1967. (The car in the picture is a Cabriolet as evidenced by a hood cover and the two sets of five louvres in the engine lid.)

style flasher. With the standardisation of the new indicator, Volkswagen also took the opportunity to increase the size of the tail pods, resulting in a larger oval-shaped lens made out of red glass. These pods housed the three functions of tail light, brake, and for the first time, indicator.

The other innovation of April 1955 specific to the American and Canadian markets was devised for entirely practical reasons, but was soon to become a popular fashion accessory throughout the Volkswagen empire. Compared to the majority of cars built in America, the Beetle's bumpers were closer to the ground; inevitably leading to bodywork

scrapes being incurred in parking manoeuvres. The answer was to increase the size of the overriders at both the front and rear of the car to support an additional bar, cylindrical in shape, above the original blade. Support braces were fixed from the front bumper through either end of the valance on to the bodyshell, and similarly at the rear, but penetrating the wings instead of the valance. To accommodate the opening and closing of the engine compartment lid, the additional bars at the rear were divided into two separate sections, both of which curved down to the bumper blade, creating a large enough gap for easy access to the car's engine. The new arrangement was attractive, became popular elsewhere, as indicated, and hence acquired a nickname bestowed by enthusiasts, this one being particularly descriptive. Enter the era of the 'towel-rail' bumper, a feature that would remain at the forefront until the summer of 1967.

Finally, in May 1955, American-specification Beetles were endowed with two chromed exhaust pipes instead of the single metal one offered previously. The redesigned exhaust sat 18mm higher than previously, necessitating a redesign of the rear valance to accommodate the two tailpipes in the form of cut-outs in the bodywork; the previous single pipe having curved under a smooth valance.

The 1956 model year Beetle, introduced in August 1955

Amidst the razzle-dazzle associated with the arrival of the one-millionth Beetle to be built, the car was quietly updated once more. As an aside, it might be worth noting that despite an enhanced specification, Nordhoff was able to offer a price cut on all Beetle models. The Standard model now cost 3,790DM, the Export 4,700DM, and the top of the range Cabrio, 5,990DM. All 1956 models benefited from the American twin-tailpipe arrangement described above. (The only downside to this would materialise many years later when single-tailpipe exhausts became difficult to source and the less particular fitted twin pipes, hacking away at the flat valance in the process, and causing a future restorer many a heartache.) Similarly, the American-specification rear pods were fitted to European market cars, although their bulb function was duo in nature; as such, cars retained semaphore indicators. The pods were moved some 60mm higher up on the wings to increase their visibility, a particularly important move for American cars that were now fitted with partially obscuring towel-rail bumpers.

On the security front, the quarter-lights were made more difficult to open from outside. The securing catch became hook-shaped and was engaged under a projection in the window channel.

The Beetle's interior was updated, the emphasis being placed on both comfort and ease. To enable the driver to read the single instrument gauge more easily, the steering wheel was redesigned so that the two spokes were positioned off centre. The tunnel-mounted heater knob was relocated further forwards for easier use, and the gear lever cranked to accommodate the benefits of this change. The front seats not only became 30mm wider, but also the backrest became adjustable to three locations, while the runner rails were modified to facilitate seven, instead of two, positions. The rear bench seat also became larger, although this did result in a reduction of the luggage space behind by some 10 litres. Trim details were changed, one such being the replacement of cloth with plastic for the rear seat grab handles.

In the front luggage compartment, the shape of the petrol tank was amended with the aim of making it less obtrusive. The revised petrol tank was flatter at its top and deeper at the bottom, the net result being an increase in luggage-carrying capacity of 15 litres, from 70 to 85 litres.

The last of the Oval models and a summary

Changes made at the start of the '57 model year and throughout its duration were minimal and mostly of a type not visible to those playing the spot the Beetle's age game. Perhaps of most significance was the decision to drop the practice of painting the VW letters in the body colour of the car where a Beetle had chromed hubcaps, selecting instead to adopt black on all cars. Inevitably, few hubcaps from this era have survived and most owners of a late-1950s Beetle tend to either paint in body colour or not bother at all, when they fit replacement chrome caps.

Oval-window Beetle production came to an end on 31 July 1957, when the car bearing the chassis number 1-0 600439 left the assembly line, although there are records of such cars having been

← The seats of a '56 model year Beetle could be adjusted more than had been the case previously. Cloth was still an option in some countries.

← The petrol tank was rather obtrusive in all Beetles produced before the '61 model year. This version was offered in the Oval era. Note the fuel cap; the diameter is 80mm, dating the tank to August 1955 or after.

← From September 1956 the VW emblems on chromed hubcaps were painted black instead of the body colour of the car.

assembled overseas after this date. Inevitably, if a CKD kit left Wolfsburg in July and took six weeks to arrive at its destination, this would be the case!

Many enthusiasts, owners, and would-be owners, have come to regard the Oval as the highpoint in Beetle manufacture. By the time of its debut, Nordhoff and his team were sufficiently down the road of making the Beetle a genuinely attractive car to all markets that any of the initial Export model anomalies were already ironed out. Fittings and fixtures were of the highest quality, and great care had been taken to produce aesthetically balanced and carefully colour-coordinated vehicles.

If the Split and Oval period might realistically be described as covering eight years, one engine upgrade, and one major body change, the later six-volt Beetles, that have never really been given a nickname by enthusiasts, cover a nine-year production span encompassing three engine upgrades and two significant body changes. Although it might appear that Nordhoff and his team were challenged to do more and more to the Beetle over increasingly short time spans, realistically Volkswagen's main aim remained one of quality and service at an affordable price.

The 1958 model year Beetle

Although the Beetle's appearance was dramatically altered both externally and internally for the '58 model year, Volkswagen's only major concession to these changes was to produce sales literature where for the first time the rear of the car featured prominently. The artist Bernd Reuters produced a clever image of the car travelling at night, with a rear seat passenger looking over her shoulder through the back window. In true Reuters style he elongated the car, conveyed an impression of speed by adding jet-style air rush lines, intensified the lustre of the paint with sharply defined shadows and, most significantly of all, reduced the size of the vehicle's occupants to give the feeling of a vehicle much larger than it was in reality.

At the front, the Beetle's windscreen was enlarged by 17 per cent, this feat being achieved by slimming down the 'A' pillars, and encroaching a little way into the roof panel; this last act more than any other helping to give the car a more modern look. At the rear the change was far more dramatic, with the old oval window being replaced by a new, and near rectangular, curved pane of glass. The 95 per cent increase in size again made the Beetle appear genuinely far more modern, while it afforded the

driver a significant improvement in visibility. Although it would be wrong to suggest that there were no longer any blind spots, the Beetle was as good as any other model of its day and would remain thus for many years to come.

One result of increasing the size of the rear window was that the engine-cooling vents, located above the compartment's lid, had to be both reduced in size and altered in shape. 50 small equidistant slots replaced two banks of 21 graduated slots. Similarly, the engine lid was revised to take into account a wider and much flatter bulb cover, but in the process it lost something, becoming flatter, and finally shedding the vestiges of the much-admired 'w' look and shape. An undoubted plus, however, was that the number plate was better positioned, being both a little higher and slightly more upright on the lid.

For the American market, the bullet-shaped indicators were replaced with an elongated teardrop style of flasher, which was mounted at the apex of both front wings. Produced out of chromed metal, with a plastic lens, and bonded to a rubber base; this new style of indicator was again unique to the USA and should not be confused with the flashers that would eventually oust the long-lived semaphore.

Seemingly another vaunted ingredient of Volkslaw, the archaic roller accelerator finally gave way to a modern, rubber-covered, and oblong treadle that had been favoured by other manufacturers for some time. Inevitably, in the light of the increase in size of the back window, the rear-view mirror was made similarly bigger, while it also became oval in shape, offset, and held by a different style of bracket.

However, such changes were of miniscule importance compared to the complete redesign of the Beetle's dashboard, with the new layout adopted remaining more or less the same to the end of Beetle production more than 45 years later (despite the foray into the world of plastic with the 1303 Beetle some 15 years or so hence). Although

← **The Beetle's looks were transformed in the summer of 1957 with the introduction of a much larger rear window. A further increase in window sizes occurred for the '65 model year, and in the final years of sloping headlamps and 6-volt electrics the emphasis turned to making the Beetle more powerful with the introduction of both a 40PS and a 44PS engine. American models at this point had a somewhat different specification.**

→ Such was the impact of the greatly increased size of the Beetle's rear window that Bernd Reuters skilfully depicted the car in a once unthinkable position. The rearward artwork not only showed the new window off to perfection but was also designed to create the usual illusion of a car larger than reality. Note the size of the lady's face looking out of the back window!

→ → The 1958 model year's new dashboard was well worthy of a full page in the latest brochure to promote the Beetle. Without doubt the most balanced of all Beetle dashboards, in one form or another the basic style would survive until the demise of the car at the end of July 2003.

→ The looks of the Beetle were transformed in 1957, for the '58 model year, when the size of both the windscreen and rear window were increased. This car dates from 1960, evidenced by a combination of the later-style Wolfsburg crest bonnet badge and semaphores.

A View of the Interior

Driving pleasure begins as you step into the car, for the interior of the Volkswagen, like the outside, is both handsome and functional. Upholstery and door and wall fabrics harmonise subtly in colour and pattern with the paint, giving you a sense of comfortable distinction. Seats and backs are softly sprung and form-fitting. The generous front seats can be individually adjusted even when the car is in motion. As they shift forward, they also rise; the backs can be adjusted to three different angles. The deep seat in the back has ample room for three, and the distance from the front seats gives them full freedom of movement. When a door is opened, the bright top light goes on automatically. The speedometer light is adjustable at will. A glance at the tasteful panel shows:

1 INDICATOR LEVER on the steering column, can be operated with one finger of the left hand.

2 Behind a tasteful grille, space to install a LOUDSPEAKER.

3 COMBINED INSTRUMENT UNIT with speedometer, odometer warning lights, neatly spotted on the dial, for generator and cooling system (red), oil pressure (green), high beam (blue), and directional signal (double arrow).

4 Hand-fitting, comfortable TWO SPOKE STEERING WHEEL, light-coloured, with the arms of Wolfsburg castle on the horn button.

5 Fast-moving WINDSCREEN WIPERS with wide sweep and firm pressure, non-dazzling, with automatic return when shut off.

6 Space for RADIO with dial and knobs, above it to the left the pull-and-twist switch for the headlights and the fully adjustable illumination of the combined instrument unit, to the right the pull switch for the windscreen wipers.

7 Handy on the driver's right the combined IGNITION AND STARTING LOCK (the ignition key is also the door key), next to this the convenient pull-out ASH-TRAY and the CHOKE KNOB.

8 Extremely roomy, wide GLOVE COMPARTMENT, the lid of which drops open automatically when the button is pressed.

Clearly visible in front of the driver is the combined instrument unit which incorporates all controls needed when driving. Immediately in this line of vision is the undistractable clear-vision area of the windscreen. Highly efficient and broad defroster warm air vents protect the windows from getting misted or iced up.

↑ This Diamond Grey model dating from 1958 appears to be in original condition and, at the time the photo was taken, was undoubtedly in the hands of an enthusiast due to its presence at the Hessich gathering of such folk. One peculiarity is the lack of overriders on the bumper.

↓ For the North American market the relatively recently introduced unique bullet-style indicators were replaced by top-of-the-wing-mounted flashers in August 1957 for the '58 model year. As illustrated, the unit was rounded at the front and tapered towards the rear. The lens was clear. European vehicles continued with semaphores, and when such Beetles finally received flashers in the summer of 1960 the style for all cars was amended once more.

↓ Compare the in-the-metal dashboard image with that depicted by a brochure artist (see opposite). The photograph depicts a dashboard of 1966 vintage, as can be determined by the extra vent located in the middle of the dash and, although hidden in this instance, the combined headlamp flasher and dip facility which had been added to the steering-column-mounted indicator arm. The biggest clue to age, however, comes in the form of the black steering wheel with a semi-circular horn ring. This feature, although absent for a year or two, had always been part of an ivory-coloured wheel previously. The 1958 dash lacked a fuel gauge, but owners of cars built during the 1962 model year and onwards benefited from this facility.

some might argue that the Oval's dashboard was aesthetically pleasing, few would deny that the latest look was a perfection of balance and style.

Volkswagen's overwhelmingly comprehensive sales literature of the day outlined in full the attributes of the new dash (perhaps it should be stressed that the information is taken from a brochure printed for a left-hand-drive market):

- Indicator level on the steering column, can be operated with one finger of the left hand.
- Behind a tasteful grille, space to install a loudspeaker.
- Combined instrument unit with speedometer, odometer-warning lights, neatly spotted on the dial, for generator and cooling system (red), oil pressure (green), high beam (blue), and directional signal (double arrow).
- Space for radio with dial and knobs, above it to the left the pull-and-twist switch for headlights and fully adjustable illumination of the combined instrument unit, to the right the pull switch for the windscreen wipers.
- Handy to the driver's right, the combined ignition and starting lock (the ignition key is also the door key), next to this the convenient pull-out ashtray and choke knob.
- Extremely roomy, wide glove compartment, the lid of which drops open automatically when the button is pressed.

In the spirit of the age, a shiny strip was run across the entire length of the new dashboard, broken only by the gauge in front of the driver. The buttons, knobs, and other fitments on the Export model continued to be produced in an up-market ivory shade of plastic.

Perhaps Volkswagen were right not to overemphasise what enthusiasts now regard as a milestone in Beetle evolution, because it certainly appeared that journalists of the day preferred to major on the car's unchanging nature. *The Autocar*, whose most recent previous test drive of the Beetle had taken place in 1954, summarises the general atmosphere:

'For 1958 the manufacturers of the Volkswagen have continued the policy of avoiding major changes and retaining the simplicity of the original design…. In its latest form, the Deluxe car has 17½ per cent more windscreen area, and the size

of the rear window has been increased to very nearly double that of the previous car…. Some three years and nine months have passed since our previous Volkswagen Road Test; the car's continuing popularity is not attributable to any one of its many virtues, but it is the combination of them all which counts. In particular it is a very pleasant little car to drive and, duties apart, if you can afford to buy and run a car you can afford a VW….'

1959 and 1960 model year Beetles

Changes made at the start of, or during, the '59 model year were few and far between. One minor modification is worthy of a mention, however. The transparent greenish plastic sun-visor was replaced by a modern padded vinyl version, at least on the Export model. Although the older item might have appeared outdated, the visor's transparency had its uses, working very much like a pair of sunglasses, and thus affording vision that padded vinyl could never do.

Without a doubt the most important modification made for the '60 model year related to a feature that was invisible! Virtually since its inception, motoring journalists and others had occasionally sniped at the car's tendency to oversteer. The combination of weight at the rear of the car, narrow rear track, and swing axle suspension, could well catch out either inexperienced, or unfamiliar drivers. The 1960 model added an anti-roll bar to the front of the Beetle, whilst lowering the pivot point of the swing axle by some 15mm, through the measure of tipping the engine and gearbox forward by two degrees. The American magazine *Road and Track* was duly impressed and reported thus:

'The chassis has been changed – not much, but to very good effect. The torsional anti-roll bar fitted on the front of the Karmann Ghia is now used, in stiffened form, on the sedan. Some unspecified changes have also been made in the rear suspension; these were not described for us, but we suspect that they involve a lowering of the transaxle assembly (and roll pivot)…. The handling of the new VW is a real eye opener for those who don't think a rear-engined car can be stable. Certainly the car is tail heavy, but we see no real analogy between automobiles and arrows with cast-iron feathers. As most automobile engineers are willing to concede, the addition of enough understeering factors to a chassis will cope with any but the most extreme rearward weight bias. The stiff anti-roll bar … is just such an understeering factor, and on the VW it does the trick.… While the new VW moves over a bit for the stronger gusts – and anything but a tank would – it doesn't try to head for the hills like the older versions did.'

Of the other modifications, would-be purchasers took their pick regarding what they deemed important. Inside the car, rear-seat passengers now had the benefit of plastic covered heel boards, the main purpose of which was to reduce the amount of noise travelling from the engine compartment into the body of the car. The front-seat passenger was endowed with a footrest, a painted metal sheet balanced between the frame head and floor pan, and covered in rubber sheeting, as per the rest of the footwells. The driver had a new dished, two-spoke, steering wheel to manipulate, this one featuring a chrome-plated semi-circular horn ring. Both driver and passenger were propped up on more steeply-angled and curved backrests. Turning to the '60 model year's exterior, the previous style of pull-out door handles were replaced with a push button, while the lock and striker plate were modified in order that less pressure was required to close the door. Finally, the Wolfsburg bonnet crest was modified; the design becoming simpler, and while at first glance appearing to have been downgraded, in reality it was a more appropriate symbol with which to adorn a car.

New decade new Beetle?

The '61 model year Beetle, launched in August 1960, was significantly different from its predecessors. For the first time in nearly seven years, the car's engine was upgraded, and while this and other changes had little or no effect on the overall appearance of the Beetle, the product offered considerably better value for money to would-be purchasers. Key amongst the developments was fully-synchronised transmission, a redesigned petrol tank and front boot, and for European owners the introduction of modern indicators at last. By this time, it is perhaps

↑ **The square push-button door handle was introduced in August 1959 for the '60 model year. Unlike the pull-out version of old, the main part of the handle was fixed to the body of the car.**

← **This simplified version of the Wolfsburg crest bonnet badge was introduced in August 1959 and was discontinued in October 1962. As an aside, the badge was reintroduced for the Ultimate Edition, the Beetle produced in Mexico as a final farewell to the car.**

↓ **With the arrival of the '61 model year and the 34PS engine, Volkswagen also took the opportunity to redesign the once obtrusive petrol tank, creating considerably more space in the boot for stowage of luggage. The filler for the new tank was now at the left-hand side of the car, rather than the right, but it was still necessary to open the boot lid to fill up at the local garage.**

'More powerful engine: engine power has now moved up to 40bhp (SAE rating). This gives more all round go … livelier acceleration in each gear … smarter overtaking … and higher maximum and cruising speeds (72mph), with modest gas consumption.

'Solex downdraft carburettor: choke control is now automatic. The choke cable goes: instead an automatic regulator controls idling speed to prevent the engine from stalling. Top economy fuel-air mixtures are automatically achieved. Driving was always smooth. Increased engine flexibility now makes it smoother than ever – especially at low speed in top. Carburettor icing is prevented by warm air ducted to the air filter.

'Fully synchronized transmission: first gear now comes into line, giving complete synchronization of all gears. Ratios have been carefully selected to give you all the power of the up-rated engine.'

Motor Sport magazine was duly impressed:

' … Wolfsburg claims an increase in top speed of only 4mph (72mph maximum and cruising) this is likely to be a modest estimate. Moreover, they claim to have clipped three seconds off the never-all-that-sluggish 0-50mph pick-up, which the VW is now said to achieve in 18 seconds.… That all these improvements are available at no increase in cost makes the Volkswagen a formidable competitor, nay the leader, where combined durability, good finish, modern design, effortless travel and economy motoring are concerned.…'

Motor magazine took a similar stance:

'… This is a car in which the excellent gearbox is meant to be used, and it is apparent that the new engine has a greatly increased ability to deliver useful power at the upper end of the speed range and to do so with a quietness and smoothness much enhanced by a stiffer crank and crankcase, and redesigned valve gear.'

Of the other changes made, the one regarded as of the utmost significance, at least to owners of European models, was the fitting at long last of modern indicators. At the rear they were more or less identical in specification to American market Beetles, with all three functions of tail light, brake

↑ **The 34PS engine was introduced in August 1960 for the '61 model year, but only to the Export specification. From December 1962 air-hoses were added, connected with the car's upgraded heating system. Although not visually obvious, this engine dates from the '65 model year, the evidence coming from the engine number stamped on the block below the generator pillar.**

understandable why Standard model sales lagged so far behind those of the Export model, equating to a paltry four per cent of total production, as the base model benefited neither from a new engine, nor any form of synchromesh.

The Beetle's new engine, a 34PS unit, had in fact received something of an airing in the Transporter well over a year earlier. Modifications, over and above the specification of the 30bhp unit, included a stronger crankcase, a more robust crankshaft, a modified fuel pump drive, a removable dynamo pedestal, and wider spacing of the cylinder barrels. Through the use of wedge-shaped combustion chambers, and valves positioned at a slant, the design of the cylinder-head was amended. Ever conscious of the charge that an air-cooled engine would always be noisier than its water-cooled counterpart, the combination of a smaller crankshaft pulley, and a larger dynamo pulley, resulted in a slower cooling fan, and hence a lower level of noise. While the bore and stroke of the new engine remained unaltered from that of its 30ps predecessor at 77mm and 64mm respectively, as did the capacity at 1192cc, the compression was raised from 6.6:1 to 7.0:1. As a result of the changes made, the new engine demonstrated a noteworthy increase in usable power. Although not loved by all owners, and perhaps somewhat unusually for a car of this size and price bracket, the new Solex carburettor (28PICT) was fitted with a thermostatically-controlled automatic choke.

The 34PS engine and synchromesh box were duly heralded as giant steps forward in a characteristically positive summary brochure produced exclusively for the American market:

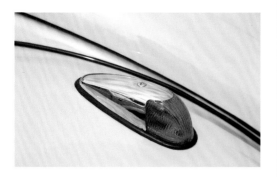

↑ From August 1960 all Beetles were fitted with wing-mounted indicators. This elegant tear-shaped style of fitment was replaced in late October 1963 by a less attractive, wider housing.

light, and indicator covered by one single lens. Both variations of car were affected at the front, with the USA's exclusive tear-shaped indicator modified to reveal less of the lens. It was this housing that was attached to all cars. One downside to the new arrangement was that conformity (in Britain, for example) suggested that the rear indicator light should flash orange rather than red; an impossibility with a single lens housing.

After one modestly successful attempt in the 1950s to increase the capacity of the front boot, Volkswagen tried again for the '61 model year, on this occasion creating much more space in the somewhat restricted area than had previously been thought possible. By making the petrol tank considerably flatter, and repositioning the filler neck from the right to the left, the boot's capacity was increased from 85 litres to 140 litres.

The fuse box, which up to this point had been located in the front boot, was moved to a concealed position under the dashboard, thereby making all eight fuses more easily accessible.

For the first time, the Beetle was supplied with windscreen washers, although many older Beetles have since had aftermarket washers fitted retrospectively. The 1-litre bottle, supplying the little nozzles that were situated on the cowl behind either side of the bonnet-mounted VW roundel, was located behind the spare wheel. The dash-mounted hand-pump button was operated by pulling it in and out.

The dashboard-mounted combined ignition and starter now came with a safety device demanding that, if the car did not start first time, the key be turned back to the 'off' position before a further attempt could be made. Unfortunately, for owners

↑ ↓ Dating from the 1961 model year, the car photographed epitomises the look of the new 34PS Beetle, for it is finished in Beryl Green – of all the colours on offer, the one with which Volkswagen took colour coordination to the extreme. Eagle-eyed observers will note that virtually every piece of internal trim has been colour-coordinated. In the two images, note particularly the running boards, the steering wheel, and the shaft of the gear lever. Other items to be given the treatment included the door cards and rubber floor coverings. Here was the aesthetic influence of Nordhoff at its most blatant. The dash-mounted passenger grab-handle was new to Deluxe saloons for 1961.

→ Although modern indicators were introduced in August '60 for a short time, the tail lights remained outwardly as they had been previously. From May 1961, however, the style of the rear tail light pictured became standard, remaining on Deluxe models in this form until the end of July 1967, and on the 1200 until the '74 model year.

↓ From August 1961 (and the debut of the '62 model), to the delight of owners, the Beetle was finally fitted with a petrol gauge. Why it wasn't incorporated into the main instrument dial remains a mystery, but nevertheless adds a curious elegance to the appearance of the dashboard.

of right-hand-drive cars, the switch was still located in a position where the front seat passenger could easily interfere with the key. Some owners chose to purchase a combined steering and ignition lock: an official accessory of the time.

The addition of a grab-handle above the passenger seat glove compartment, that had been a feature of Cabrio models for the past few years, was deemed by most to be irrelevant.

All Beetles benefited from the addition of asymmetric-dip-beam headlights, ensuring that the nearside of the road was well lit at night, even when it was impossible to apply full beam.

Beetle aesthetics have been referred to earlier, but even greater heights were scaled at the start of the 1960s. Apart from the basics of Black, plus the Standard model's lowly Jupiter Grey and Rush Green, some of the latest additions to the paintwork options lent themselves particularly well to the whims of the interior design team, and no more so than with

L478, Beryl Green – a new shade for the '61 model year. Apart from the practice of colour coordinating the running-board covers to the paint option of the body, great care was taken to match the shade of the steering wheel, the gear lever, and even the tunnel rubber to the paint.

1962, 1963, and 1964 model year changes

Although the changes made to the Beetle's specification over the model years 1962 to 1964 (inclusively) were neither overly numerous nor particularly visible to the casual observer, at least a couple were either extremely important to the driver, or of significance as far as safety was concerned.

1962

First, even before the 1961 model year had run its course, action was taken to improve the specification of the rear light cluster. With effect from May of 1961, larger tail light housings were fitted to European-specification Beetles, incorporating a separate amber section, behind which the indicator bulb was housed. This size of unit, which was added to American-specification cars at the start of the new model year, would remain in use until well into the 1970s, for the base model at least, although come August 1967, and the '68 model year, Export – and now, more correctly, Deluxe models – acquired a larger housing.

Undoubtedly of near equal importance to the owner and driver of a Beetle was the emergence, at long last, of a fuel gauge. For many years, those feeling too nervous to rely on the one-gallon fuel reserve (operated, after a cough and splutter from the car, by the flick of a lever close to the chassis tunnel) had little option but to install an aftermarket gauge – the ones produced by Dehne being amongst the most popular. Some might argue that to locate the new square and chromed gauge by the side of the main circular instrument pod, rather than within it, made the fuel gauge appear to be something of an afterthought. Others, apart from being thankful for its existence in the first place, actually believed that its separate identity helped the Beetle to appear more sophisticated than had previously been the case. As an added bonus, the gauge even accurately recorded fuel levels when

the car wasn't running! Whatever, it was here to stay in such a format until the summer of 1967, and the arrival of the '68 model year. (As a footnote, it is worth adding that the owner of a new Standard model was expected to persevere with the old tap and spare gallon of fuel arrangement.)

Standard model owners could, however, heave a sigh of relief. At long last, with effect from April 1962, mechanical brakes became a thing of the past, as the Export model's hydraulic brakes were now standard across the range; about 12 years after the first cars to receive such a luxury.

Export models benefited from the replacement of the worm-and-peg steering mechanism, in favour of the easier to operate and better directionally controlled worm-and-roller arrangement.

The original pump-action screen washer was replaced with one of a new design. This version involved a compressed-air tank, with a valve on the bottle that had to be periodically pumped up using either a foot-pump or airline. The pneumatic system operated via a press button that could be found at the centre of the dash-mounted wiper switch.

Also for the '62 model year, spring-loaded struts were employed to keep the front boot lid open, offering greater stability than the previous arrangement of a single stay plus retaining clip. The older means of propping the boot open could also lead to damage when, for example, an over enthusiastic petrol pump attendant decided, having filled the driver's tank, to close the boot without releasing the stay.

The car's interior was similarly upgraded with, amongst other items, 20mm longer seat rails for the driver and front-seat passenger, allowing greater flexibility, additional backrest adjustments for the front-seat occupants, sliding covers on the floor-mounted heater vents, which when closed propelled more hot air in the direction of the rapidly misting screen on colder days, and dedicated heating for the rear-seat passengers in the form of two cut-outs in the heel-boards through which warm air could filter.

1963

The 1963 model year saw the demise of the Wolfsburg crest bonnet badge, and the extension of the alloy trim strip to fill the gap. Similarly, the VW roundel badge was redesigned, while the metal of the luggage lid was embossed where the badge was located. These changes occurred in October 1962, and caused some disquiet amongst traditionalists.

↑ Although there is no evidence that a Volkswagen ever left Wolfsburg or any of its satellites looking like the 1963 Beetle pictured, it appears that some Australian dealers supplied cars new with additional trim and two-tone panels. Apparently, they made use of a combination of available bright-work strips and after-market materials. While no longer fashionable, in the 1960s a number of models included this style of trim as part of the specification.

← The front bonnet pull is situated under the right-hand-side of the dashboard on Australian-built Beetles.

← When the Wolfsburg crest bonnet badge was discontinued in October 1962, Volkswagen also made an amendment to the VW bonnet badge. The revised version had three locating lugs and was mounted on a new embossed circle on the boot lid designed for the purpose.

The woollen headlining, a feature of the Beetle since the early days, was replaced by a more practical perforated white plastic affair, although this could become yellow with age, or as a side-effect of the driver or his passengers regularly smoking in the car.

In December, rear-seat passengers were afforded the luxury of regulating the amount of heat entering the footwells, through the use of a lever.

By far the most significant development of the year also occurred in December, and consequently away from the traditional August revamp for the new model year. Until this point, heat for the interior had been derived from the hot air that passed over the cylinders and cylinder heads before being channelled into heater boxes that, in reality, formed a part of the exhaust system from the front pair of cylinders. Unscrewing the cable-operated knob on the central tunnel had the effect of adjusting the amount of air, by closing the cooling air outlet fan and opening the heat-control valve. The disadvantage of this arrangement was that exhaust and oil fumes could occasionally enter the car. The new system employed heat-exchangers, making it far less likely that vapours would penetrate the interior. Cars fitted with heat-exchangers were readily identifiable by the two thick 'corrugated' pipes (one to the right and one to the left) of the fan housing. One exchanger was mounted below each pair of cylinders. The heat-exchangers were sheet steel tubes, through which air from the engine's cooling fan was directed via hoses, before passing over the fins of the aluminium core encasing the exhaust pipes from the front cylinders. The heated air was then blown through large plastic pipes connecting the heat-exchangers to the car interior.

1964

Changes made to the Beetle's specification for and during the '64 model year were relatively few in number, but sufficient for those whose passion had always been for the earlier cars to criticise and carp regarding an alleged lowering of standards.

At the start of the model year, three identifying modifications were made. For many years the VW roundel present on all hubcaps had been picked out in black paint on the chromed Export version, and this time-consuming practice was now discontinued. The engine lid was redesigned once more, this time so that it might accept an enlarged and flattened-out number-plate housing. Inside the car, the steering wheel was updated, with the loss of the semi-circular horn ring and its replacement with twin chromed thumb-buttons that stood proud of the wheel's two spokes.

The Export sunroof model received its own unique update, in that a crank-operated steel sunroof replaced the old fold-back fabric roof. Still manufactured by Golde for Volkswagen, the new roof opening was considerably smaller than the old version. Although undoubtedly more advanced, the steel sunroof was much more likely to cause problems as the years passed by, and it used to be not uncommon to see daily-driver sunroof models dating from the 1960s with black tape around the opening to stop the ingress of water.

The Standard model inevitably didn't qualify to receive the new sunroof, instead soldiering on with the fold-back arrangement. However, times were changing for the base model, for not only did it benefit from a small plastic headlining (bringing it into line, albeit a little late, with the Export specification),

→ At the start of the 1964 model year, Volkswagen determined not to pick out the logo on the hubcap in black paint any more. Rightly or wrongly, many owners decided to do the job themselves!

→ →With effect from October 1963 the elegant tear-drop-shaped front indicators were replaced with the visually squatter and fatter unit in the picture.

but also the rigid adherence to black plastic fittings was finally abandoned in favour of silver-beige. The old three-spoke steering wheel of pre-Export model vintage did, however, still remain firmly in position.

A little after the general revamp for the '64 model year, in October 1963 to be precise, the delicate teardrop-shaped indicator housings on the front wings were replaced by heftier, broader pods, on all models. While offering a marginal degree of extra visibility, the new indicators undoubtedly lost a little in terms of elegance.

The final years of sloping headlamp production – bigger windows and new engines

1965

August 1964 saw a further change to the Beetle's profile that infuriated diehards; for, once again, the sizes of the windows were increased. The windscreen was extended by 28mm into the roof panel, while the rear window became larger from top to bottom by 20mm, and from left to right by 10mm. The side windows, even the quarter-lights, also became larger through a careful exercise of slimming down the 'B' pillars. The result was a lighter, airier Beetle, with the screen increased in size by 11 per cent, the rear window by 20 per cent, and the side windows by 18 per cent and 6 per cent, back and front respectively. To complete the tale, the chromed division between the quarter-light and the front side window was set at a slant, while the windscreen was sufficiently curved that the glare of the sun was no longer distracting.

The sun visors were changed in shape to accommodate the new windscreen, and could also be twisted round to stop glare through the front side windows. The front-seat backrests were both slimmed down a little; while, in a further attempt to create more luggage room, the back-seat backrest could now be folded forward virtually flat, thus extending the rear loading area considerably. Gone was the archaic rotary knob to operate the heater, its replacement being a pull up, put on lever that sat to the right of the handbrake as far as a RHD driver was concerned. A matching lever to the left adjusted heat levels in the rear-footwells of the car.

Externally, although running a poor second to the increase in the size of the window glass, the old T-handle used to open and close the engine lid was replaced by a modern push-button arrangement.

↑ The key constituents identifying a car of 1964 vintage are pictured here. Sadly out of shot, is the redesigned engine compartment lid, which looked even less like a 'W' shape than it had done previously, while the number-plate light housing had altered from a neat 'nose' to something approximating an upturned tray. This car is finished in Panama Beige (L572) and has had a number of period accessories added to the specification.

← August 1964 saw the T-handle on the engine lid replaced with a modern push button arrangement, as illustrated.

↑ By far the most important improvement to cars built from August 1964 onwards was the overall increase in the size of all the windows. The front screen was extended by 28mm into the roof panel, while the rear window increased by 20mm from top to bottom and by 10mm side to side. Increases in the sizes of the side windows were achieved by slimming down the pillars, while the metal between the quarter-lights and the main pieces of glass were slanted rather than straight as before. Although hardly visible to the naked eye, the windscreen was now slightly curved, cutting down on the glare caused by the completely flat screen of earlier times. This car is finished in Java Green.

↓ The 1965 model year saw a development in heater controls, as the rotary knob of old was replaced by a lever to the right-hand-side of the handbrake, topped off with a red plastic knob. More heat was churned through the car when the lever was pulled as near vertical as it would go. A second lever to the left of the handbrake, and topped with a white knob, opened and closed the vents in the rear of the car and below the backseat.

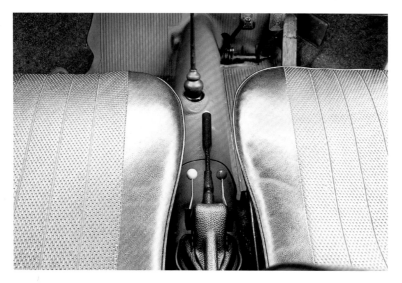

October 1964 finally saw the base model upgraded to include a full synchromesh gearbox, although its reliance on the old 30PS engine continued at least for a few more months, the last such unit being produced in July 1965 and just before the start of the '66 model year. The Standard model was redesignated as the 1200A, only to disappear briefly from the range altogether in August 1966, following the debut of the new 1500 engine Beetle. Some markets could order a 1300A, theoretically a base model 1300 (the engine available from August 1965), but this car could also be specified with a 1200, 34PS engine. Whatever form of base model was on offer, there seemed an impetus to catch up a little in specification terms. In October 1965, for example, worm-and-roller steering replaced worm-and-sector, while the seat frames were redesigned to run on tracks, banishing the old wing-nut arrangement to its rightful place in the museum of yesteryear. The recession-torn Germany of late 1966 and 1967 saw the emergence of a new base model, suitably dubbed the Sparkäfer, or budget Beetle. Despite possible attempts to kill the cheapest model off, there was undoubtedly a place for a budget Beetle and, as will be noted in the next chapter, a base model with a 1200 engine remained in production until the final cars rolled off the assembly line in Emden in January 1978.

1966

The arrival of a larger engine Beetle in August 1965 heralded more than a trickle of articles for the car

The 1966 model year saw the arrival of the larger 1285cc 40PS engine for the Beetle, although visually the only indication was a 1300 badge set at an angle on the engine lid. Otherwise, 1966 cars can be identified by ventilated steel wheels and new flat hubcaps, both items following the trend established by the larger VW1500. The car on the left is finished in Bahama Blue, while below the car is painted in Ruby Red, one of Volkswagen's most popular colours in the 1960s.

that had been around for more years than many journalists would care to remember. If the Beetle was beginning to show its age, as one or two had suggested, press comments regarding the new 1300 engine would have done much to boost its image, or at least the egos of its Wolfsburg mentors.

The American magazine *Road and Track* headed its road test of the new car with the encouraging title, 'More bite for the Beetle', before dropping in the odd phrase such as, 'a healthy increase in poke', and 'a difference in performance that is immediately discernible', amongst its general patter. That a US publication should praise the 1300 was important to Volkswagen, as in-line with previous years, American dealers were supplied with the top model in the range, at the expense of the also-rans. The 1300 engine was available as standard on both the Export saloon and the Cabriolet.

For *Motor*, in an article published some months after the 1300 made its debut, the story was similar, with their choice of heading being simply, 'A noticeably better Beetle'. 'Maximum speed,' declared the magazine, 'is up to nearly 76mph, and acceleration, now competitive with many rivals, has a new-found urgency that will impress drivers of earlier VWs, if not other people.' Although the edge is taken off by the last phrase, *Motor* soon set the record straight

with further clarification of the new engine's ability. 'Through the gears, the 1300 is appreciably quicker than the 1200 and you don't need a stopwatch to detect the difference. In fact, acceleration is now comparable with cars like the BMC 1100, the Triumph Herald and the Hillman Imp which hitherto had a comfortable edge over the VW.'

The new 1300 engine was, in fact, far from fresh in design terms. To gain its modest 6PS over its 1200 sibling, the 1300 (1285cc) engine adopted the crankshaft from the larger VW (the 1500), or Type 3 Notchback, newly-released Fastback, and the popular Variant. This had the effect of lengthening the stroke from 64mm to 69mm. The compression ratio was also increased from the 1200's 7.0:1 to 7.3:1, all of which contributed to the extra 17.5 per cent increase in usable power. The retention of single-port heads ensured that the engine remained under-stressed and would be likely to cover in excess of 100,000 miles and more before any major work was required.

The 1300 was only distinguishable both externally and internally by the addition of a 1300 badge on the engine compartment lid, but other modifications made it possible to pick out a '66 model year Beetle from its predecessors, and, for that matter, what was to come the next year.

After a brief absence, the semi-circular horn ring was reintroduced, although it was different in minor detail from the earlier version. An additional screen demister vent was added, acknowledging that 'fogging' problems still hadn't been entirely overcome. The unquestionably antiquated foot-operated dipswitch was finally ousted in favour of a conventional location on a stalk positioned to the left-hand-side of the steering wheel, and shared with the indicator function. The backrests of the front seats were fitted with a lock to prevent tipping in the case of, for example, heavy braking.

Of more significance was the arrival of ventilated steel wheels, which were again filched from the parts bin, or at least the design studio, of the VW1500. Offering slightly better cooling for the brakes, due to the larger nature of the ventilation holes, the new wheels also helped to reduce the vehicle's unsprung weight. However, sadly the much-loved domed hubcaps, a feature of the Beetle at least from the launch of the Export model some 16 years earlier, were no more. Their replacements, although in reality unique to the '66 model year due to the way they were attached to the wheel, would visually at least remain a part of the specification on most models to the very end of Beetle production in July 2003.

Finally for '66 models, it's worth noting that divergence in the specification of European and American Beetles was starting to emerge once more, the latter beginning to suffer from the demands of over-zealous bureaucrats with a health and safety agenda to administer. Hazard warning lights made their debut on American spec models in August 1965, while, just in case a driver couldn't find his or her gears, a convenient plan was added to the dashboard arrangements.

1967 – THE YEAR OF THE 1500 BEETLE, THE ENTHUSIAST'S CHOICE

As the heading implies, the 1500 Beetle launched in August 1966 for the '67 model year has subsequently become the most highly rated model of any amongst many enthusiasts. Here, at last, was a real driver's car, with improved performance at the owner's fingertips, while retaining (at least for most markets) the aesthetics that had changed the Beetle from an ugly duckling to a vehicle sought by all sectors, from blue-collar worker to the rich and famous.

The 1493cc engine was notably more powerful than the 1300 introduced just a few months earlier.

Still a single-port unit, the engine produced 44PS at 4,000rpm, while maximum torque occurred at 2,800rpm, resulting in more usable power across a wider range. While on this occasion the stroke remained unaltered at 69mm, the bore was enlarged from 77mm to 83mm, and the compression ratio was increased to 7.5:1. Not specifically connected to the new engine's performance, the air-cleaner was now twin-pronged, due to the intake pre-heating being taken from both cylinder heads and accordingly distributed to its destination through two flexible hoses.

← The picture offers a close-up of the new ventilated steel wheels in the style of those fitted to the larger VW1500 saloon and variant. This design of wheel improved brake cooling. The hubcaps, the first Beetle ones not to be domed, were borrowed from the VW1500, and while at first sight appear similar to those on all Beetles produced to the end of German production and beyond, were in reality a one-year special. This hubcap sat into the wheel, while all future ones stood proud of the steel wheel.

↓ The 1967 44PS engine remains easy to identify, thanks to the twin-pronged air filter. Pre-heated air was taken from both cylinder heads rather than one as previously, and fed through two narrow flexible hoses to the new design of air filter. The engine number stamped on the crankcase was prefixed by the letter 'H'.

↑ **The 1493cc 44PS Beetle was introduced in the summer of 1966 for the '67 model year. Not only identifiable by its 1500 badge, the car featured a new style of shorter engine lid which satisfied the demands of American legislation by allowing the number plate to sit almost vertically. Many thought that the lid was redesigned to create more room in the engine compartment for the new twin-pronged air filter, but this was not the case. Another visual difference came with the trim strips which were noticeably narrower than previously. The car pictured is finished in Zenith Blue.**

As there were a number of other improvements made over the specification of the still available 1300 car, more of which shortly, the motoring press found themselves in the position of having to find a new series of superlatives with which to heap praise on the car.

Autosport's John Bolster, more frequently behind the wheel of much more exotic machinery, nevertheless felt compelled to say that, 'compared with the original 1200 model the 1500 has appreciably more speed, very much better acceleration, and a fuel consumption which is hardly any heavier'. More was to follow with the comment that, 'on the road, the Volkswagen 1500 is definitely lively and feels very nippy in traffic', while his enthusiastic conclusion included the remark that, 'this new 1500 is sufficiently lively to be enjoyable to drive, and the handling and brakes now permit one to press on in safety'.

Although the American magazine *Road and Track* was concerned about the age of the Beetle's design, when it came to the new engine, the test drive had revealed a new breed of Volkswagen. 'The

displacement increase has been taken out in torque rather than peak power: the 16 per cent capacity increase is accompanied by an increase of 14 per cent in peak torque and only 6 per cent in power.'

Key amongst the other changes made in August 1966 was an adjustment of the third gear ratio from 1.32:1 to 1.26:1 to suit traffic conditions, while the 1500 engine model had a rear axle ratio of 4.125:1, compared to 4.375:1 of previous cars. Also relevant was a wider rear track, which crept steadily upwards from the 1,250mm, as originally offered on the 1200, to 1,349mm on the 1300, and now 1,350mm on the 1500. An equaliser spring ran transversely under the rear luggage area, adding assistance to the torsion bars when they were under load conditions. Although not relevant to the American market (more of which shortly), disc brakes replaced drums at the front of the car. These had 277mm diameter discs, and calipers with pistons of a 40mm diameter.

John Bolster, in his *Autosport* column, was particularly praiseworthy of the advances made. Writing specifically of the new 1500, he felt compelled to announce that here, 'was a safer car with far better handling, feeling less tail-heavy than its predecessor', while the disc brakes were 'powerful and free from fading'.

Of less importance, but still symptomatic of Volkswagen's enduring policy for continual improvement of its products, the 1500 Beetle fitted with disc brakes now also featured four-bolt road wheels, although the 1300 and 1200 (where available) continued with the older five-bolt arrangement. Flat rather than domed hubcaps remained the order of the day, but in the case of the disc brake 1500 the design was no longer based on that of the larger VW Notchback, Fastback and Variant. Narrower chrome trim mouldings adorned the car's boot lid, sides, and running boards, while a revised style of door-handle with a round push button was featured. For the safety conscious, the steering wheel was now finished in non reflective black, as were all the car's knobs and switches, while these were also flat-topped and made of softer materials than previously. Almost as an aside, a rotary switch, rather than a pull out affair, now operated the two-speed wipers on the 1500 and 1300 models, and single-speed on the base model. The door and side trim panels were amended, losing shiny detail in the process, while a recessed handle was now fitted with which the door could be opened. A push-down button on the doorframe and close to the car's B-pillar locked the car from the inside.

One fallacy that has developed over the years is that the '67 model engine lid was reshaped to take into account the bulk of the twin-pronged air filter. The reality of the situation was that new American legislation demanded that the car's number plate should be presented in as close a position to vertical as possible. While redesigning the lid for this reason, Volkswagen took the opportunity to make the lower lid section shorter.

Other legislative demands served to change the appearance and make-up of the American and Canadian market Beetles, as hinted previously. Curiously, the one change that would have undoubtedly benefited the driver of such a vehicle wasn't included, even though European market cars were so endowed. The reference here is, of course, to disc brakes, which would remain absent from the US Beetle throughout its remaining years of production.

All '67 model year America-bound Beetles featured 12-volt electrics and came complete with

an appropriate voltage warning sign stuck to the driver's door pillar. The sealed beam headlights were set vertically into the front wings, necessitating a re-design of the metalwork, while the sidelights, or parking lights, previously located within the headlamp were now to be found in the indicator light housings. Bumper-mounted reversing lights were positioned on the rear bumper, while racing-style seat belts were fitted as part of the standard specification. On a much more trivial level, European cars had graduated from an identifying VW1300 badge on the engine lid to a 1500 version. This wasn't adopted on American cars, the preference being for a Volkswagen script badge.

At the risk of concluding this chapter with a triviality, owners of the base model were finally offered an upgraded steering wheel. Inevitably more basic than the offering for the Export model, the new version featured two relatively hefty spokes with a deep-set hub, which in turn was home to the blank top horn button. As might have been anticipated, this new style of basic steering wheel had a good production run, still being in use when German Beetle production came to an end in early 1978.

The door handles fitted to the '67 model year Beetle are a one-year-only feature. Replacing the oblong push-button pertinent to cars built between August 1959 and July 1966, not only was the handle more bowed in design, but the new push-button was both smaller and circular in shape. From August 1967 the handle was of a trigger style.

For the 1967 model year, Beetles built for the North American market acquired much-requested 12-volt electrics. As a spin-off, chromed reversing lamps were mounted on the rear bumper, as shown here.

CHAPTER 4
VERTICAL HEADLAMP BEETLES
1968 TO 1978

Everybody, but everybody, thinks of the '68 model year Beetle as a dramatically different car from its predecessors. Clubs exist that cater for all models up to and including 1967, while books have been written with a similar cut-off date. With a new Transporter, the bay-window model, hot off the assembly line, and pressure mounting from sections of the press and a few politicians for Volkswagen to replace the Beetle, few would have questioned the guile of the marketing department when they launched the '68 model year Beetle as 'Die Neuen Käfer'. The reality of the situation, however, was somewhat different, with genuinely new Beetles only emerging in the summers of 1970 and 1972 respectively. Of course, by this time the spirit of the Volkswagen marque had changed; perfecting a single model was no longer at the top of the agenda, if an item at all. This was an age of increasing reliance on special editions to drum up business, and once the Golf and Polo had emerged the attitude towards the Beetle was one of scaling down. While many a devotee didn't regret the passing of the curved-screen 1303 in the summer of 1975, undoubtedly there was a little disappointment that the classic Beetle was more or less reduced to a 34PS power unit of 1961 vintage.

'Die Neuen Käfer'

Pick up a European market brochure for the '68 model year Beetle, and you'll find its plain purple, pink, or lime green cover will bear the words, 'The new Beetles' in whatever language the market it was supplied for chose to utter. No picture of the product graced the cover, but the implication then and now is clear; the Beetle had been sufficiently updated to warrant the prefix 'new' to be added. The internal pages qualified this burst of euphoria, for the really new model was an automatic! Only on page 18 and onwards did the word 'new' refer specifically to the other Beetles available.

'The new VW1300. The new VW1500. Just as attractive and just as well-equipped as the VW Automatic.

This year a whole heap of new ideas have gone into the VW1300 and the VW1500. More than ever before. A good dozen of these new ideas are aimed at making these two Beetles even safer. Take the dual-circuit brake system, for example. And the safety steering column. And the improved safety steering wheel. The new headlights. The two-speed windscreen wipers. The safety interior mirror. The raised and strengthened bumpers.

But we haven't neglected the comfort aspect either. Both these Beetles have the same fresh-air ventilation system as the VW Automatic. And a new fuel tank filler neck which is no longer under the front hood but in the right side panel – just the same as in the VW Automatic.

One thing which isn't new is the VW reliability. The VW quality. The VW durability. The VW economy.

These always have been basic VW ideas!'

Fundamental to the new look of the '68 model year Beetle was the adoption of the previously USA-only vertically-positioned headlamps, a decision that also demanded the universal acceptance of the redesigned front wings described in the previous chapter. Note, however, that the horn grilles were also discontinued on the 1300 and 1500 models, and for good reason, as the new bumpers fitted to these models would have obscured them anyway. At the car's rear, considerably larger light pods and lenses also helped to alter the traditionally soft lines of the Beetle. The new housings accommodated the night and brake lights, plus a separate orange section for the indicator bulbs. Today it would prove difficult to find a car on the market without the benefit of reversing lights, but in the late-1960s such items were far from common, even on luxury class

← **Only a full frontal view of a car produced after the July 31st 1967 watershed does full justice to Volkswagen's description of it as the 'New Beetle'. The vertically set headlamps demanded a redesign of the front wings, creating 'bags' under the lights, which also acted as rust traps. The larger box-shaped bumpers sat higher on the car making changes to the front valance and the shape of the boot lid inevitable, while even the bumper mounting brackets were relocated, resulting in them being more visible. The eagle-eyed will note the driver's external mirror, which had been moved from a location on the upper door hinge to a site close to the quarter-light. As the picture illustrates most clearly, the front of the Beetle took on a more purposeful, possibly even aggressive, appearance, while by the early 1970s the introduction of such colours as Brilliant Orange altered the feel of the vehicle from a quality product towards one of regaining a lost youth.**

↑ This early vertical headlamp Beetle, which could be either a 1300 or 1500 model, as the only identifying feature would have been the badge on the car's engine lid, is finished in the highly descriptive colour of VW Blue (L633), a shade that was carried over from the final days of the sloping headlamp car.

↓ Rear lamps changed dramatically in 1968 on all models other than the basic 1200 Beetle, necessitating a relatively minor amendment to the design of the wing shape. The new cluster was larger than its predecessor, but was prone to water collecting around its base, leading to rust. The example photographed here was destined for the US market as evidenced by the side-mounted reflector. As this car is resident in the UK, the lenses have been made suitable for British roads.

cars. Although not part of the standard package, throughout the years of this larger rear-light cluster, there was the option to add a built-in reversing lamp to the package.

By way of now near inevitable confirmation, the 1200 Beetle was not afforded the new rear light housings, although it was granted vertical headlamps and reshaped wings. Powered by a 12-volt system on the 1300 and 1500 cars, as per the US models of 1967, the old 1200 soldiered on with 6-volt electrics, the last such models to be so fitted for some markets at least, occurring during the model year changeover of July and August 1975. Similarly, the base model continued with both blade bumpers and decorative horn grille.

The new, near girder-like, square section bumpers, sometimes referred to in enthusiast terminology as 'Europa Bumpers', were inevitably stronger than the old type, while they were positioned higher on the car than had previously been the case. While this cancelled the need for the US towel-rail bars, it also involved shortening both the front boot and engine compartment lids. In turn, both the front and rear valances were

↓ With the arrival of the vertically-set headlamp in the summer of 1967 in Europe ('66 in North America), Beetle aesthetics suffered something of a body blow. The change was forced more by safety legislation than any other consideration. Sadly, rust tends to accumulate in the well below the headlight, but as Beetle wings aren't all that expensive to replace. perhaps the negatives are outweighed by the advantages of 12-volt electrics and increased visibility.

→ All Beetles, including those destined for North America, were fitted with stronger, larger box-shaped bumpers when the car was generally revamped for the '68 model year. Often referred to as 'Europa' bumpers, the new items were placed higher than the previous blade type. This necessitated shortening both the boot and engine compartment lids, while the front and rear valances became larger. As the front bumper was mounted on brackets attached to the outside of the inner wings rather than the inside as previously, it was no longer necessary for slots to be created in the front valance.

↓ As part of the revamp for the '68 model year, it was no longer necessary to open the boot to fuel the car. The filler cap was now located in the right front quarter panel behind a flush-fitting flap. For a short time the flap was opened by placing a finger in a recess in the adjoining bodywork. However, for the 1970 model year the flap opened via a ring-pull below the dashboard, making it more difficult for fuel thieves to help themselves but perilous for the owner when the pull mechanism failed.

↓ With effect from August 1967, the elegant door-hinge-mounted driver's mirror was a thing of the past. The new and more readily functional mirror was now fixed directly to the door of the car forward of the quarter-light. Many owners added a mirror to the passenger door; Volkswagen having arranged a suitable blanking plug specifically for this purpose.

extended, while the former one of these no longer bore the scars of slots through which the bumper brackets had previously passed. Now these brackets penetrated the wings, while they were mounted out of sight on the outside of the inner wings, rather than the inside as previously.

Incidentals to the external regime change included a set of symmetrical louvres cut into the bonnet close to its meeting with the metalwork abutting the windscreen, and the appearance of a door, more easily accessed by a finger cut-out, to conceal the repositioned fuel filler and non-lockable cap, set into the front inner wing. (This change was made to stop the need to lift the front boot lid every time refuelling

occurred.) The car's door handles were redesigned once more, this time primarily for safety reasons, the main feature being a concealed trigger rather than a protruding button with which the door might be opened. The external mirrors were now mounted on the doors themselves, rather than being fixed to the car's upper door hinges. Shorter tailpipes designed not to protrude beyond the line of the rear bumper ensured they didn't create an obstacle to passers by.

The combination of the new bumpers, vertical headlamps, and innovative rear light clusters, plus the shortened lids both front and rear, gave the Beetle a much more purposeful look. While some might say its beefier appearance lacked the elegance

↑ A quick glance at this picture wouldn't be sufficient to distinguish whether the dashboard dated from 1966 or 1968! But the tell-tale signs of a vertical headlamp model are there to detect – with a little patience. Although not all that noticeable from this angle, the separate petrol gauge was now a thing of the past, with its incorporation in the one and only instrument the Beetle was now destined to have. The control knobs also became fatter and chunkier, and each was marked with a symbol to indicate its function.

↓ 1967 saw the introduction of what was badged as an 'Automatic Beetle', in reality a semi-automatic arrangement. The car was fitted with a three-speed gearbox, with ratios corresponding to 2nd, 3rd, and 4th on a manual car. Although the 1500, and later the 1300, model was fitted with a torque converter (it had a conventional clutch), it was necessary to use the stubby gear lever to change up and down through the gearbox. As might be expected, the semi-automatic was slower than the manual, but such cars had one distinct asset; a completely new double-jointed rear axle, an arrangement that allowed faster cornering.

of the earlier models, its very chunkiness denied its critics, at least for the time being, the 'pleasure' of proclaiming that the Beetle never altered.

A photograph of the '68 model year's interior, placed alongside that of a '67, might well leave all but a dedicated enthusiast unable to distinguish between the two, serving to prove that perhaps the new Beetle wasn't necessarily quite as 'new' as Volkswagen would have potential purchasers believe. Changes such as they were, were restricted to the useful integration of the ignition switch on to the right-hand-side of the steering column, the amalgamation of the fuel gauge into the main dial, and the welcome addition of a fresh-air system discernable by two flat-topped operating switches below the radio blanking panel on the dashboard. (The works for this device were located in the car's boot, in the form of a plastic box; the fresh air being pulled in through the new louvres on the front boot lid into the box, and directed to the outlets on the top of the dashboard by means of flexible pipes.) Additionally, the rear-view mirror casing was coated in plastic and designed with a safety release to prevent injury if it was struck, while the gear lever was moved further back in the car, became shorter, and was straight once more rather than cranked.

Of considerable importance, but once again invisible as far as the internal or external appearance of the car was concerned, was the introduction of a dual-circuit brake system to replace the old single-circuit brakes, although these remained a feature of the base model. The white plastic brake-fluid reservoir was placed in the front boot, in its own securing tray on the left-hand-side of the car.

The Automatic Beetle

Inevitably designed primarily for the American market, the VW Automatic was officially launched one month into the '68 model year. Based for 12 months on the 1500 only, but then filtered down to the 1300, and later still to the base model, the Automatic wasn't quite what it seemed, in that gear-changing was still required! A three-speed gearbox, with ratios corresponding to second, third, and top on manual Beetles, was operated through a conventional clutch, plus a torque converter. Semi-automatic, in that the driver still had to change gear using the gear-lever, use of the left foot was not required, as pneumatic operation obviated the need for a clutch pedal. The characteristically large brake pedal of an automatic sat next to the traditional treadle-style accelerator, and woe betide the driver who tried to declutch using it!

Although the system worked well enough, fuel economy inevitably suffered along with attendant performance, as *The Autocar* discovered when they tested the VW Automatic shortly after its launch:

'Not surprisingly, one pays in terms of performance and fuel economy for the novelty of not having a pedal-operated clutch and the convenience of a torque converter. The manual 1500 … gave an overall fuel consumption of 27.4mpg, while this version, at 25.6mpg is only 2mpg down…. Though the actual gear change takes roughly the same time on both cars, since on both you have to shift a lever, the acceleration on the semi-automatic is reduced slightly by the churning of the torque converter, but mostly by the loss of bottom gear for getting away quickly. From a standing start to 60mph, for example, the semi-automatic takes 27.4 seconds to the other car's 21.9.… Engine power tails off so much above 60mph that up wind on a very gusty day we could not reach 70.'

Despite a hidden attribute, of which more shortly, sales were always sluggish and now, many years later, to find such a car is an uncommon feat. However, despite its potential rarity, values remain depressed, a symptom more of its automatic status, than of other issues.

The VW Automatic's great advantage over a conventional Beetle was the revised layout of the driveshafts, which were double-jointed, thus enabling the driver to take corners faster without suffering the risk of a rear wheel tucking under. To the exasperation of the European market, come the '69 model year, all US-specification Beetles benefited from double-jointed axles.

The calm before the arrival of the 1302 Beetle

The model year 1969 saw relatively few changes to the Beetle's make up, with headlines restricted to the relocation of the boot-opening mechanism from under the left-hand-side of the dash to the glove

compartment, and the substitution of the old pull-handle system with a lever. Similarly, the fuel filler was now opened via a ring-pull located under the right-hand-side of the dash, and in this new age of snapable wires, the heater vents on the sills were opened and closed by a handle under either end of the dashboard. Needless to say, such 'improvements' didn't last long! A dash-mounted switch operating the hazard warning lights became a universal feature.

Indicative of the level of change for 1969, the 1200 base model received a decorative grille in the front wing that previously had been unadorned with such splendour.

1970, too, proved a relatively uneventful year for the Beetle, despite the massive numbers that were being produced. Visually, the latest batch of 1500 Beetles could be identified by the inclusion of two banks of five louvres on the engine lid above the number plate housing, the purpose of which was to improve engine cooling. Ever thoughtful, Volkswagen fitted a steel drainage tray on the underside of the lid to ensure that rainwater didn't drip on to the engine and spoil its good looks. The 1300 Beetle and the base model 1200 continued to feature plain engine lids.

For 1970 model year cars it was the practice to paint the wheels silver instead of the traditional glossy black centre sections, with correspondingly attractive cream rims. Very much in keeping with the style of other manufacturers of the day, as the years passed the silver wheels often became particularly unsightly due to rust blemishes.

Inside, the distinguishing feature of the latest 1500 and 1300 models was the deletion of the dashboard trim strip, while the passenger sun-visor could no longer be swivelled to the side where it

↑ With effect from the 1970 model year, the Beetle lost its attractive wheels painted in cream and black. The eight-vent, four-stud, design remained as it had done, but the colour scheme was now silver; a shade that was much more in keeping with contemporary trends. The wheel in the picture dates from 2001, and although the chrome-plated hubcap had been replaced by a black centre-cap, the basic design had hardly changed.

↑ **At the end of the 1960s, Volkswagen added a further trim level to the Beetle's specification, at least as far as the 1500 and 1300 models were concerned (not available to all markets). Distinguished by an 'L' appended to the badge on the engine lid, such cars can be identified by a series of what in the day might have been regarded as extras. These included reversing lights fitted within the main rear-light clusters, and normally rubber inserts set into the central groove of the Europa bumpers. Internally, a padded dash was provided, as was an anti-dazzle mirror, lockable glovebox, and thicker more luxurious carpet than was the norm.**

had afforded protection from the sun's rays in that direction.

Although not a common sight on, for example, the British market, Volkswagen added variations to most of the models in the range. Hence, both a 1500L and 1300L existed, which included such features as a padded dashboard and black glovebox lid, an anti-dazzle rear-view mirror, a door pocket for the front-seat passenger as well as the driver, a vanity mirror on the passenger sun-visor, plus reversing lights, and a rubber nudge-strip attached to the bumper. The price for the luxury models was high in comparison to the normal Deluxe 1300 and 1500, while most features could be bought as genuine accessories.

Cars for the US market now carried side marker lights while, thanks to further State legislation, a buzzer sounded if the door was left open.

The day of the Super Beetle

Reference has already been made in Chapter One to the somewhat dubious reception the bulbous-nosed 1302S, or Super Beetle, received on its debut at the start of the 1971 model year. While this car replaced the previous top of the range 1500, the classic torsion-bar Beetle remained in production both as a 1300 and 1200. To complicate matters a little, some markets could order the Super Beetle with a 1300 engine, under which circumstances it was badged simply as a 1302.

Technically the 1302 series was more advanced than its torsion-bar siblings, thanks to its combination of MacPherson struts, with their integral dampers and coil springs, a large anti-roll bar at the front, and the adoption of the much sought after double-jointed axles – originally the exclusive preserve of the VW Automatic and latterly American-specification 1500 models. Linked to the frontal suspension changes and designed to meet the demands of some for more luggage room, the boot was totally redesigned, with the spare wheel lying flat under the lower of two load areas, and a much larger washer-bottle being attached to metalwork close to the right suspension turret. As a consequence, the newly-created boot offered owners an advantageous 86 per cent increase in the space available for luggage over that of the traditional torsion-bar models. The downside, however, was the car's appearance. Not altogether unattractive reshaped and somewhat rounder front wings nestled against a much broader, and certainly less aesthetically appealing, bonnet, while the single-skin front valance, more or less concealed by the new longer bumper merited few prizes for its designer.

The 1302S was endowed with a new 1600 engine, and both this and the revamped 1300 engine came with a revised design of cylinder head with twin inlet ports per head, allegedly to improve the engine's breathing. (The 1200 was unaffected by such changes and long-term proved to be more reliable, particularly so when tens-of-thousands of miles had

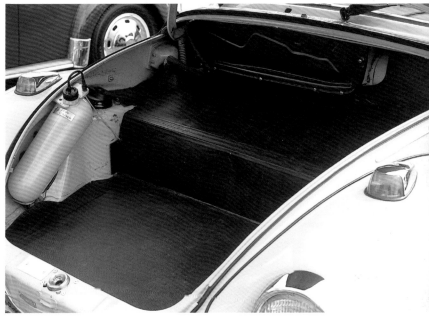

↑ One of the many improvements made for the 1968 model year was the fitting of a new style of washer bottle. This was clamped to the spare wheel in the boot of the car by means of two plastic pegs.

↓ In the summer of 1970 for the '71 model year, Volkswagen introduced a very different Beetle. Variously marketed as the Super Bug, or Super Beetle, the 1302 car featured a bulbous nose and MacPherson-strut front suspension, which made room for considerably more luggage. At the rear there were semi-trailing arms. Available in Britain only as a 1302S, the letter 'S' indicating a larger 1600 engine, many markets were also offered a plain 1302 with a 1300 engine. The car depicted is an Australian version from the State of Victoria.

↑ Compared to torsion-bar Beetles, the boot (trunk) provided in the 1302/3 is truly cavernous. The spare wheel now lies flat and, through a tube connected to the tyre valve, provides the air supply to power the windscreen washers. The screen washer bottle, formerly situated in the centre of the car on previous models, now resides on the right-hand inner wing, while the top of the right-hand MacPherson strut can just be seen next to the step covering the fuel tank in the boot lining.

↑ **In Australia, the MacPherson-strut Beetle, known in Germany as the 1302S, carried a 'Volkswagen S' badge. Note the two sets of ventilation slots on the engine lid. This feature first appeared on the 1500 Beetle of 1970 vintage.**

been rung up on the clock.) In twin-port guise, the result for the 1300 was an increase in power from 40PS to 44PS, while the new 1600 produced a relatively modest, but at least in Beetle terms suitably impressive, 50PS. The stroke of the 1584cc engine was exactly as it had been for the 1500 at 69.0mm, but the bore had increased by 2.5mm to a new figure of 85.5mm. The compression ratio remained as it had been before at 7.5:1.

All engine lids, other than the 1200 model, now boasted the ten cooling louvres, previously

the preserve of the 1500, while the lid itself was reshaped making it more sharply curved, the purpose being to accommodate the additional height of the twin-port engines.

Disc brakes were standard on the European market 1302S and could be ordered as an optional extra on the 1302. Both the 1300 and 1200 continued to be brought to a halt by drums, as did American-specification cars!

Externally, crescent-shaped air vents, situated behind the rear side windows, distinguished the '71 model from those of earlier years, this distinction even filtering down to the 1200, albeit in the form of a blank indentation in the metalwork. The black plastic vents, complete with mock brightwork, were designed to ensure draught-free, through-flow ventilation, and to this end an additional pair of air vents were added to the dashboard, and came complete with a directional control device. A two-speed electric blower could be added at extra cost.

The jack, made secure with appropriate clips, was now stored under the rear seat, and close to the battery, while the heater vents in the front footwells were fitted with levers to open and close them. There were wider backrests for the driver and front-

↓ **The rear view of a late model 1302S, or for that matter a 1300 torsion-bar Beetle of similar vintage, was normally dominated by four sets of ventilation vents pierced through the engine lid. However, the owner of this car decided that, to avoid water entering the engine compartment and spoiling the pristine appearance of the air-cooled power plant, a plastic cowl should be fitted. Note also the prominent 1302S badge, and the rear-light clusters characteristic of all Beetles bar the 1200 built after July 1967 and before the arrival of the 1303 in August 1972.**

↓ **With effect from the '71 model year, all Beetles except the basic 1200 were fitted with crescent-shaped air-extraction vents to improve circulation within the car. Initially bedecked with bright-work, latterly the vents were simply plain black. When the 1200L model was introduced after the demise of the larger-engined Beetle saloons, this also benefited from the vents.**

seat passenger, while the dashboard remained a painted metal affair for all Beetle owners, unless the Deluxe black-padded option was ordered as an extra.

The Autocar's December 1970 narrative covering the 1302S, following its usual comprehensive test drive, epitomised the relatively lukewarm response the car received: 'Even with 14 per cent more power', the author of the report complained, 'the total output of 50bhp DIN is very modest for the size of the engine. There can hardly be another engine left in production which turns out only 31bhp per litre....' From engine to fuel consumption, the response was similar: 'It will be a very careful VW driver indeed who gets 30mpg from his Super Beetle.' Handling, too, despite the struts up front and the double-jointed arrangement at the rear, was still criticised: 'As far as the driver notices, the front end behaves much the same as before, although there does seem to be a little more bump, thump, and road noise on some surfaces.' Even the fresh-air circulation system didn't acquire top marks! 'The new fresh-air system has been skimped to get it in behind the existing facia and it passes only a gentle ram breeze, never a real cooling blast.' Autocar's conclusion demonstrated how much damage Nordhoff's successor had done in his brief tenure in office. Confidence in the Beetle as the spearhead of Volkswagen's future was undoubtedly waning, with aspects of the car's make up that had rarely been criticised previously, now being openly alluded to: 'Despite all the engineering improvements a lot of the faults in the Beetle still go on … it is still a long way behind its competitors in qualities like styling, comfort, and prestige....'

Road and Track followed a similar line, and their conclusion was equally damning: 'The Beetle … has three main points to recommend it: fuel economy, workmanship, and its reputation for long life and good service. If you value those three virtues above all others, then the Beetle is for you. Otherwise it is hopelessly outdated and outdone by both Japanese and American economy cars.'

'72 MODELS

The changes made to the Beetle in August 1971, and over the next 12 months, were relatively few and far between. The 1302 range and its torsion-bar 1300 cousin were both equipped with a far greater number of cooling louvres in the engine lid, the total rising from two banks of five each, to four of unequal number, amounting to 26 louvres in total. At the same time the drainage tray was discontinued, resulting in a decent-sized aftermarket business of bolt-on cowls to prevent water penetrating the engine compartment.

The rear window was enlarged on all models, this time by 4cm from top to bottom, which equated to an 11 per cent increase. Curiously, this final enlargement would be relatively short-lived, as once the Beetle's fortunes rested on Mexican production's shoulders, inevitably it was their specification, including the older window size, which endured.

Finally, all Beetles (save the 1200) received a new style of steering wheel. The latest with a large centre-pad made of less than charming brittle black plastic, embossed with the Wolfsburg crest, had four spokes and, as reference to a centre pad implies, no need of a separate horn ring. The operation of the wipers was now controlled by a stalk to the right-hand-side of the steering wheel, replacing the previous pull-out switch arrangement.

Specials, extra – extra!

In common with many other manufacturers, then and now, Volkswagen jumped on the bandwagon of producing limited-edition, special-offer models. As virtually all of them featured a combination of accessories included at no extra cost, plus on occasion special paint finishes, there is little to describe, other than to allude to each in some sort

↓ **For the 1972 model year, all Beetle saloons except the basic 1200 received additional louvres in the engine lid, taking the total up from 10 to 26 and, thanks to a slightly differently contoured lid, the number of banks from two to four. Sadly, the water drainage tray underneath the cooling louvres was dispensed with at the same time. Fast-forwarding to the days of the 1600 engined Mexican Beetle, louvres were very much still on the agenda, as the picture of this 1999 model year car illustrates.**

↑ The first of the special Beetles, at least as far as the British market was concerned, was the June Beetle; a 1500 model finished in the rather strident shade of Signal Orange (L20E). Launched in 1970, the onus was on the dealer to add the necessary accessories to make the car special. These consisted of overriders and rubber bumper inserts, together with anodised aluminium wheel trims. Volkswagen had already fitted the heated rear window! (The car illustrated has had custom wheels fitted, and it lacks rubber inserts.)

↓ The Super Vee was something of an oddity in the world of special-edition Beetles in that it appears to have been a 'dealer-fit' accessory package intended for either Gemini or Turquoise metallic 1302S models. As each element of the Super Vee's identity could be purchased separately, examples of such cars exist in colours other than those already mentioned.

of chronological order. Some cars were only made available to a specific market, while inevitably Germany boasted more specials than most other markets.

Key to the limited-edition models is undoubtedly the changed attitude at Wolfsburg, and the lack of faith in the Beetle as its bread and butter. Although, as the years passed by and the new generation of water-cooled cars drew ever closer, there was a real need to encourage people to buy one more Beetle – this was certainly not an essential in the early days.

In the summer of 1970, Britain saw the launch of the 'June' Beetle, a 1500 model finished in the rather loud colour of Signal Orange. This purely cosmetic special featured far from common chromed overriders, complete with rubber insert, a heated rear screen and, to round things off, anodised aluminium wheel trims.

Based on the 1302S, the Super Vee was another package of trim that could easily be installed at dealer level. Available in either Turquoise metallic or Gemini (an attractive light blue metallic shade), features included 4½J Lemmerz steel wheels, and a special Super Vee badge on the boot lid. Some straightforward 1300 torsion bar Beetles were also kitted out as Super Vees, adding fuel to the theory that here indeed was a dealer-prepared special.

With the arrival of the day in February 1972 when total Beetle production overtook that of the legendary Model-T Ford, almost inevitably a very special Beetle was produced to celebrate the occasion. The car was known in Germany as 'Der Weltmeister' and was based on the 1302S, as it was in America, where curiously it was marketed as the Baja Champion SE. For the British market, the World Champion was built around the torsion-bar 1300. Australian owners benefited from individually numbered plaques to celebrate their version of the World Champion, and so the variations on the theme went on. However, there was a common denominator whatever the market, and this came in the form of a unique paint shade, Marathon Blue metallic, and special steel wheels, again manufactured by Lemmerz, this time featuring the equivalent of 10 wide silver spokes, and a glossy black centre section, plus 19mm grey covers for the wheel nuts, and a shiny alloy centre cap embossed with the VW symbol. 6,000 Weltmeisters were produced for the home market; 1,500 for Britain. The proud new owners of such cars received a

↑ Weltmeisters across the world were fitted with special ten-spoke steel wheels made by the German firm of Lemmerz. Enduringly attractive, and consequently still sought-after many years later, the wheels were painted in silver with a black centre section. The nuts were covered with 19mm grey plastic caps, while the centre hub was capped with a shiny alloy cover, appropriately stamped with the VW logo.

↑ On 17 February 1972, Beetle production finally overtook that of the legendary Ford Model T. Volkswagen produced a special edition Beetle to celebrate the occasion, a car that was branded Der Weltmeister (the World Champion). Based on the 1302S, 6,000 examples were built for the domestic market. When the extras included were taken into account, purchasers saved some 300DM over the price asked for an ordinary 1600 engine Beetle, and they also received memorabilia to celebrate Volkswagen's new record.

↓ The World Champion model of 1972 produced for the UK market was something of an oddity in that, uniquely, it was based on the 1300 torsion-bar Beetle rather than the MacPherson-strut 1302S car. Because it was finished in Marathon Blue metallic, then a shade exclusive to the special edition, enthusiasts often referred to the model as a Marathon Beetle. 1,500 examples were prepared for the UK market and the edition sold out very quickly.

→ The GT Beetle was a UK-market-only special designed to celebrate the arrival of the 300,000th Beetle on British shores in December 1972. In reality, here was a German-market 1300S, a torsion-bar Beetle with a 1600 engine, produced in three 'fruity' colours which were described as Apple Green, Lemon Yellow and, as in the case of the car depicted, Tomato Red. Most of the rest of the package was little more than dealer-fit accessories, such as a tunnel tray, sports gear lever, and crucially a GT Beetle badge on the engine compartment lid. 2,500 such cars were produced.

→ GT Beetles were fitted with 4½J sports wheels and, unusually for the time in Volkswagen circles, radial-ply tyres. With the exception of the recently introduced 1303 Beetle, the GT was the only model available for the UK market to benefit from the new 'elephant's foot' rear lights, and the redesigned rear wings necessitated by this change.

↓ Part of the standard range on offer in Germany, the 1300S never officially made its way to the UK market, much to the annoyance of traditionalists. For here was a torsion-bar Beetle with the biggest engine then available, the 1584cc, 50PS, twin-port; and disc brakes were also incorporated, replacing the drums fitted to most models. Spot a right-hand-drive 1300S and it will be a GT Beetle that wasn't appropriately re-badged by a dealer at the time.

32-page *World Champion* booklet, a certificate depicting both the Model-T and the Beetle in 1302S guise, plus a commemorative medal that read 'Der Weltmeister Wolfsburg Germany 1972'. It was intended that this last mentioned item should be mounted on the glovebox lid. German owners received a much smaller medal; the purpose in this instance being to create one very special key fob. Finally, on the subject of Der Weltmeister, because the paint shade started as a unique colour for this special edition, a practice arose of calling such cars Marathon Beetles.

In the wake of the sale of the 300,000 Beetle in Britain on 15 December 1972, a special edition of 2,500 cars, each badged as a GT Beetle, and finished in a choice of three fruity colours – Tomato Red, Lemon Yellow, and Apple Green – was launched to the delight of enthusiasts. Costing just £20 more than the 1300 model of the day, the GT Beetle was a flat screen, torsion-bar model, powered by the 1584cc engine, and brought to a halt with disc brakes on the front wheels. Externally distinguishable not only by those fruity colours (in reality, Phoenix Red, Lemon Yellow, and Cliff Green), but also by black rather than colour-coded wing beading, and 4½J steel sports wheels shod with radial-ply tyres, the GT also featured the latest style of rear light, which at the time was only available on the recently released 1303 Beetle. Inside, the car sported the latest trend of cloth upholstery, a padded dashboard, tunnel tray, and a special sporty-looking gear lever. The reality of the GT Beetle was that it formed part of the readily-available range in Germany, where it was branded as the 1300S. This special right-hand-drive batch came into the country minus the GT badge, tunnel tray, and gear lever; the onus being on the dealer to add each of these before presenting the cars for sale in their respective showrooms. Inevitably, not all followed the guidelines and the occasional 1300S could be seen on British roads.

A home-market special to the tune of 3,500 examples, the Yellow and Black Racer was based on the yet-to-be-discussed 1303S. While the majority of the car was painted in Saturn Yellow, the boot and engine compartment lids were finished in black. The bumpers, also black, were adorned with a yellow central stripe, while the lower door and rear quarter-panels of the car were trimmed with a black stripe. Predictably shod with sports wheels, although these were of the 5½J variety, Pirelli were

→ The black-painted bumpers of the Yellow and Black Racer were highlighted with centre strips, in reality nothing more than yellow sticky tape. Note the louvres in the front valance, something normally associated with US-market cars fitted with air-conditioning. Although the Yellow and Black Racer was mechanically no different from a straightforward 1303S of the time, it's clear that the designers at Volkswagen envisaged upgrades and the potentiality of fitting an oil-cooler behind the apron.

→ Chrome and general bright-work was partially absent from the Yellow and Black Racer's make up, being replaced by black trim, a feature which extended to the bumpers and door handles, while the headlight rims and indicator housings remained shiny. Black decals adorned the door bottoms and rear quarter-panels. Note how the engine lid 1303S badge was finished in yellow, a move designed to make it stand out from the surrounding black paint.

↓ Dating from 1973, the Yellow and Black Racer was a home market special designed to make the 1303S model look more sporty. 3,500 examples were produced and all were finished in a combination of Saturn Yellow (L13M) and black paintwork, the latter colour being restricted to the engine compartment and front boot lids. Beefed up with 5½J VW sports wheels, the car was originally shod with 175/70 15 tyres, specially developed by Pirelli.

↑ In September 1973, in an attempt to appeal to the young at heart, Volkswagen introduced the Jeans Beetle based on the basic 1200. Finished in Tunis Yellow (L16M), the bumpers, door handles and all the trim was painted black. For the British market, sports wheels were fitted, but some countries received the regular wheel fitted with black hubcaps.

→ The interior of the Jeans Beetle featured denim upholstery, complete with large red stitches and reinforcing rivets in true jeans style. The door cards were trimmed with vinyl matching the colour of the upholstery. Like many another surviving examples, the denim seat covers on this car have been replaced due to the original fabric becoming frayed.

→ Departing from the standard practice of fitting chrome, or anodised aluminium, the headlamps and all the exterior trim was painted black on the Jeans Beetle.

entrusted with the task of supplying 175/70x15 low-profile tyres. Inside, the Yellow and Black Racer was endowed with an especially small and padded steering wheel, plus rally seats up front, which were also trimmed in black. Mechanically, the car was no different from other 1303S models of the day, despite the fact that the total run of 3,500 cars included the kind of front valance fitted to Beetles with air-conditioning as an option; an ideal starter for anyone choosing to tune the engine and fit an oil-cooler.

The proliferation of specials was such that it is impossible to describe them all in detail, or in more than a few cases even to make mention of them. From the 'Messenger of Spring' Beetle, a home-market offering available as a 1303, 1300, or even a 1200, the 'Black is Beautiful' limited edition, with its striking red upholstery, and the later City Beetle, a special dating from September 1973 based on the 1303 and fitted with 4½J sports wheels, a padded steering wheel, deep-pile carpets, reversing lamps and a heated rear window, to the 1303S-based Big Beetle, the curiously named Herringbone Beetle, an upmarket offering with a 1200 engine, and the 1303-based Chocolate Beetle, plus the 1200 Sun Bug, appropriately with a steel sunroof for the long hot summer of 1976, these sadly must remain names to conjure with.

One further limited-edition Beetle deserves a mention, for not only was this car a popular option, but it was also a name that was to spur further German-built examples and, years later, Mexican special editions too. This car was the Jeans Beetle, finished in its own Tunis Yellow shade, shod with 4½J sports wheels, decked out with black-painted (rather than chrome) trim, adorned with black lower side panel stripes complete with cut-outs to reveal the word 'Jeans', and somewhat unusually based on the 1200 base model, rather than Volkswagen's more upmarket offerings. However, as its name implies, this Beetle was targeted at the younger, possibly even first-time, buyer. So, on reflection, perhaps the choice of the 1200 wasn't quite so odd. The Jeans Beetle's most endearing feature was undoubtedly its upholstery, which was of blue denim, complete with large stitches reinforced with rivets, just like the real thing. Carry-all pockets on the reverse of the front seats mirrored those on real Jeans. When it is considered that the Jeans package also included a dipping rear-view mirror, passenger sun-visor, heated rear screen, and a radio, all of which were extra to the specification of the standard 1200, and that the price difference between the two models was negligible, it isn't surprising that in excess of 50,000 such cars were sold in a period of 15 months.

The last major development of the German-built era

If the arrival of the 1302 Beetle in the summer of 1970 had come as something of a shock to traditionalists, just two years later there was a further one of similar proportions in store. August 1972, for the '73 model year, saw the debut of the 1303 Beetle, the first such car to feature a truly curved screen, just like those of many other manufacturers' products. Planned to meet the demands of US legislation that in the end failed to materialise, by greatly increasing the distance of the driver and front-seat passenger from the windscreen, the enlargement of the glass by some 42 per cent undoubtedly afforded far greater visibility. Achieved by encroaching into the roof panel and through the shortening of the boot lid, to many purists – already offended by the unconventional suspension and shape of the 1302S – the redesign did nothing for the Beetle's aesthetics. However, the real step too far came for many when attention was turned to the dashboard. Gone was the dash that had stood the test of time from as long ago as the '58 model year, and in its place was a padded arrangement entirely at home in any contemporary car. The single instrument was now housed in its own moulded binnacle and sat above the sweeping length of moulded black plastic, which not only curved upwards at either end to house adjustable ventilation flaps, but which also contained, close to

↑ The 1303 Beetle was introduced in the summer of 1972 for the '73 model year, and is instantly recognisable by its curved windscreen, representing a 42 per cent increase in overall size. Spurned by some enthusiasts, due not only to the window glass but also to a modern plastic dashboard, the reason for its costly introduction was straightforward. Threatened legislation in the USA would have seen the flat-screen Beetle banned, as the distance between the driver and the windscreen was insufficient.

← For the UK market, and unlike the days of the 1303's predecessor, the car was available both with a 1300 and 1600 engine, the latter being badged with the 'S' designation to denote its extra power. The car pictured is finished in Sahara Beige, one of the less sparkling options of the time. Its wheels would have been added in later years.

← Considerably larger than the light housings fitted to earlier Beetles, the new clusters arrived at the same time as the 1303, and were initially restricted to such cars. Volkswagen enthusiasts soon found an appropriate nickname for the units, christening them as the 'elephant's foot' rear light! Their shape and size demanded a redesign of the car's rear wings.

The final years of German Beetle production

From August 1973 few changes of consequence were made to the Beetle. Admittedly the 1200 was finally revamped after several years of being positively ignored by many at Wolfsburg. Europa-style bumpers replaced the chrome blades, but, this being the base model, they were painted in matt black and adorned with a silver stripe instead of the normal black one. To a point, such cars were also victim of the 'removal of chrome to cut costs' syndrome – the headlight rims were finished in black, as were the twin tailpipes from the exhaust. The decorative grilles on the front wings were a thing of the past.

The 1303 Beetle benefited from modifications to the MacPherson strut suspension to give negative steering roll radius rather than positive, as had been the case previously.

In those early days of heading towards the handover to the Golf, which was launched to the world's press in March 1974, further variations on the Beetle theme, demanding no development costs as such, emerged. The 1200 was supplemented by the 1200L – a chrome bumper, full headlining, sound deadened, and consequently more upmarket affair, a practice that was now also on the agenda for the rest of the range as and when it was deemed appropriate. Thus there was a 1303L to be had for some markets, just as there was a base model, designated the 1303A that exhibited little in the way of trim and was powered by the old faithful 34ps engine.

The distinguishing marks of a '75 model year Beetle were two-fold. For most markets, the noticeable exception being North America, the front indicators, that had been universally mounted on the top of the wings since the '61 model year, were relocated to a position towards the ends of the bumper. Allegedly more noticeable in such a place to drivers of other makes of car (but not entirely compatible with the logic behind the repositioning of the Transporter's indicators to a much higher location on its front panel just a couple of years earlier), one point was a certainty; Beetle front indicators were much more likely to be knocked or damaged in their new location. Second, the rear valance became a humped single-skin affair and thus less likely to harbour rust than the flat double-skinned arrangement that had been in place since the summer of 1967. Also at the Beetle's rear end,

↑ **The 1303S was powered by the 1584cc, 50PS, twin-port unit, first introduced with the launch of the 1302S in the summer of 1970. The 1303, like the 1302 before it, featured the 1285cc, 44PS, twin-port engine. In the autumn of 1972, just a few weeks into the 1303's production run, the oil-bath air filter was replaced by a large plastic housing containing a paper-element filter, while at the same time the original Solex 34PICT3 carburettor on the 1303S was replaced by the 34PICT4. Towards the end of the 1303's life, in February 1975 the generator was replaced by an alternator, as illustrated here.**

the screen, a continuous channel to circulate either heat or cool air on to the glass. The glovebox lid was in the shape of a shallow rectangle, while adjacent to it was space for a radio, plus, by the steering wheel, rocker switches to cover any of the functions not carried out on the dual stalks by the sides of the steering wheel. Sadly, the glovebox lid no longer folded down flat, while for all its alleged advances, in design terms some of the switchgear looked much more of an afterthought than was the case with the traditional dashboard. Open the glovebox lid and the modern device of dividing the interior into separate compartments was relatively neatly executed, if not entirely practical.

For reasons of safety, both front seats were mounted on to the equivalent of steel pyramid structures that were welded to the car's floor-pan. As the seats could now be adjusted to a greater number of fore and aft positions via the use of handles attached to the central backbone, both the gear lever and the handbrake were moved further back on the 'tunnel'.

Externally, the 1303 had redesigned rear wings to accommodate a much larger style of light cluster, no doubt introduced with safety in mind. Due to its somewhat clumsy appearance and gargantuan size, enthusiasts immediately christened it the 'elephant's foot' rear-light cluster. To the chagrin of some, the insignia on the bonnet became a thing of the past as far as the 1303 Beetle was concerned, presumably because there was less room available to devote to such minor items.

Realistically, the 1303 was nothing more than a styling update, as both the 1300 and 1600 twin-port engines continued as previously, the only genuine update being the introduction of new-style air filter fitted with a conventional paper filter, rather than the oil-bath style of old.

the number plate cover was now made of plastic and instantly recognisable by 19 small corrugations moulded into the traditionally flat top.

The basic 1200 Beetle for the home market was downgraded somewhat, as its hubcaps were deleted in favour of plastic centre caps; while inside, the glovebox lid was no more, and plain coated hardboard replaced the more expensive trimmed panels. British market 1200s were subject to this last mentioned downgrade, but not to the other two for reasons best known to those in charge at Wolfsburg, or perhaps even at Emden.

Rack-and-pinion steering replaced the worm-and-roller set-up on both the 1303 and 1303S.

The practice of upgrading the specification for an existing model, adding variations to the theme with extra luxuries for some and a Spartan specification for others, came to a dramatic halt in the summer of 1975, for the '76 model year, when all but the 1200 Beetle were hacked out of the range. As for the 1200L it became more luxurious than it ever had been, and in such form soldiered on until the last cars left the assembly line in January 1978. For British Beetle devotees at least, one final special edition was produced to denote the Beetle's demise. Built during the course of September 1977, 300 Diamond Silver 1200L models were shipped to Britain, where, at least in theory, they were sold to would-be owners with a plaque indicating that here was one of the last Beetles, and its number was X out of 300. Confusion reigned supreme in that the number on the special plaque bore no relation to the chassis number, there being no guarantee that a low limited-edition number equated to an earlier build date as depicted on the chassis. Additionally, thanks to some of Volkswagen's swansong promotional material referring to 600 such cars, dealers could also legitimately promote a selection of white, blue, and red cars as Last Edition models, their chassis numbers often being later, in production terms, than those of the silver vehicles.

Final production years in the USA

For a Beetle that was always produced in Germany, rather than assembled or built in America, the US-specification car was often at odds with what was offered to the European market. From the arrival of bullet-style indicators, and towel-rail bumpers, in the

← **For the 1975 model year, and no doubt to make their location more in line with contemporary car design trends, the front indicators were relocated to the bumper, sadly making them more prone to damage from minor parking knocks.**

mid-1950s, to the 12-volt, vertical-headlamp, drum-brake 1500 of '67 model year origins, the variations on the general Beetle theme were noticeable. With the emergence of the aforementioned 1500, and the continuation of the 1300 as a separate model, another matter became clear: American customers received whatever was at the top of the model tree, at the expense of the other cars. In this instance, then, sadly the 1300 was quietly dropped.

With reference to the period covered in this chapter, due note has been made of the VW

↓ **When it was known that Beetle production was to cease in Germany, Volkswagen in the UK organised a Last Edition model. Based on the straightforward 1200L, but finished in a colour not previously attributed to Beetles in Britain, namely Diamond Silver, 300 examples arrived in the autumn of 1977. To complicate matters, 300 other cars, finished in the standard-issue colours of the day, which included Alpine White and Miami Blue, were also marketed as Last Edition models. Owners of the Silver cars, however, were presented with a plaque to mount on the dashboard indicating the car's status, and its number in the run. However, some dealers forgot to do this! A final confusion arose when some people mistakenly described the car as the Queen's Silver Jubilee model!**

Automatic being primarily designed to satisfy the average American's desire to shift without mastering the use of the clutch. Similarly, adequate mention has already been made of the double-jointed rear axle fitted universally to the VW Automatic from its inception, but to the American-specification manually-geared 1500 only with effect from the start of the '69 model year. This pattern of special specifications for the market that was undoubtedly Volkswagen's most important in the export field continued unabated to the end of German production and, thanks to increasingly stringent state rules and regulations, the concurrent demise of all Beetle imports. There was to be no Mexican-produced Beetle in America. However, not only did the American specification vary from its European market stablemate, unique specials, too, were to be the order of the day.

For the '70 model year, American-specification Beetles were fitted with the 1585cc engine borrowed from the Transporter, and destined to replace the 1493cc unit the following year on European market cars when the 1302S was introduced. To complicate matters, according to American author John Gunnell, the torsion-bar 1600 was invariably referred to as 'the 1500' despite the new engine. 1970 model year cars also benefited from larger wing-mounted front indicators, which incorporated the previously separate side marker lights, while a buzzer sounded if the door was opened and the key left in the ignition.

With the arrival of the 1302S, or Super Bug, the American market was allocated a two-tier structure of potential Beetle ownership, thus breaking the unwritten rule of many years standing that only the best would be on offer. The newcomer was the 1300 torsion-bar Beetle, although it was invariably marketed as the Custom, or Standard, Sedan, wasn't available as a semi-automatic, and lacked a certain degree of trim.

January 1973 saw all US Beetles fitted with an alternator rather than the generator of old.

August 1973 and the new model year witnessed a change in the specification of the bumpers fitted to American cars. Although still of the same basic square section shape, the new versions were considerably heavier looking and featured plastic end caps. Key to their design, however, was their ability to withstand impacts of up to 5mph without lasting damage – yet another requirement of US legislators, and made practical by the fitting of pneumatic bumper irons. (These bumpers remained part of the specification of the American Beetle until its demise; the European bumpers containing the front indicators were never a part of the US package.) In the same vein, a device was fitted which ensured that if the front seat occupants weren't wearing safety belts, the car's ignition was inoperable.

For the '75 model year all America-bound Beetles came with Bosch L-Jectronic fuel injection as standard. Californian legislation demanded such a change, and also required all cars to be fitted with a catalytic converter. Other states weren't far behind regarding fuel injection, but only really insisted on the converter for '77 model year cars. The fuel-injected cars ran on unleaded fuel and, to ensure this was used, the petrol filler neck was altered so that it only accommodated pumps with 'unleaded' nozzles. The script on the engine lid now advertised that the Beetle was 'fuel-injected'.

Although it has frequently been written that it was essential to replace the Beetle in America as sales dwindled away immediately after Nordhoff's death, the reality is somewhat different. From a low point in 1971, when Beetle sales dropped to 318,990 compared to 366,790 the year before, in 1972 and 1973 the numbers started to increase once more. Nevertheless, by this time the pattern was established of offering sales-boosting limited-edition models to a buying public eager to snap up extras at a near standard price.

First out of the unique box came the curiosity of the Baja Bug, already referred to in relation to Der Weltmeister. Interestingly, once World Champion celebrations were out of the way, a second edition of the Baja Champion SE was launched and based

↓ **Unlike cars produced for the European market, US models retained chrome-capped front flashers mounted on the wings to the end of Beetle production. With effect from the 1970 model year, the size of the American housings was noticeably increased, and the design changed so that the lenses became wraparound in appearance. Their function was threefold in that they acted as turn indicators, parking lights, and sidemarkers.**

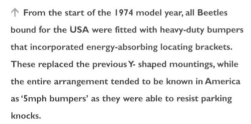

↑ From the start of the 1974 model year, all Beetles bound for the USA were fitted with heavy-duty bumpers that incorporated energy-absorbing locating brackets. These replaced the previous Y- shaped mountings, while the entire arrangement tended to be known in America as '5mph bumpers' as they were able to resist parking knocks.

↑ At the start of the 1975 model year, all Beetles received what might best be described as a single-skin but humped rear valance. For European market cars, the only advantage was that the old flat valance had always been prone to rust due to its double skin of metal. US-market valances of this new style were designed to house and conceal a catalytic converter, something that, at least in California, was now compulsory. All American cars were fuel-injected by this stage. A US-spec late rear valance had a cut-out for a single tailpipe. European models retained the traditional dual cut-outs.

once more on the Super Beetle. The package for this special consisted of Baja side stripes, what was described as a 'Superior Speed Shifter', Bosch fog lights, clip-on wheel trims, a stick-on walnut-look dashboard kit, rubber-faced bumper overriders, and a leatherette steering wheel cover.

The 'Sports Bug' of 1973 vintage was similar in appearance and specification to the home market Black and Yellow Racer, with the exception that the US-specification car featured chrome instead of the black-painted bumpers, headlamp rims, and so on – which didn't suit American tastes. Around 20,000 Sports Bugs were sold in America, and the special was even subject to its own marketing campaign, which somewhat ironically emphasised its limited, or exclusive, status with the words, 'if you don't get it now, you may never be able to get it all'.

During 1974, at a time when Beetle sales for the year slumped to 220,368 cars, special editions were thought to be invaluable, and were accordingly launched in rapid succession. There was the Sun Bug of the spring (a Harvest Gold metallic car most frequently seen as a Standard model, but available to special order as both a Super Bug and a Cabriolet), then came the Love Bug in Rallye (Phoenix) Red

and Raven (Ravena) Green, incongruously both finished with black trim and bumpers, followed by the Fun Bug, which as the name might possibly imply, consisted of little more than an accessory package.

'La Grande Bug' dating from 1975 was a Super Beetle-based special. Apart from a sunroof, this car was finished in either Ancona Blue or Viper Green metallic, the latter option being referred to as Lime Green in the United States. The interior was thoughtfully matched to the exterior with either dark blue, or bamboo-coloured leatherette and velvet cord being used. A padded steering wheel, the ubiquitous 4½J sports wheels, and a plastic wood-effect dashboard insert were also included. Like the 'Sports Bug' before it, 'La Grande Bug' was launched against the slogan, 'you don't drive in it, you arrive in it'.

As a footnote to the American story and to the chapter in general, it is worth indicating just how few Beetles were sold in the United States once the next generation of water-cooled cars started to emerge. From a disappointing 220,368 in 1974, the figure tumbled to 78,412 the following year, and a mere 23,213 in 1976. This total nearly halved again for what was to be the last year of sales, when just 12,090 Beetles were sold.

CHAPTER 5
MEXICAN BUILT BEETLES
1978 TO JULY 2003

From the demise of the German-built Beetle, and the immediate introduction of Mexican-built cars for a number of European markets, until the day in August 1985 when the last shipment of such vehicles arrived at Emden, realistically there were few specification changes. Instead, special models began to appear with what some regarded as monotonous frequency, and it is to these cars that later paragraphs in this chapter tend to be devoted. Following the cessation of imports to Europe, slowly but surely the Beetle developed, and these changes are duly noted. While Mexican buyers were delighted to know that quality budget transport was always to hand as long as Puebla produced the Beetle, their increasing affluence demanded that Nordhoff's philosophy of continual improvement was reinstated to its rightful place. The cars produced in the final years of the old millennium and the first few years of the 21st century were a far cry from the nadir of the mid-1970s. Beware the cynics who point to a Mexican Beetle that is just a few years old, but exhibits rust on a scale not seen since the bad old days, and recall that such cars were built for a salt-free land, a place were the climate was so temperate that a heater was an unnecessary luxury.

Specification changes 1978-1985

Although at first glance the initial batch of Mexican imports appeared identical to the last German-built 1200L Beetles, there were a number of variances. Bodywise, the Puebla plant had never taken on board the most recent increase in the size of the rear window that had occurred in Germany at the start of the '72 model year, in August 1971. Likewise the humped and single-skinned rear valance, a part of the German specification from August 1974, had failed to cross the ocean to Mexico, presumably because threats of catalysts linked to the American market

were irrelevant here. Other variations on the theme included the return of anodised trim on the 1200L's running boards, and chromed tailpipes instead of black-painted affairs, plus the inclusion of the 26 louvres on the engine lid, that had been part of the specification of the 1300 from the early 1970s, later 1302S models, the 1303, and 1303S German-built Beetles. Inside, the two-speed fan was deleted from the 1200L's specification, while front-seat headrests became standard. An anti-dazzle mirror was also added to the Beetle's list of essential ingredients. The AC alternator was replaced by a DC generator, and, to the delight of many, radial-ply tyres finally became standard.

With the exception of variations in the list of paint shades available, there were no changes to the Mexican Beetle until the end of July 1981, when the engine cover lost its louvres, and a brake warning light was fitted to the right of the speedometer. With effect from May 1982, all Beetles were fitted with an electric screen-washer pump, replacing the traditional pneumatic type, although a small percentage of imports had already been so endowed for the previous 12-months.

Realistically there were no further changes of significance made to the Beetle until a point past the date in August 1985 when the last official shipment of cars was made to Europe. During the next 12 months several modifications occurred, one of which was definitely of the type where it is wondered why nobody had thought of it before. Instead of fixing the seals for the engine and boot lids to the main body of the car, using a method almost guaranteed to generate rust within a few years if the Beetle in question was not particularly well cared for, now the seals were attached to the lids, a much more satisfactory option. Another modification was undoubtedly one of modern-day sophistication, as a key-operated alarm system, connected to the doors, was added. Other changes included a revised window-winder handle taken directly from the Golf

← Mexican-built cars exported for sale in Europe after the demise of German production tended to look very similar to the older models. However, after the decision had been made to cease this arrangement, the Mexican factory inevitably started to update the Beetle to meet the demands of its home market. By the start of the 21st century the external appearance had certainly moved forward, as the car in the picture demonstrates. Six paint shades were available in 2001; the car illustrated being finished in Tornado Red.

↑ Mexican Beetles exported to Germany for sale across Europe were very similar in appearance to the cars manufactured towards the end of production at Emden. Powered by the faithful old 34PS engine, the car could hardly be described as speedy, but in terms of its appointments – decent cloth upholstery, black padded dash, and heated rear window, for example – and its price, the Beetle still added up to affordable motoring for more than just a few diehards.

↓ This 1985-registered Mexican Beetle is finished in Alpine White. Other colours available included Mars Red, Atlantic Blue, and Selvas Green; all plain colours, a metallic option not then being listed. The first two shades mentioned were also standard to the Golf and other members of the water-cooled Volkswagen family. The owner of the car pictured has swapped the original wheels for the popular versions as supplied on the World Champion Beetle, and added one or two other appropriate accessories.

assembly line of the day, plus smoother door lock buttons, which again had Golf in their origins.

Perhaps of most importance in the early post-export-to-Europe era was the emergence of the Mexican Beetle with the more respectable 1600 engine. Distinguishable by its compression ratio of 6.6:1, a bore and stroke of 86.5 and 69mm respectively, the brochure writers claimed a 'net power' of 50PS at 4,000rpm, entirely in keeping with the old German-manufactured power plant. No reference was made to the engine's capability in terms of a top speed, or for that matter its acceleration from 0-60mph. Almost inevitably, the recently deleted engine louvres made a welcome comeback, more or less restoring the Beetle's looks and feel to the days of the larger-engine cars in Germany.

In October 1986 the door and side card trim became blue, and this colour scheme was somewhat controversially extended to include the headlining. Of more genuine importance, but not really catching media interest, was the news that at the same time Beetles gained an intermittent wipe system. For the '89 models, which were launched in October 1988, the passenger footrest was dropped as a less than essential piece of the car's make up, while a two-spoke steering wheel, of the design fitted to Polos during 1982 and 1983, replaced the previous rather Germanic version. October 1987 saw the decided advantages of electronic ignition introduced, while a fashionable downgrade from large painted hubcaps to unavoidably smaller black plastic centre-caps was also carried out. Likewise, the fresh-air system was discontinued, although this could hardly be described as a move to boost sales. Conceivably it was acceptable to dispense with the notion of a central warm air outlet to the windscreen when the two corner vents were still remaining, and the climate in the country was such that steaming up, or the need to defrost were far from normal occurrences. Somewhat unusually, an engine bay light was fitted, but not a corresponding one for the boot!

Whether or not the adverse reaction to the blue headlining introduced in 1986 had been sufficiently severe to demand a change; nevertheless, from October 1988 grey became the dominant colour. During the following model year, the steering wheel changed once more, this time to one borrowed from the GL trim Golf of 1984 and 1985 vintage, while alarm switches were fitted on the front and rear sections, in order that detection might be made of any lid being opened.

From October 1990, Beetles were fitted with a two-way catalytic converter, integral with the silencer, which in turn was served by a single tailpipe – all of which was in readiness for compliance with new emissions legislation due to come into effect from January of the following year. A 34 PICT carburettor was fitted and the fuel filler size was revised to ensure that the car couldn't inadvertently be filled with leaded fuel. At the same time other modifications occurred, and these included, heat exchangers without fins, and a redesign for the wheels, with the adoption of a style similar to those of many a Brazilian-produced Beetle, amounting to 20 near-square cooling slots, as opposed to the traditional eight elongated ones of many years standing. Inside the car, there was a new rear-view mirror, which dipped and, more significantly, was attached to the windscreen. Borrowing from the parts bin, Golf Mk2 headlamp and hazard-warning switches were adopted, doing little to make the dashboard appear less Spartan.

October 1991 for the 1992 model year saw further tweaking of relative insignificance, an example of which would be the relocation of the washer bottle to the side panel left of the fuel tank, when viewed from the car's front. However, of greater importance was the introduction of a Deluxe version of the Beetle in April 1992 that was branded as the Sedan GL, thus using the latest Volkswagen terminology for any model. Essentially a trim package,

no doubt based on the success of a series of special-edition models, that dispelled the rather basic feel that the Beetle had developed in the later years of the 1980s, raising more interest in importing such cars to Europe, albeit most definitely unofficially and without more than the most tacit of support from Wolfsburg, or its satellites. Chromed hubcaps made an immediate comeback, a top-of-the-range GTI style steering wheel was added, a rear parcel shelf was fitted, even speakers for the radio were included in the lower corners of the door panels. Sadly, within a very short time, some of the components of the Deluxe had been deleted, including both the rear parcel shelf and a one-piece carpet, but at least the principle of a more luxurious Beetle had been accepted.

Again in response to the threat of more stringent emission laws, the Beetle received a further engine update. On the agenda this time was Digifant Fuel Injection, which was first introduced in October 1992 in preparation for the new laws swinging into action the following January. General specification changes appeared legion, but in most instances they were not that significant. It should be noted, however, that the two-way catalytic converter of old was replaced by a three-way version, with integral silencer and lambda probe. The cylinder heads were modified to accommodate long-reach spark plugs, while the pistons were domed for higher compression (7.7:1). The electric fuel pump was fixed to the right-hand-side of the frame head, while the floor-pan was modified to lodge the fuel-injection computer. Similarly, the bodyshell was adapted to facilitate a new route from the rear luggage compartment to the engine for the main wiring harness, while the engine bay was widened a little to accept the latest engine. Visible changes were the deletion of the trim strip on the car's bonnet, and the addition of a 1600i badge on the engine compartment lid.

Updates the following year included, at long-last, the arrival of front disc brakes, an alternator to replace the generator of many years standing, larger and chunkier chromed bumpers as standard (identifiable by a much wider centre strip), and a different design of steering wheel, based on that of the Golf CL of 1990 vintage. Interior design work, although beneficial to the Beetle's cause, was limited to a new Pearl Grey shade of headlining and interior trim, while the carpets and floor mats were held in place by new plastic retainers.

→ By the year 2000, both the bumpers and headlamp rims of Mexican Beetles were colour-coded. Generally chrome and other bright-work was a thing of the past, bringing an elderly design as up to date as practically possible.

Come October 1995, the best way to summarise the changes made would be to say that the Beetle enjoyed a makeover, taking into account the trends in trim style made in recent years. Additionally, the car was re-branded with a Deluxe model known as the 'Clasico', and a standard Sedan referred to as the 'City'. While the Classic retained disc brakes, the City reverted to drums, an indication of the style of the differences between the two models.

Generally, from this date Beetles came with colour-coded headlamp trims and bumpers, plus black door mirrors, door handles, engine lid catch, boot handle, and quarter-light surrounds. Even the VW roundel on the boot lid became a black plastic affair, while the old-fashioned notion of displaying the car's credentials on the engine lid was summarily discontinued. At the same time the crescent-shaped air vents disappeared from the specification, while the Classic benefited from modern velour upholstery, and all Beetles were fitted with a remote sensor alarm.

Inevitably, more changes were made, including a further selection of steering wheels, and the abandonment of hubcaps in favour of centre caps once more. However, realistically, the Beetle of the '96 model year could be recognised as being from the same updated stable as a new millennium issue. Special editions continued to come and go, culminating in the delightfully neo-traditional Beetle produced to say farewell to a legend; the Última Edición of 2003.

Special Models

Realistically, as with their German predecessors, the special, or limited-edition, Beetles produced in the era of Mexican supremacy, were centred on trim packages, special paint colours, and additional items, on sale at what amounted to special offer prices.

The first such car, the so-called 'Silver Bug', was one of great significance in the history of the Beetle, in that it was produced to celebrate the 20 millionth Beetle rolling off the assembly line. Finished in silver, with black stripes along the lower door and rear quarter-panels, plus an identifying decal on the engine lid, the car's interior was adorned with black and white tartan upholstery, matched to similarly trimmed door and side panels, plus a special gear-lever knob carrying a commemorative plaque. Additionally, a radio came as standard, as did radial-ply tyres, and a heated rear window. The finishing touch was a key fob, also bearing a 20-million logo.

In the spring of 1982 Mexico produced its own version of the Jeans Beetle, this time available in two of the standard colours from the range of paint options. The Mars Red or Alpine White cars were adorned with stripes on the lower parts of the doors and rear quarter-panels that included the Jeans Bug motif. The same logo appeared on the engine lid and on the gear-lever knob. As with the original Jeans

Extraausgabe.

→ While the Mexican Beetle was exported to Europe, Volkswagen seemed intent on inundating would-be purchasers with a series of special edition models. One of the most popular was the so-called Winter Bug of 1983 vintage. Finished in Ice Blue metallic, the 1200L Beetle's package included discreet lower side stripes, chrome trim rings on the wheels, and the interior featured special blue-grey upholstery and carpets, plus a radio.

Beetle, the majority of the trim was finished in black, a story that included the bumpers, headlamp rims, door, boot and engine lid handles, tailpipes, quarter-light surrounds, exterior mirror, hubcaps, and more. The car's upholstery was of denim material; with matching blue side trim panels. On this occasion a leather Jeans patch was sewn onto the sides of the seat backs.

In the autumn of the same year, the Special Bug made its debut, and was available in Mars Red or Metallic Black, the latter option being more commonly seen. Like the Jeans Beetle before it, the catalogue of trim finished in black was extensive. On this occasion the side stripes were finished in gold, as was the motif 'Special Bug' that appeared on both the engine and boot lid. The gold theme extended to the car's interior, with black and gold tartan upholstery. Remaining interior trim was finished in black; while the car's wheels were sprayed with gold, rather than the normal silver, finish. As with the Jeans Beetle, a radio came as part of the standard package.

1983 saw too further specials, the 'Aubergine Beetle' in the spring, and the 'Winter Beetle' later in the year. As with preceding specials, both cars featured special exterior and interior trim, a radio, and little else, but of all the Mexican specials built in the era of exports to Europe these two were undoubtedly high on the list when it came to Beetle aesthetics. The Aubergine Beetle featured unique Aubergine paintwork that extended to the car's wheels, which in turn were decorated with 'chrome' trim rings. Silver stripes adorned the Beetle's sides, while, inside, the upholstery was of an aubergine-coloured cloth with matching door and side panel trim. The Winter Bug was finished in Ice Blue Metallic paint, featured chrome trim rings, black and silver side stripes, blue grey upholstery, and grey blue carpets, this last feature being extended into the luggage area behind the rear seat. Finally, for 1983, a special version of the standard colour Alpine White Beetle appeared. Once again, its extra features majored on side stripes, wheel trims, and a special interior cloth, on this occasion being blue-grey in colour.

1984 saw a revival of the Winter Bug, the appearance of the 'Sunny Bug' in February and, later in the year, the debut of the 'Velvet Red Beetle'. Inevitably the Sunny Bug was finished in Sun Yellow paint and, apart from featuring narrow black and white side stripes and chrome wheel trims, its most striking attribute was its cord-ribbed upholstery

which was of a revolting curry shade! Fortunately, this colour wasn't extended to the door trims or side panels. By contrast, the Velvet Red Beetle's upholstery was the epitome of good taste; being finished in red and blue striped velour, with matching Mauritius Blue vinyl trim elsewhere. Externally, apart from its special paint shade, the car could be identified by the now ubiquitous chrome wheel trims and lower body stripes, on this occasion of blue vinyl. However, the stripes on the rear quarter panels burst into life, developing into a not unattractive flower motif.

As with many of the Beetles already described, the only special to be produced in 1985 was supported by its own sales brochure. Commonly referred to as the Jubilee Beetle, as its decals contained this message, and its arrival in Germany more or less coincided with Wolfsburg's gigantic gathering to celebrate the Beetle's 50th Birthday. In reality, and as the brochure was headed, this was 'Der letzte Käfer'. The final edition of Beetles to be exported to Europe totalled 3,150 cars, and all were finished in 'Zinngraue Metallic'. Without doubt this was one of the most attractive specials produced so far; its specification outclassing anything issued previously. Apart from the '50 Jahre Käfer' motif fixed to the engine lid and left front quarter panel, and the twin silver stripes on the lower door and rear quarter panels, this special featured a mass of chrome or bright-work reminiscent of the good old days, sports wheels boasting 165 SR15 tyres, and green-tinted heat resistant glass.

↓ **When the decision had been taken to cease imports of Mexican Beetles for consumption on the European market, a final special edition was conceived. This was the '50 Jahre Käfer', a car also designed to commemorate the 50th anniversary of the Beetle, dating its origins back to 1935 and the first running prototypes. 3,150 such models were produced and they arrived at Emden on 12 August 1985. Many were snapped up by enthusiasts who thought the end of the road for the Beetle had finally been reached.**

↑ → Like most other limited editions, the Jubilee Beetle was offered in a special paint colour which was described in the special brochure produced to promote it as 'Zinngraue metallic'. The general specification was high, in that the Jubilee model also featured green-tinted heat-resistant glass, 'silver' decor lines along the lower side panels, sports wheels shod with 165 SR15 tyres, a Brunswick Radio, particularly attractive striped cloth material for the seats, a four-button steering wheel purloined from the Golf, and 50-year decals.

← To confirm its special identity, the Jubilee Beetle was adorned with '50 Jahre Käfer' branding on both its engine lid and, as depicted in the photograph, on the left-hand front quarter-panel.

↓ September 2002 saw the launch of the Sedan Summer, yet another special edition Beetle, although in this instance production was limited to just 800 examples. The car was available in Azul – a relatively bright shade of mid-blue – and in Amarillo, as illustrated. The Sedan Summer featured colour-coded upholstery, and sported logos on the rear quarter-panels and, again as shown, on the engine compartment lid. Like many a special edition model, the Sedan Summer represented excellent value for money, being only slightly more expensive than the standard models of the year.

Inside, the hardwearing cloth upholstery was finished in grey with discreet red and grey stripes running through the central panels. The door cards and quarter panels were trimmed with well-matching vinyl, while the carpet was similarly of a tasteful grey hue. Finally, the four-spoke steering wheel, very similar in style to that fitted to a contemporary Golf GTI was a big improvement on the rather dated affair that had made its debut in the early 1970s and had been standard issue on all Beetles since.

Free from the restraints of supplying Europe with cars, Volkswagen in Mexico could concentrate on its home market for which, at least initially, there seemed little need to produce specials. However, come May 1989, a 'Celebration edition' was launched, followed in the autumn of 1991 by 'El Auto del Siglo', or the Car of the Century Special, which was debuted simultaneously with a 'Wolfsburg Edition' model. By 1994, specials were once again dominating the scene, with no less than four such cars available. These were the 'Edition 1' that was finished in Aubergine metallic, the curiously-named, considering its paint hue of black, 'Fire Beetle', a revival of the ever-popular Jeans trim, and the 40th Anniversary model (referring to four decades of Beetle sales in Mexico) finished in Kansas Beige. Specials came and went virtually to the end of production in 2003, one of the last such being the Sedan Summer. Limited to a run of just 800 cars, this special was available in two exclusive colours, namely Azul (an attractive shade of mid-blue), and Amarillo (a light yellowish green). Colour-coded seats, with fabric interpretations of the car's exterior colours, contrasted with grey adjoining

← The 'Última Edición' was limited to 3,000 cars and was available in two colours, Harvest Moon Beige (or 'Beige Luna' to crib from the special brochure produced to promote the last cars), and Aquarius Blue ('Azul Aquario') as reproduced here. The emphasis was firmly placed on offering a final-fling Beetle that was loaded with as many 21st-century comforts as possible, while also recalling some of the highlights of German production from much earlier years (spoiler non-standard).

material, were this particular special's other highlight, the package being more or less completed by the application of Summer logos on the rear quarter panels and the engine lid.

Recalling the words of Dr Jens Neumann on the day he announced that Beetle production was finally set to end, his emphasis centring around the car bowing out at its best. If by that he meant that the 3,000 'Última Edición' Sedans produced to bid the Beetle farewell were the most magnificent such cars ever made, many would concur with such sentiments. Combining the latest developments in Beetle styling with some of its most treasured attributes of yesteryear, the Ultimate was available in two attractive colours, both of which were thoroughly modern, yet successfully hinted at shades available at a time when production outstripped any other single model anywhere in the world. Although Aquarius Blue and Harvest Moon Beige were also paint options for the Puebla-manufactured New Beetle, somehow they seem to have been designed solely for this very special classic Beetle. Continuing this nostalgic theme, chrome and bright-work trim reappeared in a big way, with an anodised aluminium strip adorning the bonnet, the running boards, and the waistline, while door handles, engine and boot lid catches, plus the hubcaps and bumpers once more luxuriated in full chrome. The jewel in the crown, though, had to be a final airing for the modified version of the Wolfsburg crest badge; over 40 years after it had last appeared on the boot lid of a Beetle. A similar gesture to Beetle days of old was the inclusion of whitewall tyres, while interior trim and the addition of a radio, CD player, and four speakers demonstrated that the Beetle had been equally at home in the new millennium.

The very last Beetle, an Ultimate Edition finished in Aquarius Blue, was despatched to the Automuseum in Germany; a permanent record of 58 years of continuous production of a single model.

↑ Without doubt, the definitive item in the retro feel of the 'Última Edición' was the reappearance of the always greatly-coveted Wolfsburg crest bonnet badge. The version selected for reproduction had previously been fitted to Deluxe models, including Cabriolets, dating from August 1959 through to October 1962.

↑ For the 'Última Edición', not only did chrome hubcaps make a welcome reappearance, but that fad of the 1950s and 1960s, whitewall tyres were also firmly back on the agenda. Chrome bumpers, headlamp rims, door handles, and shiny door mirrors, plus bright running board, side and bonnet trim strips – features long since abandoned on Mexican-built Beetles – evoked the spirit of production from earlier years. One quirky addition came in the form of a chrome bezel between the rear light clusters and the wings.

↓ The interior of the 'Última Edición' featured, amongst other items, colour coordinated seating fabric, a glovebox lid and corresponding metalwork around the speedo dial finished in the body colour of the car, a rear parcel shelf, and a radio and CD player complete with four speakers.

CHAPTER 6

THE VOLKSWAGEN BEETLE CABRIOLET

With the Beetle's lengthy history already outlined, and the changes it underwent from the early post-war days to the end of German production and beyond having been explained, much of the Cabriolet Beetle's story has also unknowingly already been told.

It was always Ferdinand Porsche's intention that, together with the saloon and a sunroof model, the convertible Beetle would be an integral part of the Volkswagen programme. From the earliest of days, open-top prototypes featured heavily in the many test programmes designed to bring the Beetle to production. Such a car was predictably present at the ceremony surrounding the laying of the factory's foundation stone, its purpose on that occasion in part being to transport Hitler to the nearby station once the festivities were over. Similarly, on the occasion of his 50th birthday, the Führer was duly presented with a Cabriolet. This vehicle was regularly used, if not by Hitler; it survived the war years and is now resident in Volkswagen's museum at Wolfsburg. Once the British were in control at Wolfsburg it wasn't long before experimental work with open-top Beetles recommenced, the most famous of these being the Radclyffe Roadster, so-named as it was built for the use of Colonel Charles Radclyffe, the senior officer at CCG headquarters. However, interesting though these vehicles might have been, none was produced for commercial sale, and it is to the Nordhoff era we have to turn to find the true origins of the Cabriolet that formed part of Volkswagen's Beetle range until January 1980.

Once established, there was one golden rule applicable to the Cabriolet for many years, encompassing the majority of markets, until the end of production. Just as the USA was scheduled always to receive the Deluxe, or, in later years, most powerful Beetle, so too was the open car forever based on the specification of the top of the range saloon, offering would-be owners the latest and finest in Beetle technology and styling.

However, lest the Cabriolet's significance appears all-embracing to the Beetle's good fortunes, reality is such that between the debut of the Karmann-built model in July 1949 and the last example leaving the Osnabrück assembly line in January 1980, 331,850 such cars had found their way on to the world's highways. This total, a result of 30-years production, equated to less than the number of Beetles built in 1957 alone, and accounted for just 1½ per cent of total production when this figure could finally be calculated in 2003.

But for a quirk of fate

Unable to meet the current and anticipated demand for the Beetle saloon, while recognising that investment in the basic product was essential to long-term success, Nordhoff was painfully aware that resources were not available to be sidelined for a niche market, open-top version of his Volkswagen. Key to any soft-top project's success was that Wolfsburg must not be involved in building the car, although marketing a cabriolet as an integral part of the Beetle range was not an issue. As more than one firm of coachbuilders were not only eager to be involved, but had already dabbled with prototype work in the British era, a solution to perceived difficulties was at hand. Wilhelm Karmann, whose Osnabrück coachworks had a history dating back to 1874, was one such; Wuppertal-based Josef Hebmüller and Sons (of 1889 pedigree) was the other.

Nordhoff eventually awarded Karmann the licence to build a four-seater cabriolet, and Hebmüller a two-seater coupé. By the end of 1948, three prototypes, each based on saloons of 1945 or 1946 vintage, had been completed by the latter firm. The greatest problem the company faced was one of chassis flex, noticeable through the poor alignment of the doors within just a few miles

← **More or less handcrafted, and certainly so in the case of the many layered, glass-windowed hood, the Cabriolet Beetle naturally cost considerably more than the equivalent saloon. However, for the money paid, owners enjoyed all the advantages of open-air motoring, but also completely watertight travel when the weather was inclement, as well as a mechanical and trim specification at least as comprehensive as that of the top saloon in the range. The Cabriolet shown in this photo dates from 1964 and is finished in Java Green.**

↑ **This red Hebmüller has been treated to a series of period accessories, including fender skirts, Bosch horns, a bonnet-mounted bug deflector, large rear stone-guards, and spotlights. Most would argue that the large-logo hubcaps are wrong for a Hebmüller, in that smaller VW roundel versions appeared in May 1949 just before the launch of the coupé edition of the Beetle. The car is finished in Coral Red, paint code L50, and dates from either 1949 or 1950.**

of road tests. Similarly, the glass of the windscreen would crack as the windscreen surround flexed. By the time Nordhoff gave his seal of approval in the summer of 1949 by ordering 2,000 open-top coupés, such difficulties had been ironed out. General flexing was countered by strengthening the car's sills with a box-section pressing, welded underneath each; while at the Hebmüller's rear, extra side panels, and strengthening plates were welded in. A large cross-member found a place under the rear occasional-use seat, while the engine compartment was also home to two box-section reinforcing panels. Likewise, the front bulkhead was reinforced through the expedient of welding in panels adjacent to the driver's and front-seat passenger's legs respectively. To solve the windscreen issue, the production Hebmüller incorporated a heavy tubular frame in the squared-off windscreen surround that, in turn, was complemented by a steel plate welded across the base of the windscreen, noticeable in the front luggage compartment.

However, to would-be purchasers of the Hebmüller, the most important aspect was its stunning design, highlighted by a specially-crafted engine lid cover, reminiscent of the boot lid, but incorporating a magnificently sculptured scoop that

terminated above the number plate and was home to the single brake light in the manner of production saloons of the time. Hebmüller's skills were also such that the whole roof, in itself an expensive and thoroughly waterproof affair, folded away behind the occasional rear seat, making way for a tonneau cover to take its place.

Available in a variety of single colours – black, red, and white being the most popular – the Hebmüller was also offered with two-tone paintwork, a couple of the most attractive combinations being black and red, or red and ivory. Despite the hefty difference in price of some 38 per cent between that of the ordinary Export Beetle and the near-handcrafted Hebmüller, the prospects for its success looked extremely rosy. Sadly, this was not to be the case, as on 23 July 1949 a fire broke out in the paint-spraying department of the Hebmüller factory and spread rapidly. Although production restarted just four months after the fire, with a healthy 104 cars being produced in November, 119 in December, and 125 in January 1950, it became increasingly apparent that Hebmüller was experiencing mounting financial difficulties. Numbers dwindled rapidly, so that by April the firm's output was down to a miserly 17 coupés. During 1952 Hebmüller was registered as

↓ The Karosserie Hebmüller badge was positioned towards the bottom of the right front quarter-panel.

↓ ↓ All Hebmüller Cabriolets featured semaphores positioned ahead of the doors in the front quarter-panels, and all were identical in design and size to those fitted on contemporary saloons. Note also the Karosserie badge and a proud owner's decision to fit a coveted 100,000 kilometre badge.

↑ The key to the Hebmüller's elegance was undoubtedly the graceful contours of the engine compartment lid. Although, at first appearance, this might have looked like a reworked boot lid, in reality this was a special handcrafted panel. Additionally, and unlike the Karmann, the Hebmüller coupé's hood folded completely out of the way when open-air motoring was prescribed.

↓ Black was undoubtedly one of the most popular choices when a Hebmüller was ordered, but many owners also opted for a second side colour. The choice was large, with Coral Red, Yellow, Beige and, as here, Ivory being on offer. Viewed from the front, the Hebmüller might almost be mistaken for a Karmann Cabriolet, hence most enthusiasts' pictures being taken of the rear of the car.

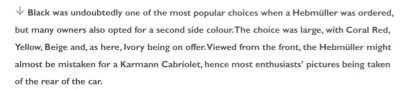

bankrupt, while Karmann completed 12 coupés on their behalf at its own works. Volkswagen's records indicate that 696 Hebmüllers were built in total, although figures have been produced indicating a higher total of 750 cars. The remaining vehicles are undoubtedly the most coveted in the Beetle enthusiast's world.

Karmann's story starts in a similar way to that of Hebmüller, with a first prototype having been built around the 10,000th Beetle to be manufactured after the war, a car that dated from November 1946. This first car lacked some of the ingredients of the Beetle Cabriolet that would eventually be put into production, most notably the absence of a rear-view window, and the lack of a wind-down facility for the rear side windows. Following the development of both a second and third prototype, a series of 25 pre-production Karmann Cabriolets were subjected to extensive testing that they duly passed with flying colours. Nordhoff accordingly placed an order for some 2,000 later in the same month of August 1949. Production initially amounted to two cars per day, but within a few months this had increased to six, while during April 1950 the 1,000th such vehicle had left Karmann's Osnabrück premises. For his part, Nordhoff had placed a second

↑ **The Cabriolet depicted dates from either 1951 or the first nine-months of 1952, as evidenced by the ventilation shutters in the front quarter-panels, and the charming paint colour combination of Dove Blue and Beige, an option offered until October 1952. Many Cabriolets left the factory with two-tone paint, and the main body colour of Dove Blue could be specified with the optional side colours of Ivory or Beige. The owner of this example has been particularly careful to retain originality, as can be seen from the wheels, which, as shown in the picture, would have left the factory with Dove Blue rims.**

↓ **The two-tone paintwork option of Black and Coral Red was one of the first to be offered on a Karmann Cabriolet, and was subsequently withdrawn at the beginning of 1951. The owner of this Cabriolet is using the car as Karmann intended – with its hood down. The operation to lower the hood was a simple one, although rearward vision was a little restricted for the driver, as the material and its frame didn't drop into the car's body.**

The last year of the decade accounted for 10,995 Karmann Cabriolets, and the 1960s got off to an equally promising start, the high point being 1962, when 12,005 cars were produced. From here, annual production hovered at around the 10,000 mark, until the recession years, with 1967 proving to be the low point, when just 7,583 Cabriolets were built. Despite the oft-repeated call that the Beetle was past its sell-by date as the 1970s dawned, Cabriolet production boomed, with the car's best-ever year being recorded in 1971 when 24,317 vehicles were produced. However, by 1975 such numbers had dwindled to 5,327 cars and, just like the saloon, the end was in sight. This seemed to stimulate additional interest, as before the Beetle Cabriolet bowed out in January 1980 to make way for an equivalent Golf, numbers had jumped back up in leaps and bounds. From 18,511 such cars in 1978, the last full year of production saw an extremely healthy 19,569 Cabriolets built.

← ↑ **The rear view image and interior shot are of the same vehicle, a 1964 Java Green Cabriolet. Although cars of this vintage still boasted no more than 34PS they remain much sought after today. Volkswagen went to considerable lengths to ensure that the fittings were well designed and of exceptional quality, while also maintaining the highest standards of aesthetics.**

Cabriolet upgrades

Having established already that the Cabriolet was based on the top of the range model – unless by some quirk of fate a specific market demanded an 'economy' engine or suchlike – the car's evolutionary process is easy to track. From straightforward Export specification for many years, the Cabriolet first adopted the 1300 engine, albeit briefly, then the 1500, followed by a new body shape and power unit attributable to the 1302S, and finally, and possibly most successfully of all, the soft-top was built around the 1303S. Classic in its appeal in the 1950s and 1960s, the hood, its chief distinguishing feature, blended more than adequately with the Beetle's

order in February, once again for 2,000 cars. Like Hebmüller's product, the Karmann Cabriolet needed a number of strengthening measures to stop flexing in a vehicle without a roof. (Press images of an early car with its doors out of alignment would have done little to convince would-be buyers of the Cabriolet's attributes.) Rails were welded on to the bottom plate of each sill, while an inner strengthening panel was added to the rear of the front door pillars, and to the base of the 'B' posts. Further measures centred round transversely-mounted metalwork under the rear seat, a weightier panel above the engine lid, in part devised to provide a fixing point for the hood, and much stronger rear quarter panels than those offered on the saloon.

The Karmann Cabriolet's instant appeal was such that from the 364 vehicles that were built in the first few months in production, the number had increased to a run of 2,695 in the following year, 1950, while in 1951 3,958 four-seater Cabriolets followed. This pattern of ever-increasing numbers continued throughout the 1950s, the sole exception being 1954, when a drop of some 500 vehicles occurred.

↑ The Karmann Cabriolet's hood was complex in its make-up, and consisted of layers of combination rubber and horsehair. Almost without precedent, the rear window was made of glass from the start of production. The style of hood depicted, and the size of the window, was current from October 1952 to 1958.

↑ The new look of the 1968 model year Beetle somehow didn't lend itself to the Cabriolet version, even though the basic components were the same. Unfortunately the hood now looked ponderous, if not blatantly top-heavy. Sales, however, were unaffected, and indeed were higher than those of the two preceding years, with in excess of 13,000 being sold in the first year of the car's new look.

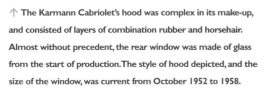

← Once larger engines were offered in addition to the 34PS unit, Volkswagen created something of an unwritten rule that the Cabriolet would always be based on the highest-spec saloon model; a car that inevitably had the largest engine. Hence, when the 1302 shape arrived and the car some called the '13 oh dear' was endowed with a 1600 engine, with its roof removed it became the obvious choice for Cabriolet status. Sadly, if the 1500 version of the Cabriolet looked cumbersome, this car looked even worse. The 1302 pictured is finished in Iberian Red, although the effects of a lack of polish seem to have taken their toll on the paintwork.

↓ Although, in later years, engine lid badges became much simpler in style, in the lifetime of the 1302 the Cabriolet received all the letters to which it was entitled. Accordingly, this car has a larger than basic engine – hence the 'S', and was endowed with the best trim level possible – hence the 'L'.

↓ Owing to the absence of air intake slots between the hood and the engine compartment lid – reference the metal-roof Beetle – all early Karmann Cabriolets were endowed with 18 air slits cut into the lid vertically. In the summer of 1957, when the saloon received a much larger window, the design of the engine lid slits changed, becoming horizontal and in two banks of five either side of the lid's central spine.

↑ Other than the change in design of the bumpers (which took effect in October 1952) there is little externally, at least with a frontal shot in mind, to distinguish between a Split and an Oval era version. By 1953 the last of the remaining two-tone colour options were on their way out.

sloping headlamps and gracefully proportioned engine lid and boot lid. However, a little was lost with the arrival of the new '68 model year saloon, and by the time of the 1302S, the hood had started to look more like a straightforward, but ill-fitting, wig. Somehow, the curved nature of the 1303's windscreen and the particularly neat fixing of hood to metal transformed the Cabriolet's looks; the elegance of earlier years was fully restored.

Key to the Karmann Cabriolet's existence was its hood, a masterpiece of the craftsman's skill. For many years beautifully assembled on a wooden and metal frame, it comprised three separate layers, the outer of vinyl (or in some instances mohair), the inner of cloth or, later, plastic, and the centre a blend of rubberised fabric mixed with horsehair. From 1972 the frame became all-metal in construction, resulting in an ability to fold it some 5cm flatter than previously, although, unlike the Hebmüller, the Karmann's hood was never intended to disappear completely. Towards the end of production, the traditional horsehair padding was superseded by equally effective, but undoubtedly less expensive, foam.

Unlike the saloon, the Cabriolet always had cooling louvres stamped through the engine lid. Initially comprising two sets of 18 vertical openings, their purpose was instantly apparent when it was realised that the soft-top Volkswagen lacked the essential row of cooling apertures afforded to the saloon under its rear window. For the '58 model year the arrangement changed, with vertical slits being replaced by horizontal ones; still in two banks, but now totalling just five in number in

↓ Although the picture depicts a full view of a Cabriolet, two areas are of particular interest. The first, and rather irrelevant to the soft-top car specifically, is to note the side-fenders fitted to the rear wheel arches. The second concerned all European Cabriolet owners purchasing a car before the summer of 1961. Without a fixed upper body, it was necessary to position the semaphore indicators elsewhere. After a short period of residency in the front quarter-panel, with effect from late 1949 the semaphores were sunk into the rear quarter-panel just to the rear of the driver's, and front-seat passenger's, door.

→ The Karmann badge of a pre-1961 vintage was a simple rectangular affair. Curiously, it was to become more elaborate, rather than less so, with the advent of later models.

→ → The Karmann badge illustrated was fitted to all Cabriolets manufactured in 1961 or after, and continued to be positioned towards the bottom of the right front quarter-panel.

↓ Although a significant number of aspects of the Cabriolet were distinct to the car, the dashboard was not one of them. The example portrayed dates from October 1952 to the end of Oval production in the summer of 1957. The owner of this Cabriolet has been to town on the accessory front, and the lengthy list of items extends to a Petri 'Pealit' steering wheel, dash-mounted auxiliary gauges, a useful extension designed for easy operation of the reserve tank control, a Dehne petrol gauge, period radio, chromium-plated window-mounted tax disk holder, a green Perspex 'cover' for the interior mirror (designed to cut glare from following drivers' headlights), not to mention a screen-mounted fan and picnic tray!

each instance. For the '70 model year, two banks became four and the openings increased to 28 in number. When the 1300 Beetle saloon and above also received four banks of cooling slots, totalling 26 in number, the Cabriolet's were accordingly standardised with those of its metal-top brethren.

Initially located in the front quarter panels, in January 1951 the Cabriolet's semaphore indicators were moved to the rear quarter panels, in a position just behind the doors, a place they remained in until the abandonment of such devices in favour of flashing indicators.

The Cabriolet not only always had a rear window, but also one made out of glass – an almost unheard of feature in open-top cars in those days. No attempt was made to emulate the split rear panes of Beetle saloons built before March 1953, although the tiny area of glass apparent in the first years of production must have afforded drivers very little in the way of visibility. For the '58 model year, the point when the saloon received its much larger rear window, so too did the Cabriolet, on this first occasion the enlargement amounting to a generous 45 per cent. 1966 saw a further increase of 30 per cent, while 10 years later, with what was to prove

↑ ← Despised as it might have been by some elements of the VW fraternity, the 1303 model lent itself wonderfully to the soft-top version. As the photograph illustrates, the hood blended particularly well with the new model's curved screen. Towards the end of Beetle Cabriolet production a change was made regarding badging, with the near universal adoption of a simple VW1303, no matter what the size of the engine or the level of trim. This proved particularly useful on the Italian market, where the 34PS engine was added to the options primarily for tax purposes! This car is finished in Viper Green metallic, a favourite for Golf owners.

↑ The curved screen and much deeper dashboard gave the 1303's interior a spacious and modern feel, almost in line with its contemporaries. Some dashboards featured a full-width wood-effect inlay for the rocker switches, radio, and glovebox, although the rather brittle four-spoke steering wheel was not to everyone's taste.

↓ The Mars Red paint works well on this late model 1303S Cabriolet, which also carries sports wheels, and a white interior. The large wing-mounted indicators with integral side lights, the bumpers with energy-absorbing brackets, and the plastic end-caps for the rubber protection strip, all identify it as an American-specification car, as would the single tailpipe for the fuel-injected engine if it was visible.

to be the final change to the specification, a heated rear window became almost universally standard, the home market missing out on such luxury, while American owners had to wait until 1977.

More minor changes exclusive to the Cabriolet are relatively few and far between, but there are one or two that merit a mention, while it's also worth noting that throughout its illustrious existence would-be soft-top owners had an additional, attractive, and desirously exclusive range of colour options to choose from.

The vehicle's Karmann origins were noted via a rectangular enamel badge attached to the body of the car on the right-hand front quarter panel, bearing the words Karmann Kabriolet. During the course of 1961, this was replaced by a more attractive version, more delicate in shape, and complete with a decal, while simply bearing the word Karmann. Engine lid badge strategy changed in the later years, with 'Fuel Injection' being emblazoned on an American-specification car, while for the European market it was felt unnecessary to label a vehicle as a 1303LS, when the simple designation of 1303 was just as effective.

To conclude this round-up of the Cabriolet Beetle, one or two special models, directed towards the American market, emerged in the final years of soft-top production. Of these, the Triple White Cabriolet tends to be the one most frequently seen at enthusiast gatherings. Distinctive in that not only the car's paintwork, but also its hood and interior, including door cards and seat coverings, were finished in white, this also has to be one of the least practical soft-top Beetles ever made. The Champagne model was first produced in 1977, and, for reasons best known to Volkswagen, was created to celebrate the sale of the one-millionth Rabbit (Golf) in the USA! The first series of cars were finished in Alpine White, had an 'opal' interior, and a pale sand hood, plus other luxuries such as deep-pile carpet. A second edition of the same car was available in either Ancona Blue Metallic, or Red Metallic. This special edition had an ivory hood plus interior trim, a wood-panelled dashboard, whitewall tyres and the ubiquitous sports wheels. The final special was aptly named the 'Epilog' and, perhaps appropriately, was a sombre affair finished in each and every respect in black. A true limited-edition, just one example was available to each Volkswagen dealer.

↑ ← The Triple White Cabriolet – white paintwork, white hood, plus white seat-covers and interior trim panels – was just one of a series of special editions designed to boost sales in the latter days of the Cabriolet's production. Created especially for the American market, where the majority of sales were engendered anyway, keeping the interior pristine was something of a nightmare for the more fastidious owner.

CHAPTER 7
CHOOSING AND BUYING YOUR BEETLE

That the Beetle was and remains a phenomenon is unquestionable; the world's most produced car of a single type could hardly be anything other. However, beware, for all that glitters is not necessarily gold. Some Beetles aren't anywhere near as desirable as others, and here the reference is to cars of the 1970s, and particularly to the 1302 and 1303 series, excluding the Cabrio in the latter instance, of course. Then there are the Mexican Beetles, almost modern-day cars, and consequently attracting a double dose of depreciation. The first measure is simply the same as that of a four-year-old Golf being worth more than a ten-year-old one. The second centres on the idiosyncrasies of a car built for a left-hand-drive market running about on right-hand-drive roads, and the equally potentially dubious nature of a car switched over from one to the other to placate the whims of the British motorist. Fortunate for them, American drivers are not faced with such a dilemma, as woe betide anyone trying to bring a Mexican Beetle into the States.

In summary, it is fair to say that the older the car the greater the possibility that it will be worth more money, but in practical terms it will be increasingly unsuitable for regular driving on ever-busier roads. Pre-1961 model year European specification cars lose points on their outmoded semaphore indicators, as nobody knows where to look for such a primitive indicator of intentions these days. Later German-built models lose out on twin-port cylinder heads, while many a 1200 Beetle of a similar vintage is simply too basic to attract enthusiastic buyers. Fuel injection on an American-specification Sedan or Cabrio can be suspect, as the system employed was known to be both somewhat unreliable and complex to work on. Older cars gain points in terms of build quality and aesthetics; Mexi Beetles score a plus with their velour upholstery. The 1303 loses out on both counts, except in Cabrio form, while the 1500 Beetle of 1967 vintage may have it all, with earlier model aesthetics and a real driver's engine. As for Cabrios, they are

in a class of their own, expensive when new and inevitably still carrying a premium price for open-top luxury now!

The conclusion, then, has to be that 'you pays your money and takes your choice'; but, of course, you should part with your cash wisely, and be sure that the Beetle in question is not being offered at an overinflated price. Conversely, if it's undervalued, beware – it might be genuine, or it might be a quick sale rot box! Finally, if the list of woes that ensues tends to put you off, remember that minor mechanical defects to components such as steering joints, wheel bearings, brakes, and wiring are easily and cheaply rectified, and the Beetle's general survival rate is one of the best.

The Beetle for you

The question of which Beetle you want should be a relatively easy one to answer, even to a novice in the field. Without doubt, it has to be the very best example of the type of car you want, from restoration project to Concours entrant and prize-winner; at the kind of money you can both afford and believe to be appropriate in terms of today's market place.

If a would-be owner's main aim in life is to prepare a vehicle for Concours competitions, which model he or she chooses is more or less immaterial. The same might be said of the person who derives more enjoyment out of restoring or renovating a vehicle than actually driving it; while someone proposing to customise a model, likewise merely requires a suitably cheap donor vehicle on which to work.

As far as everyday use goes, most would suggest that a late model of Mexican origin would be best and, as mentioned, these cars still appear to be depreciating like any other modern Volkswagen at the moment, so it's possible to pick up a low-mileage

← **The process of selecting, and subsequently purchasing, a car can be both stressful and painful if anything goes wrong. New and shiny paint can conceal many a maggot. On the other hand, the delights of finding a really solid car of enduring character are plentiful.**

→ To consider or reject out of hand? The reality of the matter is a car's rarity value. A 1970s Beetle in this kind of condition would be dismissed out of hand. A 1949 Hebmüller, on the other hand, found abandoned to the elements would not only be worth buying but should also be snapped up quickly before anyone else discovers its existence.

↓ A fully-fledged Concours winning Beetle isn't going to be all that cheap to purchase. Of recent years, the Beetle's popularity has seen something of a downturn, at least compared to the all-conquering Transporter. However, the Beetle will make a comeback, and many would opt for a Concours model that is up for sale, rather than a cheaper car that will cost money to restore to pristine condition.

example at a good price. Perhaps the only doubt is one of rust treatment, bearing in mind the lack of such needs in Mexico, and the necessity of adding the same before running the car around on the salty roads of a British winter.

Buying a Beetle – from whom?

It is a known fact that a Beetle bought from a specialist dealer is going to cost more than one purchased from an individual. Rogue traders do exist, and a buyer needs to be wary, but on the whole a transaction is safer when a 'professional' is involved, and a dealer might offer a warranty, or guarantee. There might also be the possibility of a finance deal.

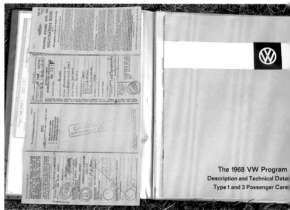

↑ A mass of surviving paperwork, including the original registration document and service booklet usually indicates that a car has been in good hands.

On the other hand, sadly, many Beetles on specialist dealers' forecourts lack detailed history and paperwork. This can be where a private sale is best, providing the seller can offer details of lengthy ownership, or at worst a list of previous owners, service bills, MOT certificates, and all the other documents associated with vehicle ownership. Individuals should also be able to furnish a potential purchaser with their reason for selling the car.

It is normally wisest to view any car on the dealer's forecourt, or at a private individual's home. A

thorough test drive should be regarded as essential, and a vehicle rejected if the seller is not prepared to comply with this demand. It almost goes without saying that you should never view a vehicle in the dark, or in adverse conditions, such as wet weather.

Assessing a Beetle for purchase

PAINT

Amazingly, there are some 1960s Beetles around that are still wearing the coats of paint applied by Wolfsburg, Emden, or wherever. Finding a Split or an Oval in such condition is certainly more difficult, but well-looked-after 1970's models, particularly Cabrios, in original condition are relatively commonplace. Later model Mexican Beetles should be as they left the Puebla factory, or something is amiss.

For the potential Concours entrant it is important that a vehicle, whatever its age, is finished in a shade correct to the year of manufacture. There must be no evidence of other colours present, but a silver sticker bearing the colour code and description would be ideal. The vexed question of original paint compared to a top class, professional respray occurs at this point, and, to be honest, both are acceptable. Concours rules don't as yet stipulate which a judge should prefer. Inevitably, to many people a deep gloss shine with a life of under 12 months appeals more than a 30-year-old coat of paint, complete with the occasional well-touched-in stone chip and the unavoidable slight degree of fade. But there are those who take the point of view that it is better to reward genuine care for originality than it is to shower points on those who have sufficient funds at their fingertips to pour gloss on a vehicle.

On the general issue of resprays, potential purchasers should be wary of a freshly painted vehicle. A quick coat of glossy paint can disguise a whole host of flaws, ranging from blatant panel rot, to bubbling, and all sorts of other horrors. An honest seller with a recently resprayed vehicle is likely to have kept a photographic record of the preparation work carried out. Paintwork bearing a resemblance to orange peel, showing obvious runs, or transparently dull and flat, even though recently applied, should be avoided.

A flat, dull, and sorry looking Beetle that hasn't been repainted recently should not be dismissed out of hand. Providing there are no signs of rust, or

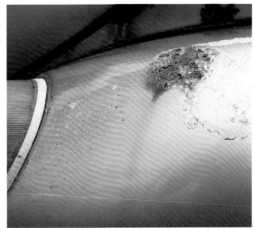

other forms of decay, an application of 'T-cut', or other proprietary brands, followed by a couple of coats of decent polish, can often work wonders. The exceptions to the rule, however, are metallic-painted vehicles that have lost part or all of the clear lacquer coat applied on top of the colour. Nothing can be done in such cases, other than to repaint the vehicle. Early 1970s Beetles were particularly prone to this problem, although the chances are that such an issue will have emerged before now, and that the problem will have been rectified.

BODYWORK

Starting at the top, the Beetle's roof is a robust affair, but look out for creeping rust where the gutter is folded back on to the main section. Likewise, check the gutters near the bottom of the rear window, as this area of metal is particularly vulnerable. Inevitably, sunroofs – either canvas or, particularly, the metal wind-back versions of later years – are prone to leaks and should be thoroughly checked in appropriate conditions. Canvas is relatively easy to replace, but a rusted or rotted metal sunroof is best regarded as

↑ **Cal-look cars are often painted in garish colours. While the option selected would obviously have appealed to its creator, when the time comes to part with the car, the chosen colour, in this case pink, may not be to everyone's taste.**

← **Beetles produced in the 1970s and coated with metallic paint often deteriorate badly if routine cleaning and polishing has been neglected. The lacquer coat fails after prolonged exposure to the weather, causing the vulnerable metallic paint to fade and eventually break up.**

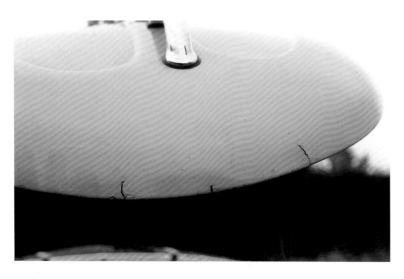

someone else's problem. Beware, also, aftermarket sunroofs, as not only can these weaken the car's structure, but they may have been fitted in an amateurish way. Finally, the Cabrio's roof is not only costly to replace, and such soft-tops do deteriorate with age, but also consider the inherent damage to the rest of a car if the roof is leaking.

As the Beetle lacks a conventional radiator grille, predictably the boot lid is particularly vulnerable to stone chips, which if not treated cause unsightly blemishes. Some owners have fitted bonnet bibs to limit the damage, but these hold their own problems as water runs down inside the material, collects at the base, and is likely to cause rust. One other option is a Perspex bumper-mounted stone-guard, although some enthusiasts regard such devices as unsightly. A further consideration has to be the boot lid where the metal has split at the tip.

Some Beetles have been known to develop blemishes under the windscreen caused by rust creeping out from underneath the rubber seal.

↑ Bonnets aren't cheap to replace, although as they are not particularly prone to rust a second-hand one could well be an excellent choice. However, keep an eye open for torn, or split, metal. It's both unsightly and difficult to repair.

→ Door hinges can wear with age, causing the door to drop and eventually scrape on the running board. Similarly the door might have been accidentally forced back on itself, causing the metalwork adjoining the hinge to crumple. Neither problem is terminal to a Beetle's existence, but is best avoided when making a purchase, as remedial work is time-consuming.

Beetles built after July 1967, or July 1966 in the case of American-specification models, are referred to as vertical headlamp cars. The wings of these cars tend to rust in the area at the base of the headlamp rim, although replacement panels are both relatively cheap and readily available.

With the exception of the larger-boot 1302 and 1303 models, all Beetles have a well at the front of the boot that is home to the spare tyre. The bottom of this is another vulnerable area, well known for attracting damp and, consequently, rust – and cutting out, replacing, and welding is quite costly because of the amount of work involved. The 1302 and 1303 Super Beetle models are fitted with MacPherson strut front suspension, the top mounts of which are attached to the front inner wings, making them an important area to check for corrosion. The struts also need to be removed before the body can be separated from the floor-pan, making them more inconvenient to work on when compared to the torsion-bar equipped models. The inner wings on all cars can rot close to where they meet the visible wing. Although welding resolves this problem, a Concours judge will frown on visible signs of remedial work.

Doors tend to rust at the bottom, and a good test is to open the door and check the condition of the metal lip underneath and by the rubber seal, while also confirming that the drain holes are clear. Damage in the form of an ugly crease can appear on the door due to seized hinges. Doors also tend to drop with heavy usage, straightforward age, or the neglect of one or more owners. Imbalanced trim lines tend to confirm whether a vehicle has experienced such problems. Doors can be replaced, although care will be needed to select one of the right age for the car, as there were a number of changes made over the years. Replacement of the hinges is a much more tricky issue and, if this is needed, the car, unless rare, is best avoided!

The rear quarter panel is another rust hot spot, and all would-be owners should check the car thoroughly for signs of filler, or bubbling. Rust here is symptomatic of even more serious problems involving the sills, or heater channels. Looking under the car, behind the running board should give an indication of the condition of the sills. Also, check the jacking points for solidity, although no self-respecting Beetle owner would ever consider lifting the car using this method. Then, with the doors open, squeeze the area between the running board outside and the floor of the car inside. If it gives, or creaks, there is rot to contend with, and the sills will need replacing. Heater channels are readily available, but the surgery involved in cutting out the old and fitting the new is quite protracted.

Next, check the car's floor-pan, particularly in the vicinity of the battery located under the rear seat on the right-hand-side of the car. Again, new pan halves are available, but welding and painting is linked to replacing old with new. Look under the rear wings in the vicinity of the torsion bars. Rust here is serious, while for the Concours judge badly-welded panels invariably lead to a heavy deduction of points.

At the rear of the interior of the car, the luggage compartment behind the back seat should be examined, as rust can often be found where the wings meet the floor, the result of a leaking rear window seal. Externally, look carefully at any car fitted with crescent-shaped extractor vents behind the rear side window. Rust might have bubbled through the bodywork below these, and will be costly to eradicate with any degree of professionalism.

The rear bumper mounts need checking, as the area tends to attract mud, salt and other problem materials, while the double-skinned engine lid of pre-1968 model year cars can easily bubble and rust at its base. The valance of these cars and those produced up to the '75 model year are similarly double-skinned and prone to rust, the later single-skinned variation on German-built models being infinitely preferable. Mexican cars despatched to Germany in lieu of the original product sadly reverted to the double skin. Finally, beware the pre-August 1955 car with a valance that has been hacked and adapted to receive the twin tailpipes of later models. Replacing this panel will be extremely costly; that is providing you can obtain one in the first place.

Last of all, check out the retaining strips that hold the rubber seals in place in both the boot and engine compartments. These are notorious rust attracters, and once established it's virtually impossible to get rid of. In some instances it's likely that the seals are held in place by little more than imagination. The Mexicans had the answer when they attached the seals to the lid rather than the body, and this can be a remedy for owners of earlier cars, providing Concours entry is not on the agenda.

← Rear quarter-panels have always been noted as one of the most vulnerable places for rust. Beware a car with rust here. In many instances the cause could be attributed to rusting of the sills allowing an ingress of water. A perfect repair was, and is, a relatively costly business.

← With effect from the 1971 model year, all Deluxe versions of the Beetle were endowed with crescent-shaped air-extractor grilles situated behind the rear passenger side windows. Although they did serve a useful purpose, the vents tended to attract rust in the metalwork below, and for an individual it is almost impossible to defeat. Beware the car with bubbling bodywork in this vicinity.

↓ The potential rustiness of the rear valance depends entirely on the age of the Beetle. In practice, all valances fitted before August 1974 were double-skinned and, as such, are prone to rust. Post this date, the valance's shape changed, becoming humped in appearance, while also single-skinned. The early example shown here with a raised 'H' pattern is particularly difficult to source. The 'H' section, concealed when the lid is closed, rarely rusts, unlike the exposed lower part of the panel. Consequently, a restorer might well cut the 'H' section from the rusty original panel and graft it into a later version of a new double-skinned panel.

↑ Nobody would contemplate using semaphores on a daily basis, and only a few would consider conveying a Concours car to a show without some additional means of notifying fellow drivers. Semaphores, new-old-stock or otherwise, still seem to be readily available. Early ones varied from those fitted to later models.

→ Although somewhat unsightly and giving the impression of a Beetle with ears, these accessory indicators go some way to solving the problem of near-invisible semaphores.

↓ The four-stud wheel finished in cream with a black centre section, a product of the latter part of the 1960s and first fitted to the 1500 Beetle of 1967 vintage, suited Volkswagen's image of the day. Less prone to the surface rust that plagued the silver-painted wheels of August 1969 and onwards vintage; even if they were so afflicted, repainting wouldn't have been too onerous a task.

EXTERNAL TRIM, WINDOW GLASS AND LIGHT FITTINGS

Unless contemplating the purchase of a really early Beetle, trim will be readily available and not prohibitively costly. Chrome bumpers, unless of Brazilian origin (which should be avoided), are relatively expensive, although they will last for many years, and hence rusty ones shouldn't prohibit the purchase of a car. (Even stainless steel examples are available nowadays.) Hubcaps, both the earlier domed variety and later flat ones are available, while sports wheels without hubcaps can easily be sandblasted and resprayed if they look unsightly. Replacing pitted handles, doors, bonnet, and boot will be expensive if the car is a 1950s model. Genuine window-seals are available for most later models, while there are good-quality copies available, at a price, for just about every Beetle. Beware cheap rubber seals and window surrounds imported from South America as they are of very poor quality, and will split and crack quickly.

Tarnished, or otherwise dulled, headlight reflectors of any age will result in an MOT failure!

Semaphore indicators were fitted to home and European models until the '61 model year, and most owners would consider them at best ineffective and at worst dangerous on today's roads. If contemplating purchasing a Beetle of this age, check whether panel-damaging and inappropriate indicators have been added, or if bumper-mounted, acceptably discreet additions have been fitted.

WHEELS AND TYRES

For classic Concours purposes it is essential that the wheels fitted by Volkswagen at the time the Beetle was first registered are still in place, and many judges consider it preferable for a vehicle to run on the type of tyre it would have had originally.

Five-bolt wheels until 1967 and four-bolt thereafter, 16in wheels with 5-00 x 16in tyres before October 1952, and 15in wheels with 5-60 x 15in rubber from that point. Allegedly that simple, only the 1303S-based Big Beetle of 1973 vintage broke the rules, being allocated fatter wheels shod with 175/70 HR15 radial-ply tyres.

Wheels were minus cooling slots for many years, these first appearing in August 1965, while until the 1960s gathered pace there was a great emphasis on painted wheels with an attractive combination of two colours, one for the rim and the other for

the centre part. Much later, as the 1970s dawned, glossy paint gave way to rust-prone silver spray, a finish also allocated to the so-called sports wheel, as fitted, for example, to the GT and Big Beetle, and the sought-after wheels that formed part of the package associated with the World Champion Beetle of 1972.

While under ideal circumstances all tyres should be of the same make, it is dangerous to mix sizes, and both illegal and potentially lethal to run a combination of radial and cross-ply tyres. Care should be taken to spot buckled rims on steel wheels, which might imply damage to suspension components. Badly rusted and pitted steel wheels cost a reasonable amount to refurbish, although it is fairly easy to acquire ones in good to excellent condition on the second-hand market.

Beetle interiors

HEADLINING

For many years made of woollen cloth, for the 1963 model year the headlining was of white vinyl stamped with a polka dot kind of pattern. This, in turn, became plain; while in the later years of Mexican production the headlining tended to be colour-coded to the general appearance of the product, if not the specific trim of the car. Base model cars always featured just the basic roof headlining, while other cars were favoured with a covering that extended around the rear window.

Cloth headlinings tended to darken with age and be prone to rot, particularly around the rear window. Replacements are costly and usually require the services of a professional to fit. A vinyl headlining may become stained, particularly if the driver or passenger is a smoker, but can usually be cleaned with proprietary cleaning aids. Torn or split headlinings cannot be effectively repaired.

FLOOR COVERINGS

There are many variations in colours of carpets and, for that matter, just how much of a car is covered in such material. However, rubber mats in the footwells were applicable to all German-built Beetles at least, and to find a car with carpet in this area without rubber underneath is simply incorrect for the Concours judge. The rubber footwell mats are hardwearing, but can become tired around the driver's foot pedals. Replacements are available, although some late 1950s and earlier 1960s cars with colour co-ordinated rubber are a much trickier

↑ As far as the British market was concerned, 4½J x 15 steel sports wheels made their first appearance on the GT Beetle of 1973 model vintage. A number of vehicles received them subsequently, while some cars, such as the Big Beetle, a special of the 1974 model year and based on the 1303S, were fitted with a 5½J version of the same wheels, albeit that the brochure produced to promote the edition referred to them as Rally Wheels!

← A rotten, discoloured, or torn headlining is both relatively costly to replace and difficult to fit. This example is of Australian origin and from the days when the Clayton factory was manufacturing Beetles, hence its unusual corduroy-style appearance.

→ Although the cloth seats illustrated have survived remarkably well, most early cars needing a full restoration will require replacement covers. The original pattern material, although expensive, can still be sourced from suppliers in mainland Europe.

↓ Leatherette seats tend to be fairly robust, but be careful if they have split, as new covers can be costly to fit, and matching isn't always straightforward. On later models, particularly the basket-weave examples of the late-1960s, a note of caution is necessary. Black holds no issues, but heavily-soiled 'cream' examples take many patient hours to clean satisfactorily, while some can acquire an unsightly yellowish tinge that no amount of perseverance will remedy.

proposition. Carpet on the 'walls' of the front foot compartments, on the heater sills, and over the back seat in the luggage area can become worn with age, or rot due to sunlight or damp. Later carpets are easy to match, earlier ones not so, and it is surprising to see just how many Concours entrants fail to take the trouble to get this right. For daily drivers, or non-show cars, carpets should not present a problem.

The general rule in the case of the rubber mats referred to earlier, is to lift them. This should reveal rust-free and damp-free metal. Be extremely wary of water clinging to the back of the rubber, or bright orange rust stains.

SEATS

For many years, leatherette was the standard covering for the seats in all Beetles, although some early cars, notably Splits and to a lesser extent Ovals, could be found with cloth upholstery. In the 1970s, cloth began to reappear alongside basket-weave vinyl, while by the time of the Mexican Beetle, hardwearing

fabrics were not only universal but also particularly attractive in many instances.

Hardwearing though leatherette and vinyl is, the more elaborate the covering, notably those fitted to Deluxe models, the more stitching involved, and the greater the chance of splits occurring. While the black vinyl of the late 1960s and 1970s is easy to clean, some of the creams or off-whites of this period discolour permanently, while the attractive duo-tones of earlier years can prove difficult to restore to an acceptable Concours condition. Fortunately, help is at hand in the form of excellent reproductions that are readily available, albeit at a hefty cost.

Curiously, cloth from the 1950s has tended to stand the test of time much better than that fitted in the 1970s. Beware rot caused by sunlight on the backrest of the rear seat, the almost inevitable wear and tear visible on the driver's seat, plus stains on any of the upholstery. Finding appropriate upholstery for a 1970s car is difficult, while 1950s patterns will be costly. Also, be cautious of the Cabrio with cloth upholstery, as it certainly wasn't an option when the car was new! To reiterate, Mexican Beetles, even those dating from the earlier years of the 1980s, were fitted with hardwearing but attractive cloth upholstery, and this pattern continued through to the very last such cars. Tinted glass, of course, helps preserve the upholstery of such vehicles.

DASHBOARD, STEERING WHEEL, HANDLES AND WINDERS

Although the main elements of a Beetle's interior have been covered, without the sundry elements discussed below an owner wouldn't get very far.

Until the arrival of the 'L' versions of the 1500 and 1300 in the late 1960s, all dashboards were of painted metal, ensuring longevity, and ease of restoration if necessary. Only one factor can present a problem, and this relates to the fitting of a modern radio necessitating hacksaw work to the original opening, or holes made in a similar way to fit auxiliary instruments. Unless the rest of the car is pristine, which is unlikely, such a vehicle is best avoided.

Padded coverings for the flat-screen dash and the plastic dashboard of the 1303 Beetles can be more of a problem – inescapably, with the effects of age and sunlight, cracks and splits are likely to appear as the material becomes more brittle. Regrettably, these days not all that many new old stock (NOS) fitments, or good second-hand examples, are to be found.

← If a period radio hasn't been fitted, or if it has subsequently been removed, the radio blanking panel should be in place, or at least available. Beware the car with damage to this area caused by the decision to fit a modern and bulkier stereo system.

Auxiliary, or accessory, period instruments don't necessarily detract from a car, while in the case of a fuel gauge fitted to a pre-62 model year car, it's a positive bonus.

Early steering wheels can either be replaced or refurbished without too much difficulty, although it won't be cheap. Later wheels should require little, if any, attention, even though the Deluxe version fitted from 1972 onwards on German cars and for some years on Mexican vehicles, tends to rattle, the horn pad area being made of unattractive and brittle plastic.

Door-cards, handles, internal locks, and window winders; the remaining components of a Beetle's interior, all tend to be robust. However, beware the warped door card that can be a sign of water ingress, and therefore potentially serious. Also look out for the rather more flimsy nature of later fittings, as a broken door button for example can be extremely irritating if not replaced. Ensure that the window winders don't creak and groan, a sure sign that the mechanism isn't far away from failure.

← If the car has a painted door handle, it should be a Standard model. The argument, however, lies in whether it should be painted in a sort of greenish silver-grey, or in the body-colour of the car. The knowledgeable enthusiast's money would be on the former option!

↓ Apart from not having to rely on the reserve fuel tank operated by a tap on pre-1962 cars not fitted with a fuel gauge as standard, the Dehne accessory item is both attractive to look at and worth a reasonable amount of money.

↓ The door-card on this 1961 car is in good condition. However, if the plastic membrane within the car's door is damaged when a handle is replaced or similar, water that would normally drain out of the base can affect the hardboard structure of the door card; the result being a wavy, wrinkled appearance that would irritate most and lose points in a Concours event. Broken clips tend to have the same long-term effect. Replacement cards are available, but they aren't cheap.

↑ The position of the wiper arms varied from year to year, and between left-hand and right-hand models. This ungainly arrangement is correct for a mid-fifties left-hand-drive Beetle.

Electrics and wiring

Until 1967, all European-market Beetles were fitted with 6-volt electrics, while US-specification cars were similarly supplied until the summer of 1966. Headlight units for the earlier models, featuring the VW logo on the Bosch or Hella lenses, will command a premium compared with the later asymmetrical-beam sloping headlights. The 12-volt upright headlights fitted to models built after August 1967 are readily available, as are H4 units fitted during the late 1970s. Over the years the rear lights evolved to feature more functions, and, once more, those for the early models will be expensive to replace. The larger rear light mounting pods fitted from 1968 through to 1972 on all but the basic 1200 are also more prone to suffer from rust. The large round rear lights made entirely of plastic ('elephant's feet' in Beetle parlance) were first introduced on 1303 models, and continued to the end of Beetle production. As previously indicated, until the summer of 1960, European models were fitted with semaphore indicators, while American

↓ Although the wiring on this customised Beetle might be neat, the fact that all the cables are of the same colour would prove a nightmare when endeavouring to trace any electrical faults.

owners enjoyed bullet-style flashers mounted low on the front wing from 1955. In 1958 narrow indicators with clear lenses mounted on top of the wing were introduced for the American market. These appeared on European models during 1960 when the lens colour changed to orange. The design changed again in 1964 when a wider flasher unit was introduced. This design endured until 1974 when the flasher migrated to a position within the front bumper. American models received a final change to the wing-mounted indicators in 1970 when enormous front-wing-mounted flasher units, featuring side lights, appeared.

Check the operation of all lights and pay attention to the condition of the headlight reflectors. Also operate the wipers, checking that the screen washers and the two-speed function are in working order on the later Deluxe models. The wiper spindles and connecting rods are difficult to find for the early models and can be expensive to replace. Badly worn wiper spindles tend to wobble during operation. The fuse box and wiring are all easily accessible from within the front boot, situated behind a fibreboard panel to the rear of the dashboard. However, after August 1960 the fuses are behind a plastic cover accessible from the driver's seat. Be very wary if this area contains a tangle of non-standard wiring colours connected using crimped pre-insulated spade terminals or, worse still, using the hinged terminals containing a tapered slot to cut through the insulation. 1303 models have the wiring under the dashboard, and is inaccessible from within the front boot. Wiring in the engine compartment is subject to a lot of heat, which can cause the insulation to become brittle. This applies particularly to the wire low down on the engine connected to the oil pressure warning light switch. The voltage regulator is situated in the engine bay, mounted piggyback-style on the generator of most 6-volt Beetles. In 1966, the regulator was moved to the left-hand footwell beneath the rear seat. The ignition and oil warning lights should extinguish immediately after starting the engine if all is well.

Steering and suspension

With the exception of the 1302 and 1303 models, all Beetles are fitted with twin-beam torsion bars at the front. The torsion bar tubes of the early models are mounted 120mm apart and contain eight

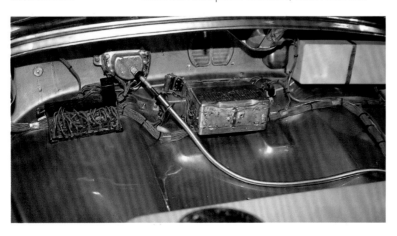

← The floor-pan illustrated is from an Australian-built Country Buggy. It is virtually indistinguishable from a pre-1965 Beetle floor-pan, the only exceptions being the use of king- and link-pin front stub axles, taken from the Australian version of the Transporter, and always referred to as a Kombi, plus reduction boxes on the rear swing-axles common to the same vehicle.

leaves. Steering was achieved with a king and link pin assembly. The design changed for the 1966 model year, when the tubes were mounted 150mm apart and the quantity of leaves increased to ten. The stub axles were then fitted with robust ball joints to provide the steering swivel. These are strong units, but the torsion bar tubes should be thoroughly checked for corrosion, particularly where the shock absorber turrets are joined to the transverse tubes, as well as the damper mountings themselves. This applies particularly to the post 1966 models. The large heavy-duty section at the front of the chassis on which the torsion bar tubes are mounted should also be checked for corrosion. Pay particular attention to where the aforementioned section is welded to the tunnel, and also to the bottom plate that can be viewed from below. Many customised Beetles have been lowered in keeping with the latest trend. In most cases this has been achieved by cutting sections from the centre of the torsion bar tubes to accommodate the adjustable lowering device, or Sway-away as they are often known. This area should be thoroughly checked for competent welding and structural integrity. The internal leaves of the front torsion bars are bound together by a central block mounted within the tube and by the torsion arms mounted at each end. These leaves have been known to break but it's a very rare occurrence. Severe head-on accident damage can also bend the tubes back, but again this is very rare. Beetle rally cars were fitted with safari kits that consisted of a bracing bar between the torsion bar tubes and the two large bolts at the front of the chassis and heater channel. These were fitted to prevent the torsion bar tubes bending, and were developed for the demanding conditions of the East African Safari Rally.

With the car safely supported, spin each front wheel to check for worn wheel bearings by listening for grating noises. Grip the wheel at the top and bottom and rock it to detect any free play. Play in the wheel bearings can also be detected by gripping the wheel each side and then rocking. Wheel-bearing play can be adjusted, and so is not a problem unless the bearing proved to be noisy when spun. On pre-1966 models, free play can be attributed to one of two things; link pins which are adjustable to eliminate free play, or the king pins, which will require replacing if movement is detected. The steering ball-joints fitted to the torsion arms of later models can be checked for excessive wear by levering with a pry bar. To further enhance road holding, an anti-roll bar was fitted in 1959. The sleeves that attach the bar to the lower torsion arms are prone to corrosion. The shock absorbers on all models should be examined for leaks, and checked for excessive bounce. In this latter instance the car should return to its normal ride height without further bouncing after pressing down each corner. From March 1960, a steering damper was fitted between the top torsion bar tube and the long track rod to help damp out shocks through the steering. The piston should move smoothly in and out without any loose points in its travel.

Two types of steering gear have been used, worm-and-sector until 1960, and worm-and-roller for later models. Some overlap occurred with the worm-and-sector steering gear being used on the Standard model until July 1965. Both types are fully adjustable but should be checked for excessive wear. The steering wheel should have no more than 25mm of free play at the centre position. With the car supported there should be no tight spots when the steering wheel is turned from lock to lock. This is also

→ The MacPherson strut illustrated is on a 1303S that has been stripped of its wing ready for restoration work. The steering on this example is controlled by a steering box. The lower steering swivel ball-joint on the base of the strut was modified on later vehicles to give negative scrub radius. This assisted stability when braking on uneven, or unmade, surfaces, wet mud, or even ice. Later 1303 models benefited from rack-and-pinion steering gear.

a good time to check for play in the track rod ball-joints. If there are tight spots between the central position and the right, or left, lock positions then the steering gear will need replacing. The steering column shaft is joined to the steering gear with a circular rubber spacer, which should be checked for damage.

1302 and 1303 Beetles are completely different at the front, as they are fitted with MacPherson strut front suspension. The frame head at the front end of the chassis was completely redesigned for this model, being shaped like the front end of a Hammerhead Shark, and is more prone to corrosion than the torsion-bar version. A track control arm is connected to the frame head with a rubber bush, and a swivel ball-joint at its outer end, and provides the steering movement at the base of the strut. This ball-joint should be checked for wear and excessive free play by rocking the road wheel, with the car safely supported on axle stands, and by using a suitable pry bar to check for movement between components. Another way of detecting unwanted movement in the steering ball-joint at the bottom of the strut is to raise the vehicle so both wheels are clear of the ground, and then watch the joint as a helper turns the steering from lock to lock. This joint was redesigned during 1973, providing negative scrub radius steering geometry for more stability under braking when one or more wheels are on a loose or slippery surface. The coil springs should be checked for damage, and the shock absorbers examined for

leakage plus damping efficiency. As the top of the strut is attached to the body of the car, check for corrosion within 300mm of the top strut mounting point. This arrangement makes separating the floor pan of a 1302/3 from the body during restoration more difficult, as the chassis cannot be wheeled about once the top strut mount has been detached from the body as it can with other Beetles. In August 1974, the steering damper was deleted from the 1303 parts list when the steering gearbox was replaced with a steering rack.

The rear suspension consists of torsion bars mounted in a substantial tube forward of the rear axle. The round torsion bars are held by splines into a point at the centre of the car and can be removed individually when adjustments need to be made to the ride height. Spring plates held by splines to the torsion bars locate the rear axle tubes on swing-axle cars, plus the double-jointed rear axles on Automatic Beetles and 1302/3 models. Swing-axle models were fitted with an equaliser spring, or Z Bar, from August 1966. This helped soften the rear suspension, and suppress roll during cornering. The rear shock absorbers should be checked for leakage and wear. The rubber axle boots on swing-axle models should be checked for signs of leaking gearbox oil. The constant velocity joints fitted to double-jointed axle models need replacing if a clicking noise can be detected during cornering. Damaged rubber boots, protecting the constant-velocity joints, will hasten wear due to dirt entering the joint.

Brakes

Without dismantling the drum brakes, fitted to the front of most and the rear of all Beetles, it is difficult to assess the condition of the linings. Excessive pedal travel will indicate that the brake shoes need adjusting to the drums. The brake back-plates are fitted with rubber bungs, with the inner pair being used to gain access to the adjusters, and the outer pair to examine the lining thickness. These inspection holes only give access to the adjuster end of the brake shoes, so the linings could be badly worn at the wheel cylinder end if regular adjustment has not been carried out. To access the internals of the rear brakes it is necessary to undo the 36mm nut on the rear axle, which on completion of the work must be tightened to 217lb ft or 294Nm.

replacing. Leaking rear oil seals are often due to the rear axle nut not being tight enough.

HANDBRAKE

The handbrake should hold the car with only four or five clicks of the ratchet. Check the handbrake lever for one cable being longer than the other. This usually indicates that one cable has been recently replaced and the other is overdue to fail. Beware the car that has long brake pedal travel but short handbrake movement, as this usually indicates that the handbrake has been adjusted without first adjusting the shoes to the drums. To conclude this scenario, when the shoes are eventually adjusted, the handbrake will either be too tight, or may even prevent proper adjustment.

Gearbox and clutch

The clutch free play should be between 10mm and 20mm when measured at the top of the pedal. No free play will result in the clutch slipping, causing premature wear, whereas too much will give rise to gears crunching during changes. If the clutch slips and the pedal adjustment is correct, the clutch unit will need replacing. The split case gearbox on the early models has some straight-cut gears and is likely to whine, especially in the lower ratios. Beware of excessive noise from the gearbox and transmission, as this will certainly prove expensive in the long term, although noisy final drives have been known to go on for many years. The box shouldn't jump out of any forward gear during hard acceleration, or when in reverse.

AUTOMATIC GEARBOX

The automatic box fitted to Beetles after August 1967 is, in reality, a semi-automatic arrangement consisting of a manual three-speed box, a servo-operated clutch, and a torque converter. The car should not jump out of gear during acceleration. The operation of the clutch can be checked by carrying out a torque converter stall test. First, the engine is run to operating temperature, an electronic tachometer is connected, and with a foot planted firmly on the brake pedal, and driving range 2 selected, the accelerator is depressed until maximum revs are achieved. The reading should be between 2,000 and 2,250rpm. Do not prolong this test, as the

← Disc brakes were only fitted to selected cars in the Beetle range, starting with the 1500 of the '67 model year vintage. Both the 1302S and the 1303S followed in the same mould. It is not beyond the realms of impossibility for a gifted amateur to contemplate a conversion to discs for any Beetle. American-market Beetles were never endowed with discs.

The brakes of early models with five-bolt wheels are adjusted through holes in the brake drums. The rare Standard model was equipped with cable brakes until April 1962, instead of the hydraulic system fitted to all other Beetles from April 1950 onwards. As well as adjusting the shoes to the drum, the cable variety also requires adjustment to the sleeve on the outer cable when setting up the brakes. Original specification brake pipes are made of steel and should be checked for corrosion. Some owners have opted to fit copper, or Kunifer brake pipes, which are usually trouble free, though copper pipes can be damaged by stones thrown up from the road surface. The rubber flexible hoses should also be checked for splitting and corrosion on end fittings.

The European 1500 Beetle of 1967, the British market limited-edition GT Beetle of 1973, and the non-American 1302S and 1303S models were all fitted with disc brakes at the front. Compared to drum brakes, these give much better stopping distances without any of the tendency to pull to one side. The brake pads can be checked through the wheels, though it's easier with the wheel removed. Faulty seals within the caliper (rare), or a sticking piston, are the only likely faults. Maladjustment and brake fluid or oil on the linings, are the usual reasons why the brakes pull to one side, and this can be easily checked during a road test. Brake fluid on the linings requires immediate attention, while oil may indicate that the rear oil seals need

↑ This engine from an 'Última Edición' Mexican Beetle is equipped with Digifant fuel-injection and an alternator.

torque converter fluid will overheat. A higher reading will indicate a slipping clutch, and a lower reading a poorly-tuned engine.

Engine

With so many variations of engine introduced during the production period, it's almost impossible to provide a full list of faults. The general rule is that the older the engine, the more difficult it is to obtain genuine replacement parts, and those that are available are likely to be more expensive than the equivalent part for the more popular later units.

A badly-worn engine can be identified by the amount of end-float present at the crankshaft. With the engine switched off and the key removed from the ignition switch, grasp the crankshaft pulley with both hands and push and pull to detect movement. Any significant forwards and backward movement

→ The earliest models of Beetle were fitted with a single tailpipe exhaust that emerged from under the rear valance. Cars built after July 1955 were fitted with a rear valance that included two half-round cut-outs for the redesigned exhaust with twin tailpipes. Although simple in construction, the single-tailpipe system will cost considerably more than later exhausts due to their comparative rarity.

indicates the engine is past its best. The play on a new or rebuilt engine is 0.1mm, or .004in. Sometimes smoke will appear on start up if the car has been parked with the engine tilted to one side, due to oil being on the cylinder walls. On Beetles fitted with 34PS and later engines the automatic-choke should engage after pressing the accelerator pedal prior to starting the engine. The automatic-choke will normally disengage after about three minutes and the engine should settle down to a smoke-free steady tickover. The tappets should not be excessively noisy, but remember that a slightly ticking tappet is better than one which is too tight, as this can lead to burnt-out valves. Rev the engine a few times to check for any knocking or rattles not detectable at tickover speed. A low rumble may indicate trouble with the main bearings, whereas a knocking noise could be a big end bearing, or a broken piston. Broken pistons or piston rings are usually accompanied by smoke from the exhaust. A Beetle engine will even run with a broken crankshaft, but this can be very noisy. The cylinder head can work loose, especially on the larger capacity engines, due to the head studs pulling out of the relatively soft magnesium-alloy crankcase. This can usually be detected by a chuffing sound. Another rare occurrence is a loose flywheel. This can be very noisy, sounding like a stick on railings as the teeth rattle against the bell housing.

Exhaust system

Depending on model, the exhaust should ideally be the single- or twin-tailpipe system supplied by Volkswagen, as this is more efficient than some folk would have you believe. They are also relatively cheap to replace, unlike the aftermarket extractor systems currently in fashion. The pipework on some of these systems runs so close to the rear valance that the paint can be stripped off by the heat.

Fuel systems

The earliest models have a bulbous petrol tank that filled most of the front luggage compartment and, due to the absence of a petrol gauge, was controlled by a three-way tap under the dashboard. The central position is 'off' and the left position 'on'. The right-hand position gives access to a reserve gallon of petrol. This system continued on the Standard model well into the 1960s. The carburettor is a simple downdraft Solex with a manual choke for cold starting. When the 34PS engine was introduced for the 1961 model year, a flatter style of petrol tank was part of the improvement package, although the petrol tap continued until the next year when a fuel gauge became available on Export models. A 28PICT carburettor with automatic choke was introduced for 1961.

To check operation of the choke, either press the accelerator pedal once, or pull back the throttle lever on the carburettor and the stop should sit on the highest stop of the automatic choke cam. Also check that the wire is connected between the coil and the choke element. Later models also have an additional link on this wire running to the fuel cut-off valve. The engine won't tickover if this wire is disconnected. With the introduction of ever-more stringent emission laws in the United States, the carburettors became increasingly complicated as the 1960s progressed. By the time the 1303S was introduced, the standard 34PICT 4 carburettor was so tedious to set up without flat spots during acceleration, that many owners replaced them with the more-forgiving Weber replacement. These later models should be road-tested to check for flat spots during acceleration. Beetles destined for the North American market received an allegedly troublesome fuel-injection system and a catalytic converter in 1975. Mexican-built models received a different fuel-injection system and catalytic converter during the early 1990s.

Battery

The battery is situated on the right of the car under the rear seat, and, due to its relative inaccessibility, can often be neglected. It is usually a good sign if the battery is clean with well-greased terminals. Older models have an insulated metal lid secured with a strap that is essential to prevent the seat springs causing a short circuit and possibly a fire. Some owners of 6-volt Beetles have fitted the taller battery designed for the MGB that can be even more deadly if the lid is missing. 12-volt Beetles don't have a lid, but the positive terminal should be protected with the often missing plastic flap attached to the battery.

↑ With a late-model Mexican Beetle in place on a service bay ramp, the exhaust system and underside of the engine are clearly visible. The catalytic converter is to the right behind the rear valance, and the relatively recently introduced spin-on oil filter can be seen forward of the single tailpipe exhaust pipe.

↓ This late Mexican exhaust sits under a bulbous rear valance to allow room for the catalytic converter. Note the single tailpipe.

← Before the somewhat overdue introduction of a fuel gauge to coincide with the 1962 model year, owners relied on a fuel tap situated between the front foot-wells and above the Beetle's central tunnel. When turned to the appropriate position, the driver knew he had one gallon of fuel left.

CHAPTER 8
CARING FOR YOUR BEETLE

The Beetle has an enviable reputation for reliability and build quality, and the horizontally-opposed four-cylinder engine is famed for its legendary longevity. Although somewhat unconventional, it is a relatively simple vehicle to maintain using the tools found in the toolbox of most home mechanics. With a few simple procedures it can be kept in tip-top condition, only needing the skills of a specialist in the unlikely event of a major fault occurring with the transmission or engine.

Engine

The oil plays an important role in the cooling system of the engine, as it's pumped through an oil-cooler mounted in the air flow within the fan housing. The engine doesn't have a modern-style oil filter, instead relying on a wire gauze screen surrounding the oil pick-up tube to remove any large particles. Because of the lack of an efficient oil filter, and to prevent premature engine wear due to contamination, the oil should be changed every 3,000 miles, or more frequently in a dusty environment. The oil drain plug is situated in the centre of the engine within a plate covering the aforementioned strainer gauze. During an oil change this plate and gauze should be removed and cleaned with petrol, before being replaced using new gaskets and washers on the six retaining studs. If the gauze is showing signs of being clogged with dirt, the oil strainer should be replaced. It is worth noting at this point that the earliest 25 and 30PS engines have a smaller plate and gauze strainer than all the later units, so be sure to obtain the correct gaskets before embarking on this task.

The jury is still out on which oil is best to use. The original recommendation from Volkswagen was to use SAE 30HD monograde oil and some owners stick doggedly to this. Modern thinking, however, suggests good-quality SAE 15w40 multigrade oil as an acceptable alternative, as this covers a wider

range of ambient temperatures. The capacity of the engine is 2.5 litres, or 4.4 pints, and it should not be overfilled. This is because the crankshaft does not have an oil seal at the fan pulley end, instead relying on a concave thrower plate and helical groove on the pulley, to keep the oil within the engine. Failure to heed this warning will result in oil being flicked around the engine compartment. The Beetle is renowned for not using oil between oil changes, but it's best to check the level weekly on a car in regular use.

To give the air-cooling the best possible chance to do its job efficiently, the drive belt for the generator and cooling fan should be checked regularly. The deflection of the belt measured at the mid-point between the pulleys should be between 10mm and 15mm when pressed firmly with your thumb. Adjustment is achieved by first positioning a screwdriver in the cut-out at the back of the generator pulley, and wedging it against the head of one of the generator through bolts. This prevents the pulley from turning while the nut is being released. The nut, washer, any shims present, and the outer pulley half are removed. A shim is then extracted from between the two pulley halves, and placed between the washer and outer pulley half. The pulley is then reassembled in reverse order, taking care to correctly locate the lugs on the pulley halves. Tighten the nut on the generator shaft and re-check the belt tension. Do not make the belt tension too tight as it could shorten the life of the generator bearings. Early generator pulleys don't have locating lugs, instead relying on the shape of the shaft to prevent the pulley halves slipping.

The valve clearances should be checked every 3,000 miles, and adjusted according to the specification indicated in the handbook, unless superseded by a silver sticker on the right-hand-side of the fan-housing. They should be checked when the engine is 'stone' cold Again, 25 and 30PS engines have a slightly different arrangement from

← **Beetles have a reputation for simply running and running. While this might well be the case, even the newest of Mexican models are now a few years old, while some daily drivers could easily be well over 30, and all such cars will benefit from a regular regime of maintenance. Beetles are not a part of the modern 10,000-miles-or-more intervals before the next visit to the garage is due!**

↑ **The damaged piston illustrated was the result of overheating, probably caused by incorrect ignition timing. Weak fuel mixture, an incorrectly tensioned fan belt, coupled to high motorway speeds, could also be likely factors in this kind of scenario.**

late engines, although the adjustment procedure remains the same. With the 25 and 30PS engines, the tappet that acts as a follower on the camshaft is an integral part of the valve pushrod, whereas later engines have cam-follower tappets and pushrods that are separate parts. To adjust the valve clearances, first remove the distributor cap and observe the timing mark cut into the rim of the distributor body. Revolve the engine using a spanner or socket wrench on the generator pulley nut until the centre of the rotor arm aligns with the timing mark for No. 1 cylinder on the rim of the distributor, and the top dead centre mark on the crankshaft pulley aligns with the join in the crankcase. Remove the right-hand valve cover by pulling the spring retaining clip downwards. Take care not to spill oil retained in the valve cover.

You are now ready to check both valve clearances on No. 1 cylinder located at the front right of the engine. Adjust the clearance, if necessary, using a screwdriver to turn the adjuster after first loosening the locking nut with a ring spanner. When satisfied that the clearance is a drag fit on the feeler gauge, tighten the lock nut while holding the screw to prevent it turning. To adjust the clearances on cylinder two, three and four, turn the engine anti-clockwise, moving the rotor arm 90° for each cylinder. It is useful to mark the rim of the pulley in some way at a point opposite the top dead centre mark, thus aiding alignment when working on cylinders two and four. When checking cylinder three, the rotor arm is pointing directly opposite the timing mark on the distributor rim, and the same timing mark on the pulley used when adjusting

cylinder one is aligned with the crankcase split. Cylinder three is located at the front left, and cylinder four is situated at the left rear of the engine. Adjust the clearances of each cylinder in the order 1, 2, 3 and 4, rotating the engine anti-clockwise each time.

Routine maintenance should be carried out on the distributor and ignition system every 3,000 miles. First, remove the rotor arm and place one small drop of oil on the felt pad located in the centre of the distributor shaft. Next, place no more than the merest smear of lithium-based grease on the contact breaker cam, taking care not to contaminate the contact breaker points. With the rotor arm removed, and the heel of the contact breaker arm resting on the highest point of the cam lobe, check that the points gap is 0.04mm, or .016in. If adjustment is required, loosen the screw holding the points, then, use a screwdriver to move the contact breaker plate using the lugs provided. If there is a build-up of material on the contact breaker surface it may indicate that the condenser needs replacing as well as the points. After any work on the distributor it's advisable to check the ignition timing with the engine stone cold.

First, remove the distributor cap and align the rotor arm with the timing mark for No. 1 cylinder on the distributor rim. Align the timing mark on the crankshaft pulley with the join in the crankcase. Some engines have a depression in the crankshaft pulley rim to indicate TDC (top dead centre), and one or more timing marks indicating either 7.5° or 10° before TDC. Other engines have V-shaped notches for TDC and timing marks, while a few have just one notch to indicate the ignition timing mark. Providing the original distributor is still being used, some late model engines are timed at 0°, while others are timed at 5° after TDC. Refer to your handbook for guidance regarding which mark to use. It's not unusual to find aftermarket all-centrifugal advance distributors fitted to Beetles. These are either numbered as Bosch 009 or 050 series, and are timed at 7.5° before TDC. With the correct timing mark aligned with the crankcase join, connect a simple timing light (not a strobe) to No. 1 terminal on the ignition coil. Connect the second wire of the timing light to an earth point on the engine. Loosen the clamp around the shaft of the distributor body and turn on the ignition. Rotate the distributor body clockwise, and then slowly rotate the distributor anti-clockwise until the timing light illuminates. Tighten the distributor clamp and rotate the engine to check the adjustment. Repeat the above if needed, as the ignition timing is fairly critical to the health of the engine. Finally, warm up the engine and remove the spark plugs. Clean and re-gap the plugs, or replace them if the electrodes are worn. Plugs are best removed from a warm engine to prevent stripping the thread in the cylinder head.

In addition to the above, the following engine procedures should be carried out as part of the 3,000-mile service. All wiring, hoses, fuel lines and breather pipes should be checked for condition and replaced if damaged. The fuel filter should be replaced and all fuel hoses should be secured with proper clips. The carburettor should be checked for leaks and adjustment.

Finally, the exhaust system, including heat exchangers, should be checked for damage, corrosion and leaks.

↑ ↓ **These two pictures illustrate the result of insufficient maintenance. The exhaust valve has broken resulting in a holed piston. The head of the broken valve can be seen in the left-hand chamber of the cylinder head. It's advisable to replace exhaust valves between 60,000 and 75,000 miles, and pay attention to valve clearances during routine servicing.**

Clutch and transmission

The Beetle transmission and gearbox is a robust unit, although it's not unusual for an older model to become fairly noisy, while remaining reliable for many more years. When noisy it is probably advisable to drain and replace the SAE 90 Hypoid oil and add a suitable additive to prevent further wear. A transmission oil change should be performed every 15,000 miles. A 17mm Allen key is required to remove the drain and filler plugs. The clutch is easily replaced once the engine is removed, although adjustment of free play, while not difficult, is a fiddly procedure. The adjustment point is located high up on the left side of the transmission casing, and working space is fairly limited. Early models are fitted with an adjusting nut that is locked in position with a lock nut. Later models have a cam-shaped wing nut that clicks into place every half turn of the adjustment. Working under the car, the cable should be held with grips to prevent it turning, while the lock nut of early models is loosened from the adjusting nut. All models then require the adjusting nut, or the wing nut on later models, to be turned until 10mm to 20mm of free play (measured at the top of the pedal) is achieved. When the correct setting has been obtained, tighten the lock nut to the adjuster to prevent losing the required free play.

Suspension and steering

With the steering in the straight-ahead position, there should be no more than 25mm, or 1in, of play at the steering wheel. If more play is apparent, then refer to a good workshop manual to learn how to adjust the steering gear. Early models use king and link pins on the steering swivels, while later models are fitted with steering ball-joints. All models have four grease nipples on the torsion bar tubes to keep the torsion bar leaves greased, while early models have several grease nipples on the king and link-pin assembly. Very early models have grease nipples on the track-rod ball-joints and, in some cases, the pedal cluster. All grease nipples should be lubricated with general-purpose grease every 1,500miles.

Wear in the steering swivels, and/or wheel bearings, can be detected when the car is supported on axle stands. The wheel should be gripped top and bottom, and then rocked back and forth. The wheel bearings should be adjusted first to allow play in the steering swivels to be detected. If there is play in the king-pins of the early models, the only option is to replace them. Play detected in the link-pin can be adjusted out. This is achieved by loosening the locking bolts and turning the link-pins using the spanner flats provided. Play can be detected on the later models fitted with steering swivel ball-joints by using a pry bar. The steering ball-joints can be replaced by removing the torsion arm and taking it to a Beetle specialist to have a new joint pressed into place. The steering ball-joints and the track-rod end ball-joints often fail due to the rubber gaiter surrounding the joint perishing and allowing the ingress of dirt. Check the boots during a routine service and safety check, as a split gaiter will fail the yearly roadworthiness inspection.

The shock absorbers can be checked by pressing down on each corner of the car. The car should return to its original position without bouncing. A visual check to detect leaking fluid should also be performed, replacing both dampers on the axle if one is found to be defective. From 1959 the front axle was fitted with an anti-roll bar. This was attached to the lower torsion arms using two clamps for each side. These should be examined for security and corrosion.

Brakes

Until the 1500 Beetle was introduced in August 1966, all Beetles were fitted with drum brakes on all four wheels. The 1500, the GT Beetle of 1973, (or home market 1300S), plus the Super Beetle 1302S, and 1303S models were fitted with disc brakes on the front axle. The exception to this was US-specification cars, which retained drum brakes to the end of production. The Deluxe or Export model was fitted with hydraulically-operated brakes, but the Standard model used mechanical brakes operated by cables. The handbrake of the Standard model also operated on all four wheels. The efficient

front disc brakes are self-adjusting, but the brake shoes of drum brake models require adjusting to the drums to retain braking efficiency. All hydraulically-operated Beetle drum brakes use star wheels acting on threaded adjusters to achieve the optimum clearance between the shoes and drum, necessary for efficient brake operation. These star wheels are accessed through a hole in the drum on the earlier models, and through the back-plate on later cars. The star wheels are each turned clockwise until the brakes start to bind, and are then backed off three clicks. The brake shoes should be adjusted to the drums before any attempt is made to adjust the parking-brake cables adjacent to the handbrake lever. Periodically, the brake linings, or pads, should be checked for wear and replaced as necessary. The brake fluid level should be examined during the weekly check to prevent a nasty surprise when applying the brakes. The brake fluid container is located on the panel behind the spare wheel on the early models. When the dual-circuit brake system was introduced, this was relocated to the left rear of the front luggage compartment.

Miscellaneous

The often-neglected battery is located under the rear seat, and the electrolyte level should be checked and topped up monthly, unless a 'maintenance-free' battery is fitted. The battery terminals often become corroded and covered with a deposit of white powder. This can be removed by immersing the terminal in a hot solution of washing soda. The battery posts and terminals should then be cleaned to provide a good connection and coated with a thin film of petroleum jelly.

A thorough inspection of the bodywork and chassis should be carried out periodically, and any damage or corrosion dealt with appropriately. Small paint scratches can often be polished out or touched up whereas rust in panels or seams should receive remedial attention to prevent, or at least delay, expensive repairs in the future. The chassis and underside should be coated with one of the many products available to protect against water, stone-chips and corrosion. In addition, check that all drainage holes at the bottom of doors and sills are clear and consider having enclosed panel sections injected with a proprietary corrosion inhibitor.

Although most Beetles have been resprayed, some are still sporting their original coat of paint. The paint finish used has proven to be durable, with the exception of certain metallic colours available during the early 1970s. These faded badly when the original clear lacquer coat deteriorated owing to the action of sunlight. Due to the large amount of painted panels at the front of the car, Beetles have always been susceptible to stone chips. These should be touched in as soon as possible to prevent further deterioration, or if very bad consider respraying the affected panel. The area of the floor pan immediately under the battery is the most susceptible panel to rot out on the floor-pan. Most Beetle corrosion occurs on the lower 150mm (6in) of the bodywork and usually involves the heater channels. The sill, which is commonly referred to as the heater channel, runs along the side from the front bulkhead to just forward of the rear wing, and is the fixing point for the running-boards. It overhangs the floor pan so is susceptible to the ravages of salt and water. Care should be taken when cleaning the car to remove any build-up of dirt from behind the running-boards, and under both sets of wings.

The front wings of models featuring vertical headlights fitted since 1967, or 1966 in the case of American-specification cars, are also susceptible to corrosion around the lamp units, as is the spare-wheel well of the torsion-bar front suspension models. The areas around the rear bumper mounting brackets are also worthy of extra attention to prevent a build-up of corrosion-attracting mud. Beetles built in the 1970s seem to be more prone to rust than the earlier cars. This was particularly true of the models fitted with 'elephant's feet' rear lights, which often developed holes in the wings, an occurrence previously unheard of. This may have been due, to some extent, to changes in paint technology, as the offerings from other manufacturers built around this time suffered the same fate. It's not unusual for the paint finish, particularly red, to lose its gloss, this can usually be rectified with an application of a cutting polish, followed by a good coat of wax polish. Special products are available from Volkswagen, and other manufacturers, to remove insects and tar spots. There are dedicated cleaning products designed to keep every part of the car in top condition.

Before October 1952 split rear window models featured 16in wheels fitted with 5.00–16 tyres, after which 15in wheels fitted with 5.60–15 cross-ply tyres were used. Before August 1966 the wheels were attached with five studs, after which four studs were used until the end of production. With a few exceptions, most models were fitted with cross-ply tyres at the factory. One such model, the 1303S Big Beetle of 1973, was fitted with special 5½J sports wheels equipped with 175/70–15 radial-ply tyres. The two-tone paint finish used on the wheels into the late 1960s proved to be durable, but the black and silver finishes used later on were less so, often becoming corroded after a short length of service. The cross-ply tyres should be inflated to the correct pressure as indicated in the handbook. Most owners have opted to fit radial-ply tyres and Michelin recommend 19psi front and 28psi rear for theirs. Periodically check the tyres for unusual wear, particularly at the front. If the tyre wear is uneven, check the track-rod end joints and other suspension components for wear, and have the tracking tested and adjusted by a tyre-fitting depot.

↑ **Hidden away under the rear seat, there has always been a temptation for less diligent owners to regard the battery as out of sight and, therefore, out of mind. Earlier cars should come complete with a cover to cut out the risk of contact with the structure of the rear seat, and, when purchasing a Beetle, a thorough check of the metalwork around the battery should be made.**

For many years, one of the few criticisms made of the Beetle concerned its relatively feeble headlights. When, in the summer of 1967, 12-volt electrics became standard as far as the Deluxe models, the 1300 and 1500, were concerned at least, owners of older vehicles started to consider an upgrade. [In]evitably, as the years went by and car lights [gene]rally became ever more powerful and potentially [blind]ing to an owner of a candle-power Beetle, [the t]rend accelerated to such an extent that few, [othe]r than dedicated Concours exhibitors, wouldn't [con]sider such action nowadays if contemplating the [pur]chase of a 6-volt Beetle. An additional irritation [to t]would-be diehards has been the increasing [sc]arcity of 6-volt bulbs, batteries, and accessories.

The easiest, but relatively expensive, method is [t]o have the original starter and generator rewound [t]o accept 12 volts. At a stroke, this eliminates all the problems associated with the modifications made by Volkswagen as the years rolled by. Those owners lucky enough to own a 6-volt 1300, or 1500 Beetle manufactured between August 1966 and the end of July 1967 will have a 130-tooth flywheel as used on the 12-volt system, plus a generator stand with the correct curvature to accept the 12-volt unit. It is also relatively easy to change the windscreen-wiper motor assembly, voltage regulator, horn, and bulbs, as they are similar in dimension to the pre-1970 12-volt items. However, in most cases the motor and linkage to the wiper spindles are not interchangeable due to the larger diameter of the wiper-shaft spindles, and the connecting-rod bearings of the 12-volt items. Again, it's not possible to fit the 12-volt wiper motor to the 6-volt linkage owing to variations in shaft bearing dimensions. The easiest solution to overcome these problems is to use the original 6-volt parts with a 12v to 6v voltage drop relay.

Another worthwhile improvement when changing from a 6-volt to a 12-volt system is to fit an alternator and stand from either a 1600cc Bay Transporter, or a late model Beetle. However,

a specially-made 25mm spacer will be required between the carburettor and the inlet manifold flange, as this prevents the throttle linkage binding against the alternator when fully open. The fuel pump will also need replacing with the angled type used on later engines fitted with an alternator. A carburettor from a later 12-volt car will be required, as the auto-choke element and the fuel cut-off valves are not interchangeable. Some of the earlier alternators used a separate voltage regulator, while later models incorporated the regulator into the brush assembly. The wiring connected to the original generator-mounted voltage regulator will require adapting, to join up with the built-in regulator on the alternator, or the separate one fitted to earlier examples. The wiring will have to be diverted to the engine compartment when the original regulator is located under the rear seat.

Earlier 6-volt equipped engines have a 109 tooth flywheel, whereas the 1967 6-volt 1300 and 1500cc engines, and all 12-volt units use a flywheel with 130 teeth. Additionally, the 12-volt starter is fitted with a smaller diameter shaft, necessitating the use of a different starter motor bush in the gearbox. An adapter bush enabling a 12-volt starter to be mated to an early 6-volt gearbox is available from some specialist suppliers, or can be specially made by an engineering workshop. However, a 12-volt starter cannot be used with the 109 tooth flywheel fitted to the earlier 6-volt engines, or vice-versa. As an alternative, some owners carry on using the 6-volt starter by simply swapping the starter solenoid for a 12-volt unit. Using a 6-volt starter is acceptable if the ignition system is in good condition and the engine starts almost immediately. The 6-volt starter is liable to burn out if turned over for a prolonged period when used on a 12-volt system. The bell housing on an early 6-volt gearbox may require machining to provide clearance when fitting a later engine equipped with a 12-volt, 130 tooth flywheel and clutch assembly. This can make the metal around

← This Beetle was fitted with a re-worked engine by the now-defunct tuning company Autocavan. With the crankcase bored out to receive 1679cc pistons and barrels, a Sig Erson camshaft, re-worked heads with larger valves, and a Holley-Weber carburettor, the engine would have produced close to 100PS.

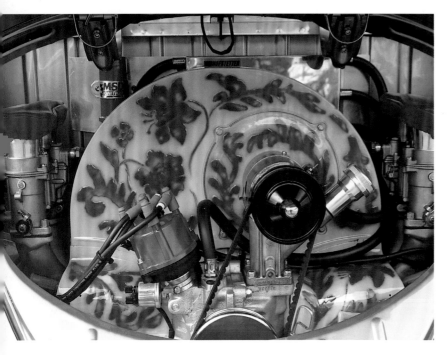

↑ **This very individual engine, featuring floral graphics on the tin-ware, also boasts a lot of bolt-on horsepower, including two twin-choke carburettors, electronic ignition, as well as, no doubt, internal components hidden from view.**

the starter motor support bearing dangerously thin. Be aware that where the flywheel meets the crankshaft there are detail differences between 6-volt and 12-volt engines, preventing a 130 tooth, 12-volt flywheel being fitted on to the crankshaft of a 6-volt engine originally equipped with the 109 tooth variety.

If the intention is to fit a later engine, such as a 1600 twin-port, to an early car, the easiest solution is to fit the matching gearbox as well. This eliminates problems with the starter motor and the gearbox bell housing. The driveshafts from the earlier car may need to be used due to the increase in track of the later transmissions. The gearshift housings may also need to be swapped over, as the front gearbox mounting changed several times during Beetle production. Alternatively, a homespun gearbox mounting may be the easiest solution. The twin-port motor will fit the earlier cars, but the heat exchangers may need to be bolted on after the engine is fitted, due to clearance problems.

The advantages of the standard 1600cc engine include a wider, high-capacity cooling fan and a larger oil cooler, known as a 'dogleg' cooler, mounted in a separate compartment behind the fan housing. This allows more cooling air to reach the allegedly hotter No. 3 cylinder. Due to the position of the dogleg oil cooler, the 1600cc twin-port engine is built with a captive nut to receive the top left mounting bolt. The original bolt for this

position has either a hexagon head or a D-shaped head to hold it captive. Gearboxes designed for use with a D-shaped headed bolt will require the use of an Allen bolt, as there is insufficient clearance to allow the use of the hexagon headed bolt normally used on engines equipped with a captive nut.

The 1300 to 1600cc engines with a 69mm-throw crankshaft are highly tuneable, with kits readily available to increase their capacity in several stages up to and beyond 2 litres. When increasing the capacity beyond 1641cc, the crankcase and the cylinder heads require machining to accept larger diameter cylinder barrels. Forged pistons are a stronger option than the cast variety for the larger capacity engines. To achieve the larger capacities a longer stroke crankshaft, known as a 'stroker crankshaft', is required. These are manufactured Scat, CB Performance, and others, and are availa with 76, 78, 82, and 84mm strokes, and are usua supplied with eight dowels. When using a standar crankshaft, it's advisable to locate the flywheel usir eight dowels instead of the usual four, due to the increase in power and torque. The work to provide the extra dowel holes should be entrusted to a competent engineering workshop. As a result of the longer throw of the stroker crankshaft, the crankcase will need machining to allow extra clearance for the connecting rods. Again, special crankcases, some made from stronger aluminium instead of the usual magnesium alloy, are produced by various manufacturers. Cylinder heads fitted with bigger valves to improve breathing, and a high-lift camshaft from Engle, Scat, or Eagle, profiled to extract the maximum power, will be needed to get the most out of these larger capacity engines. When fitted with twin Weber or Dellorto carburettors, considerably more power can be achieved.

One of the main things to consider when fitting a larger engine is the inevitable increase in oil temperature. It's advisable to use a higher capacity oil pump coupled with a full flow oil filter and an external oil cooler controlled by an oil thermostat. Remote all-in-one oil cooler fan units, controlled by an inline thermostatic switch in the oil supply pipe, are now available from specialist suppliers.

When a more powerful engine has been fitted, both the brakes and suspension should be reviewed as a matter of some urgency. Disc brake conversions from the Volkswagen and Porsche parts bin are available for all models, including those with five-bolt

Inevi
gene
dazzl
this tr
othe
con
pur
for
sc

wheels and king-pin stub axles. High-performance shock absorbers from Koni, Spax, and others, help keep the car firmly planted on to the road surface. Stronger front anti-roll bars, rear anti-roll bars, and other suspension components are now readily available from independent VW tuning specialists.

Another option worthy of consideration is the VW Type 3 1500S engine that came equipped with twin-carburettors from the factory. Along with the later 1600 twin-carburettor and the electronic fuel-injected 1600 engine, these units produce 54PS. There is no extra performance to be gained by using the rarer single-carburettor engine from lowlier Type 3 models as they are only rated at 45PS. In the case of the fuel-injected 1600 engine, all the components from the fuel-injection system will be needed. All these engines are known in Volkswagen enthusiast parlance as 'suitcase' engines, due to the cooling fan being mounted on the end of the crankshaft in a housing at the rear of the engine. Type 3 engines can be fitted directly into a Beetle, subject to modifications being made to the rear valance – however, they are better suited to Beach Buggy and Baja Bug applications.

The oil filler tube fitted on Type 3 engines is also the location for the dipstick, and must be removed before fitting the unit into a Beetle. This tube should be replaced by a specially-made cover and gasket obtained from one of the Beetle engine-tuning specialists. The engine will need to be stripped down

for rebuild before fitting, as the hole for the Beetle dipstick, absent on a Type 3 engine, will need to be drilled out. This would not be practical unless the engine is completely taken apart, due to swarf from the drilling process contaminating the internals. To fit this unit in a Beetle, the best option is to strip it down to a short engine by removing the fan and its housing, the oil cooler, tin-ware, indeed everything excepting the twin-carburettors, and replace each with Beetle items.

The final air-cooled option from the Volkswagen parts bin comes from the Type 4, or all four-cylinder units from the VW-Porsche 914, and the similar 1700, 1800, and 2-litre engines from the Bay-window Transporter. The 2-litre unit from the air-cooled T25 Transporter can also be used. These are also suitcase engines, so unless it is fitted in a Beach Buggy or Baja Bug, the cooling system will need to be converted by using a Porsche 911 fan kit, available from most tuning companies. However, care should be taken when choosing these kits, as although they are expensive, some have very poor instructions, and additional parts are often needed to finish the conversion. Some machining work is also required to the raised oil filler platform on the case, to allow the Porsche alternator to fit snugly. These kits also have no provision for supplying air to the oil cooler. Some owners rely on using an external aftermarket oil cooler with an electric fan actuated by an in-line thermostat. This can prove insufficient

↑ Due to the cut-away bodywork at the rear, both the Beach Buggy and Baja Bug lend themselves to receiving an engine from either the Type 3 or 4. With only a few extra PS to gain from the Type 3 unit, most, as in the buggy shown, have opted to use a Type 4 engine.

↑ Before a Type 4 engine
can be fitted into a Beetle,
an alternative to the
crankshaft-mounted fan
unit must be found. This
example, originating from
Germany, uses a cooling
system reminiscent of the
917 racing Porsches. The
horizontal cooling fan,
mounted in a carbon-fibre
housing, is driven from the
crankshaft via a specially-
made adaptor using two
pulleys, allowing the fan
belt to turn through 90°.

↑ This Type 4 engine is fitted with a fan and alternator
from a Porsche 911, mounted in a fibreglass housing. Also
emanating from Germany, this is undoubtedly the route
most people go down when fitting a Type 4 into a Beetle.

when stationary in heavy traffic. One solution is
to fabricate ducting from the Porsche fan-housing
to the original oil cooler. The flywheel from an
early 1700cc Type 4 engine will need to be fitted,
as later engines were equipped with a modified
flywheel requiring a clutch too big for Beetle
applications. Another consideration is the interior
heater, as the heat exchangers for this engine
require an electric fan unit and pipe assembly from
a Type 4 or Transporter to push the warm air into
the vehicle.

Over the years, air-cooled Porsche engines
have also found their way into Beetles, with the
most practical being the four-cylinder units from
the Porsche 356 and 912 ranges. While at first
glance the water-boxer engine from the post '83
T25, or T3, Transporter appears to be an easy-fit
option, ingenuity is required to fit the radiator and
associated plumbing. Some owners have fitted the
radiator at the front of the car in the spare wheel
well, and have cut holes in the boot lid to allow
air to pass through. A neater solution that doesn't
spoil the original lines of the Beetle design is to cut
away one side of the luggage area behind the back
seat, leaving the rear inner wing section intact.
Half of the luggage area floor, and rear bulkhead
is removed. A box to house the radiator and fan
assembly, plus a narrow strengthening section
between the floor and the inner wing, is then

→ In order to control oil
temperature, this Beetle
sports a long narrow oil
cooler mounted under the
front bumper. This style of
oil cooler is prevalent on
Beetles from Germany,
especially when they
have been fitted with a
Type 4 engine.

← This Beetle is fitted with a Ford V6 unit known as the Essex engine. The radiator for the large water-cooled engine is mounted in a specially-constructed box, situated in front of the power plant, taking up half of the rear luggage area behind the back seat.

↑ The most charismatic and sought-after engine to fit into a Beetle is a unit from the Porsche 356. Revised over the years, it is relatively easy to fit, while it undoubtedly provides more power than any stock Beetle engine.

welded in place behind the rear seat. The radiator and fan unit are then fitted at an angle that allows the cooling air to pass through it from under the car. Once in place, most owners will choose to trim the box with original-type matching carpet.

Custom-made adaptor plates are produced to allow the fitment of engines from VW Golfs manufactured before the advent of the 16-valve Mk3 in late 1993, by which time the increase in electronics and the advent of the catalytic converter make fitting beyond the scope of the average DIY person. The Golf engines fitted with dual-mass flywheels are also unsuitable. Appropriate plates can be made for a selection of models produced by other manufacturers, options including the flat-four from the Alfa Romeo Alfasud, and various offerings from Subaru, as well as the Ford V6 Essex engine and the trusty Rover V8. An 8-valve engine from the first two generations of GTI, or a 16-valve engine from a Mk 2 Golf GTI, Corrado, or Passat is a good choice, but requires a specially made-up flywheel from an Audi 80 using a Beetle ring gear to mate with the starter motor. This can be supplied by some tuning specialists. Research and ingenuity would be required when fitting engines from other manufacturers. This often involves an engineering company building a bespoke flywheel, using the outer part from a Beetle unit and the inner section from the donor engine. The two parts are then precision-welded before being machined to provide a flat surface for the clutch.

↑ ↓ With a bit of a squeeze this Beetle has been fitted with an engine from a Rover V8. Despite its size, the engine is lighter than expected due to its aluminium construction. However, with all its ancillaries, plus the substantial rear protection bar, it weighs considerably more than a Beetle unit. The bonnet has been louvred to scoop cooling air into the radiator located in the spare wheel well.

CHAPTER 10
A MATTER OF PERSONAL TASTE

As long as the Beetle has been in production, owners have been customising them. For much of the 1950s this might be more accurately described as personalising their vehicle, as the emphasis was upon adding accessories, enhancing the appearance or driving pleasure.

In the early days, a heater (standard equipment on the Beetle) was a luxury item on many contemporary cars, with only top-of-the-range models being so endowed. The radio has been a taken-for-granted part of a car since Japanese manufacturers came on the scene, but it was very much an expensive luxury in the 1950s. Fender guards to hide the rear wheels were standard on some upmarket models from other manufacturers and were considered a desirable addition to the '50s Beetle, as were sunshade peaks over the front window. The latter are still produced in Australia where they are an essential accessory, especially in the interior bush regions.

Additional chrome trim accessories have always been desirable, and these include chrome-plated or aluminium guards to protect the wings from stone damage, trim to fit between the tailpipes (now commonly nicknamed the cheese-grater), and embellishers for the grilles on and above the engine lid. A chrome trim was also available for the fresh-air grille forward of the windscreen on post-1968 models. Alternative horn grilles, consisting of three horizontal bars, were produced, as were alternative bonnet badges. Various designs of external rear-view mirrors have been produced, as have aerials for the radio.

Deflectors attached to the side windows prevented draughts, and provided adequate ventilation, while also reducing the noise and drumming associated with having the side window down. The German manufacturer Kamei (taken from the name of the founder Karl Meier) was a prolific producer of accessories, ranging from front spoilers and roof racks to interior goodies such as front parcel-shelves made of bamboo, a luggage-compartment lid cover, and headrests for the seats. Rarely seen curiosities included a tunnel positioned wastepaper bin, leg, knee and calf supports, plus a metal frame mounted close to the headlining designed for storage of a gentleman's trilby!

Before Volkswagen made the fuel gauge part of the standard specification for Deluxe models, introduced at the start of the '62 model year, various manufacturers produced accessory add-on versions. Of these, by far the most visually attractive was the one produced by Dehne, which sat neatly in the dashboard, looking as though it was original equipment. Another fairly regularly seen device was the specially-made extension which enabled the reserve fuel tap to be easily turned on or off from the driving position. For the more practically minded owner, Hazet produced a comprehensive toolkit in a metal case that fitted in the spare wheel, as did a similarly designed fuel can. The toolkit, particularly, is much sought after and can easily command high prices, especially if the tin's contents are both complete and pristine. Although modern replica tins are available and quite acceptable, beware of the individual who might wish to sell such an item as an original.

For those wanting a bit more power, the German firm of Okrasa, founded by the engineer Gerhard Oettinger, produced a series of tuning kits, the first of which was launched in 1951 in the days of the 25PS engine. These invariably included a camshaft with an improved profile, twin carburettors with branched induction pipes, and modified twin-port cylinder heads to raise the compression ratio and smooth the flow through the inlet ports. In the case of a kit produced in the Oval era, the 30PS engine could be developed to achieve output exceeding 40PS, resulting in an increase in the top speed from a nominal 68mph with the engine in standard guise to a suitably impressive 80mph. As the years went by, a whole host of tuning companies emerged.

← **Personal taste implies all things to all men, and can range from a highly-accessorised car to a violent chop job with lowered suspension and non-VW paint. The Cabriolet shown here dates from the earlier years of the 1950s and externally sports a bonnet-mounted bug deflector, powerful Bosch horns, period badge-bar-mounted Bosch spotlights, fender skirts, a chromium-plated cowl for the exhaust tailpipe, and reversing lamps. Inside the car the story is similar. See pages 115 and 116 for rearward and interior pictures.**

← Although sometimes seen fitted to Beetles based in Britain, this metal-gauze peaked sunshade, fitted to an Australian Beetle, would be of genuine benefit to its owner on many more days of the year!

↓ Stand alongside a cluster of Beetle enthusiasts examining a car's fender guards and it won't be long before the authenticity of the accessory comes into question. Nevertheless, a small band of dedicated owners continue to streamline the look of their 1950s or 1960s cars with such devices.

→ Although in-car entertainment is taken for granted today, before the Japanese manufacturers entered the market in the late 1960s, a radio was an expensive accessory. This 6-volt Blaupunkt radio in full working order is a desirable and much-coveted addition for any early Beetle.

↓ Of Swedish origins, the Jungle Green Oval pictured was once a regular visitor to British Volkswagen shows, where it always attracted a crowd of onlookers due to the abundance of authentic period accessories.

← Not seen all that often, some owners decided to add status to their car's appearance with an enhanced VW badge, very much in the style of Austin models produced in the 1950s and before.

↓ The rear air intake grille embellishers fitted to this Oval remained a popular accessory throughout the Beetle's production run in Germany and beyond. After the days of the Oval, most were formed out of a single piece of anodised aluminium which encased the area, rather than the individual strips pictured. Many aftermarket copies were produced too, hence those stamped with the VW symbol being particularly coveted. Beware age or model variations as, for example, there were different-sized trims for a 1303 compared to a 1200 or 1300 model of the day.

→ When cooling slots began to appear in the engine lids of saloons, owners decided they would like to trim these in the same manner as the air intake grille above. Both Volkswagen and the aftermarket responded in a positive manner.

↓ Suited to Beetles with twin-tailpipe exhausts, this embellishment is known amongst enthusiasts as a cheese grater. It serves no practical purpose.

→ Designed originally in 1953 by Karl Meier, who traded under the famous Kamei brand, this style of spoiler, perhaps understandably, didn't go into serious production. The other accessories shown – a Hazet spare wheel tool kit, and a luggage case shaped to fit the Beetle's boot – fared better.

↓ The somewhat limited space in a Beetle's boot was always going to suggest that a roof rack should be on Volkswagen's list of official accessories, which indeed it was. For some time now there has been a trend to add a roof rack to a Beetle, and adorn it with period advertising cans. As a result, both the tins and the roof racks have appreciated in value, while in the latter instance many copies of the original product are now readily available.

← Hinged side-opening windows were available as a genuine accessory for many years. As the size of the side windows changed over time, it would be important to source fittings of the correct age and dimensions if contemplating a dose of fresh air circulating through the car.

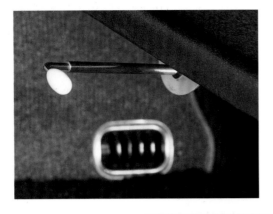

↑ As a Beetle of pre-1962 vintage without a fuel gauge coughed, spitted and spluttered, the owner of a fuel-tap extension didn't have to struggle with foot or hand close to the car's floor to release the reserve gallon necessary to ensure a smooth journey to a convenient filling station.

↑ The well-known firm of Okrasa was one of the first to tune Beetle engines. Basic work carried out included fitting replacement heads with twin-inlet ports and larger valves, plus a pair of Solex 32PBI carburettors. More extensive modifications involved forged longer-stroke camshafts and resultant substantial increases in performance. Such engines, with a capacity of 1293cc, developed 48PS.

← The Judson Supercharger, a popular add-on from the mid-1950s, boosted both PS and torque, in turn cutting 0-62mph times substantially, whilst increasing the overall top speed.

↓ A spare-wheel-mounted petrol can was probably more useful to a Beetle owner than a tool kit, but somehow the item doesn't command such high prices today.

↓ One of the most popular and sought-after accessories, both when the car was in production and now, has to be the Hazet spare wheel tool kit. If complete, and above all genuine, enthusiasts are prepared to pay considerable amounts to add a kit to their collection. Purists insist that the right content for the year of the car's manufacture is in place.

↑ Beetle rear wings were always vulnerable to chips from stones thrown up as the car travelled. The style of stone-guard depicted was designed in the early days, but sadly required the wing to be drilled in the process of fitting. Nevertheless, both genuine and reproduction guards of this nature are still much in demand.

→ The early Standard model's bumper-mounted horn was deemed unsuitable for the Deluxe version; such items were for concealment behind an appropriate wing. Not so for the accessory market, as this three-bar horn-grille-cover indicates. Bosch and Hella, amongst others, also produced similar items.

→ Certainly not to everyone's taste, the Thermador air-cooler was an American-made device for the purpose of scooping air into the car's interior.

↑ Whereas overriders clad with rubber mouldings to suit Euro-style bumpers are comparatively well-known, and all pre-1967 models featured chrome or painted overriders as part of their make-up, the rubber fixed to this curved overrider is a rare beast, although there is no indication that it was made at home.

↓ Clever thinking! The boot-lid-mounted bug deflector helped considerably in deflecting the number of insects determined to commit suicide on the Beetle's windscreen!

The 1970s produced some of the most flamboyant customised Beetles. These ranged from wild paint jobs with air-brushed pictures or graphic designs, to huge spoilers replicating the ones used on the racing cars from the Jackie Stewart era. One car that won many trophies in the custom Concours events was the Darth Vader Beetle. This was a sinister black Beetle with a sunshade over the front window and a Darth Vader mascot on the bonnet.

As the Beetle became increasingly used for rallying and autocross, a highly organised tuning industry was spawned. This in turn produced a desire to customise a Beetle to replicate the look of a rally car. Companies such as Autocavan and

↑ This Beetle was the last to make an appearance in the Lombard RAC rally. Specifically entered as a Fusca, the Brazilian version of the Beetle, in order that homologation regulations might be circumnavigated, the car successfully completed the event.

→ When Porsche attached a stubby spoiler to the rear of some 911 models, it quickly became known as a Ducktail. This was soon copied by Beetle owners who could purchase a ready made fibreglass extension to add to their engine lid. As shown here, some owners used this as a convenient location to house an oil cooler.

Cartune were among the leaders in the UK, while EMPI and Gene Berg were at the forefront in the USA.

From the early 1960s, big advances were made in increasing the power output, especially after Volkswagen introduced the 1500cc unit. Companies produced rally brackets to mount enormous spot and fog lights above the front bumper, and wider wheels started to appear, often shod with chunky-tread mud and snow tyres. Along with increased power outputs came a desire to lower the oil temperature, and special coolers appeared on the scene. The German tuning firms favoured a long narrow oil cooler mounted under the front bumper, while British companies preferred a more square-shaped design under the rear wing, or above the gearbox. Additionally, sump extensions holding more oil appeared, while larger oil pumps were produced to increase the flow.

When Porsche produced the 911 with a little rear spoiler not unlike a duck's tail, and later produced the turbo model with a huge flat rear spoiler resembling a tea tray, an opportunity arose to produce similar products for the Beetle. In the latter case, complete body kits were produced, including wide fibreglass wings that flowed into the Porsche-style moulded bumpers replicating those found on a 911 turbo. Both styles of rear spoilers presented yet another opportunity to neatly house an auxiliary

oil cooler. Incidentally, an English company, Day Mouldings, produce excellent replica fibreglass Beetle wings that are an exact copy of the original offerings from Wolfsburg. Although frowned upon by Concours judges for not being original equipment, they are so good that nobody would notice in

general use, unless they felt the thickness of the wing edges. In the early days of production they were even self-coloured, with pigment being added to the gel coat, using original Volkswagen colours. With the current vast range of colours, and a limited market, they are now supplied in grey primer.

Following on from the Rally-car theme was the Baja Bug, replicating the Beetles used in the annual Baja 1000 race across the Baja peninsula in Mexico. The fronts of these cars are shortened, using replacement bodywork to allow more ground clearance, while the rear bodywork and wings are cut away and replaced with a partial skirt over the engine, thus eliminating the need for an engine lid. A buggy-style exhaust is used, with the tailpipes curling around to exit above the sides of the engine. Alternatives include an extractor exhaust with a silencer mounted above the rear of the engine for road use, and a stinger megaphone tailpipe for off-road use. A steel cage often partially encased the exhaust system to prevent damage when used off-road, while discouraging bystanders from approaching too closely. Highly tuned large-capacity engines were, and are, used up to around 2.1 litres.

Larger engines derived from the Type 4 unit are available now with capacities of up to 3 litres. This is achieved with larger than standard pistons and barrels, and longer stroke crankshafts. Enormous

↑ ↓ **When Porsche introduced the 930 turbo models, yet another trend appeared on the Volkswagen scene. The first examples to incorporate this development were driven by enthusiasts from mainland Europe. Many had been fitted with a Type 4 or Porsche 914 four-cylinder engine, the temperature being controlled by an efficient long, but narrow, oil cooler which was located in the air stream under the front bumper. It wasn't long before the kits became available in the UK; the red 1303S pictured being an early example of such a car.**

↑ The Baja Bug illustrated has been fitted with a highly accessorised engine, which includes a lot of chrome-plated parts. A quick scan would reveal aluminium rocker covers, aluminium custom fan housing without provision for a standard oil cooler, and enormous twin pipes topped off with twin bugpack air filters feeding the centrally-mounted carburettor. The exhaust system, vee-belt guard, and engine firewall lining are all chrome-plated, and the rear suspension is assisted by coil-over shock absorbers.

↑ Appropriately named the Giraffe by its owner, this Baja-style Beetle bucks the general trend, in that it has been built with higher ground clearance in mind, primarily in order that it might compete successfully in classic trial events.

↓ This heavily-customised Beetle features a chopped roof, twin-headlamps, and wide wheels. The standard bumpers have been replaced with California-style Nerf-bars.

Holley, Weber, or Dellorto twin-carburettors are required to feed these greedy large-capacity engines. Modified cylinder heads fitted with larger valves and double springs, coupled with high-lift camshafts and/or high-ratio valve rockers, allow yet more fuel into the cylinders.

During the late 1970s, the California look (later shortened to 'Cal-look') became a popular choice on the customising scene. Cal-lookers are usually painted in non-standard garish colours with all bright trim removed. The suspension is lowered – or 'slammed' in modern VW enthusiasts' slang – at both ends, often with the front lower than the back. Sometimes the bumpers are replaced with nerf-bars. These consist of upright chrome-plated rods fitted on modified bumper mounting brackets. Large capacity engines, usually dressed up with a lot of chrome, are used, with the exhaust system being of the aftermarket extractor

→ During the 1970s, Formula 1 racing cars carried huge wings. This Beetle, with the curious name of Can Can Am, emulated this trend, while also sporting larger rear wheels in continuance of the theme. The bodywork and fittings were presented to a very high standard, earning the owner several trophies in the Custom Concours of a number of Volkswagen events.

← The creative juices must have overflowed when the design for this project came to mind. The only parts still to appear as Volkswagen had intended are the boot lid and the original bonnet badge, but even this has been painted red!

↓ As well as being lowered, this typical Cal Looker has had every trace of original bright-work removed, and the hinges have been moved to the rear of the opening to create what is known as a suicide door. Aftermarket smooth running boards have been fitted and painted in the same metallic red as the rest of the car. Inside, the seat and door-card colour complements the exterior finish, while a full roll-cage protects the occupants.

style. The so-called cool wheels to use on a Cal-look are either Speedwell BRM Magnesium-alloy, or the EMPI five- or eight-spoke designs.

With most early chrome trim becoming both rare and desirable, a lot of owners opted to follow the Resto Cal-look trend. This is essentially the same as Cal-look but retaining all the bright work, and can be painted in an original Volkswagen colour scheme as well as custom non-standard finishes. The interiors are usually replaced with non-factory upholstery trimmed by one of the companies specialising in this work. A state-of-the-art ICE system is now almost essential to complete the picture, with an array of gigantic speakers replacing the rear seating.

Another option available during the 1980s was the Wizard Roadster. The roof section is removed to make way for a convertible soft top, while rounded fibreglass panels, apparently lacking the necessary

↑ The Resto-Cal look is epitomised by retention of much of the original trim while lowering the car to an inch of its life. The original wheels have been replaced by meaty BRM alloys, and the engine has been beefed up with a Weber carburettor, while the exhaust has been taken care of by a reasonably throaty quiet-pack extractor system.

↑ The German look is hard to define. Such cars are usually lowered in a logical way and fitted with wheel-arch-filling wide wheels and tyres; the result being a car with a purposeful stance. This example is fitted with aftermarket headlight units, probably 12-volt, using upright lenses behind the sloping outer cover. The interior is kitted out with high-quality seating and fittings giving the whole car an up-market feel. The engine, quite possibly a Type 4-based unit, while not actually seen, sounded powerful as the car drove away.

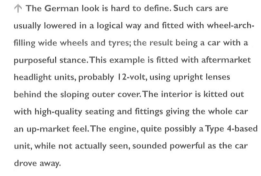

← This heavily-customised open-top Beetle has been shortened to Noddy Car proportions, with access to the driving seat being accomplished by clambering over the welded up doors.

OPPOSITE PAGE: The Wizard Roadster was a popular Beetle-based open-top kit featuring modified doors, moulded plastic skirts – which replaced the running boards, and a rounded rear panel – which played substitute to the original bodywork. The boot lid and all four wings remained largely untouched. Lacking traditional cooling slots, air to cool the engine was ducted from under the car.

→ The EMPI 5-spoke was always a popular choice for those owners wishing to fit customised wheels to their pride and joy.

→ → These German-made ATS wheels were another popular fitment. The example pictured is fitted with a 175/70-15 Michelin tyre.

→ A number of Beetle-based kit cars have been produced with the aim of replicating classic sporting designs from a bygone era. The example pictured imitates the look of a Bugatti, but the car's true identity is revealed by its front axle.

↑ The Nova pictured was by far the most popular kit-car to make use of a Beetle chassis. Gaining access to the pseudo super-car wasn't that easy, as it was necessary to tilt the whole front cab section, including the windscreen, forward. However, thanks to its lightweight and low-profile body, providing a suitably beefy engine was fitted, compensation came in the shape of performance that could be quite exhilarating.

↑ The Berkshire-based firm of UVA operated in the late 1970s, producing this futuristic-looking sports car kit, as well as the components for a typical Beach Buggy, and a van-like body to graft on to the back end of a Beetle.

↓ The Charger was another Beetle-based kit-car from the 1970s. The picture was taken at VW Action in the early autumn of 1980, at a time when the show was held at the Royal Showground in Stoneleigh.

vents for engine cooling, replace the bodywork at the rear. That the engine is cooled is attributable to air being scooped through a duct under the car that leads to the air intake on the fan housing.

Many kit cars have been produced for mounting on a Beetle floor-pan, ranging from replica early MG models to reproduction modern exotic super-cars. The most enduring design produced over many years has been the Nova, a vehicle that bears more than a passing resemblance to a Ferrari or Lamborghini. Many designs of Beach Buggy and Sand Rail have been produced, with the former being mounted on a shortened Beetle floor-pan in most cases. A Sand Rail is usually assembled using a purpose-built tubular steel chassis with Beetle suspension components, engine, and transmission.

↑ There have been many variations on the Beach Buggy theme over the years and, as a result, wide differences in style exist. The majority of such vehicles require the floor-pan to be shortened, although a few make use of the full-length chassis. Due to the lightweight construction of the body tub, and an ability in most instances to accept any type of air-cooled Volkswagen engine, Beach Buggies have always made excellent classic trial vehicles. This one was captured on camera while competing in the Exmoor Clouds Trial during the autumn of 1990.

↑ This Beach Buggy has the ultimate power-unit for a Beetle-based vehicle, as it has been taken from a Porsche 911.

↓ This lowered and squat Beetle-based roadster appeared recently at the Vanfest Transporter show. However, the question has to be, where is the petrol tank and filler? A possible answer could be that it was behind the driver but forward of the engine.

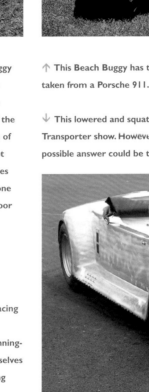

↓ The Sand Rail owes its origins to the dune-buggy racing scene in the United States. Built using a tubular-steel chassis and body, fitted with Beetle suspension and running-gear, plus a tuned VW engine, such vehicles lend themselves to both an exciting and relatively cheap way of entering into motorsport.

The most recent trend to appear is the Rat-look Beetle, a vehicle that, on the face of it, seems to be the lazy man's restoration project. In simplistic terms, the ideal appears to be to find a sun-faded Beetle imported from California or Australia, complete with a light dusting of surface rust, on an otherwise sound body, and merely to put it back into everyday use. This is not entirely fair, as closer inspection will reveal that a lot of effort and work has been carried out on the floor-pan and suspension components. As well as lowered suspension, the front beam is often narrowed to allow clearance for wider wheels. A further look will invariably reveal a floor-pan and suspension components that have been painted to a very high standard. Immaculate alloy wheels, a well-

→ ↓ The two roadworthy Beetles shown could well be just tired cars in need of a bit of TLC in the form of cosmetic paintwork. Conversely, they may have been deliberately aged to comply with the increasingly popular Rat-look fashion, particularly prevalent on the Transporter scene. In such cases the vehicles tend to be spotless under the skin, with new chassis parts, often lowered and, when running with wider wheels, use a front beam that has been narrowed.

detailed high-specification engine and an aftermarket extractor exhaust might well complete the picture.

One way of arresting the progression of rust in our wetter climate is to spray the entire bodywork with clear lacquer; another is to coat everything with a product called Anchor Wax. Sometimes, to achieve an in-vogue look, a perfectly sound Beetle is artificially aged by rubbing through the topcoat of paint exposing the primer, and by using similar techniques to deliberately dull the surface.

When the Cal-look made its debut, one of the essential ways to achieve it was to adjust the suspension, often with the front lowered more than the back. In the early days the only way to lower the front was to use Sway-Away beam adjusters fitted to the front torsion-bar tubes. These allow the central support for the torsion-bar leaves to rotate within the beam once the locating dimples have been drilled out and a slot to allow adjustment cut into each beam. A toothed adjusting plate is then welded to the beam. Next, a bolt is fitted to the central collar that holds the leaves in place, while a matching toothed plate fitted over this allows the suspension height to be altered at will, with any point between stock height and 4in lower being easily achieved. This modification is still the most frequently used method to lower the front beam.

To allow wide wheels and tyres to turn within the wheel arch, the beam is often narrowed at the same time as the Sway-Aways are fitted. This requires precision welding and should be entrusted to an expert, as your life may depend on the integrity of the beam. The downside to this method of lowering is that, apart from ruining an original front beam, the steering geometry is altered, causing problems such as bump-steer to arise. There are several components that have been designed to reduce these problems, one of which, the bump-steer kit, consists of two bushes that relocate the track-rod ends into the underside of the steering knuckle. Caster shims are often required behind the lower beam of the torsion bar assembly to restore the correct caster angle. The standard steering ball-joints are under extreme stress on lowered post-1965 models, and extra-long-travel joints have been developed to address this.

A better way to lower a Beetle is to fit Drop-Spindles. These are either king-pin or ball-joint stub-axle assemblies with the stub axle mounted 2½ inches higher than usual on the carrier. This allows the ride height to be lowered by an identical amount. However, that is not sufficient to satisfy some owners, who therefore use Drop-Spindles with Sway-Aways to create an extra low 'In the weeds' stance that causes insurmountable problems when speed bumps and potholes are encountered.

Drop-Spindles are often supplied with ready-to-fit disc brakes from the Volkswagen or the Porsche parts bin, even to king-pin assemblies. There are also a lot more options available to up-rate the brakes. CB Performance produces kits to convert all models to disc brakes, both front and rear, four- and five-bolt wheels. These are available on stock-height front stub-axles as well as the Drop-Spindle versions. A six-pot caliper, allowing either Beetle, or Golf, or even Porsche discs to be used, is available for the front of all Beetles except 1302 and 1303 models. A lightweight Porsche four-pot caliper conversion is also available for the front brakes. Cool Air also produces kits to convert both front and rear brakes to discs from drums at a budget price.

Altering the angle of the rear spring plates is the usual method for lowering the rear suspension. This can also cause problems due to the angle of the plates

being changed from the factory settings, necessitating the replacement of the original equipment shock absorber with shorter non-standard items. Stepped spring plates are available, allowing the suspension a 2in drop without altering the factory settings. Adjustable spring plates are also available from EMPI that are stronger than the standard items. 1302 and 1303 models with MacPherson struts can be lowered at the front by simply changing the stock front coil springs for shorter aftermarket replacements. The IRS rear suspension used on these models and the Automatic Beetle can be lowered by the methods already outlined.

← In order to retain full steering lock on a Beetle that has been lowered, some custom-car builders resort to narrowing the front axle beam.

↓ This is the standard set-up for a later model with swing-axle rear suspension, showing the spring plates, axle, and the equaliser bar, sometimes referred to as a Z-bar. Lowering is usually achieved by rotating the solid torsion bar one spline in each direction, thereby altering the angle of the spring plate. As an alternative, it is possible to fit an aftermarket laser-cut spring-plate with an upward kink allowing the car to be lowered by 50mm, without upsetting the factory spring-plate angle.

APPENDIX
CLUBS, TRADERS AND SHOWS FOR THE ENTHUSIAST

With over 21½ million examples built through many decades of enduring popularity, it is inevitable that there are a great number of suppliers of aftermarket parts and panels, while in some instances NOS (new old stock) goods are still available. Additionally, there are a number of clubs that offer support, advice, camaraderie, and more, to both owners and would-be purchasers. One of the best ways of becoming involved with the Beetle scene is to attend one or more of the shows held each year for enthusiasts, or where there is a large presence of the type.

The list below is not intended to be exhaustive and doesn't imply recommendation, but merely recognises some of the better-known names in the world of the Volkswagen Beetle.

CLUBS

Historic Volkswagen Owners Club
c/o 5 Gresley Close, Sutton Coldfield, West Midlands, B75 5HT
Tel. 0121 308 3693
www.historicvws.org.uk
For owners or enthusiasts of all pre-August 1967 Beetles.

The Mexican and Brazilian Beetle Register
c/o 24 Green Acres, Ludlow, Shropshire, SY8 1LU
Tel. 01584 872186

VW Cabriolet Owners Club GB
c/o 6 Station Road, Verwood, Dorset, BH31 7PU
Tel. 01202 820093
www.beetlecabrio.co.uk

Volkswagen Owners Club (Great Britain)
c/o PO Box 7, Burntwood, Staffs, WS7 2SB
Tel. 0121 707 9071
www.vwocgb.com
For all Volkswagen enthusiasts – this club has a large number of Beetle-owning members.

TRADE

VW Heritage Parts Centre (Parts)
9-11 Consort Way, Victoria Business Park, Burgess Hill,
West Sussex, RH15 9TJ
Tel. 0845 873 8328
www.vwheritage.com

Cool Air (Parts)
Unit 6, Bilton Road, Erith, Kent, DA8 2AN
Tel. 01322 335050
www.coolairvw.co.uk

Karmann Konnection (Parts and some car sales)
6 Grainger Road,
Southend on Sea,
Essex, SS2 5BZ
Tel. 01702 601155
www.karmannkonnection.com

GSF Car Parts
Branches all over the country.
Mail Order Hotline 0208 917 3800
www.gsfcarparts.com

Volkspares (Parts)
104-106 Newlands Park, Sydenham, London SE26 5NA
Tel. 020 8778 7766
www.volkspares.co.uk

Henley Beetles (VW Beetles rebuilt to order)
Northfield Road, Lower Shiplake, Henley-on-Thames, Oxon. RG9 3PA
Tel. 01189 403464

RCC Import/Export
(Beetle sales and imported parts)
Rhiwlas Farm, Llanbedr, Denbighshire, LL15 1US
Tel. 01824 702768
www.rccimport.co.uk

← The Volkswagen Owners Club of Great Britain was formed in 1953, the year the Beetle made its official debut on British soil. Since then, many others have come and, in some instances, gone. The same applies to traders in Beetle accessories, body and engine parts, and many other aspects of the whole Beetle story which began almost as soon as the car was first recognised as more than a mere whim of the Nazi government in Germany. Shows continue to proliferate, one of the latest being an event designed to captivate enthusiasts of the oldest cars. The cult of the Beetle remains, and long may it continue for all concerned.

Beetlelink (Servicing, restoration and sales)
Unit D2, Preymead Farm, Badshot Lea, Farnham,
Surrey, GU9 9LR
Tel. 01252 326767
www.beetlelink.co.uk

Volksheaven (VW salvage and import specialist)
Tel. 01302 351355
www.volksheaven.co.uk

Status VW (Parts)
Unit 2C, Old Station Yard,
Kirkby Lonsdale, Cumbria, LA6 2HP
Tel. 0870 143 1445
www.status-vw.co.uk

Volksgoods (Electrical parts)
Tel. 01522 751941

Cogbox (Gearbox rebuilds and repairs)
Tel. 0208 842 2580 (London area)

Richard Hulin Motor Engineers
(Volkswagen and Porsche specialists)
Tel. 01452 502333

Stateside Tuning
(Engine machining and tuning specialists)
Moreton-in-Marsh, Glos
Tel. 01608 812438

Mega-Bug (Spares and salvage)
Unit 3, Whitehart Road, Plumstead, SE18 1DG
Tel. 020 8317 7333
www.megabug.co.uk

Bernard Newbury (Auto interior trim and
performance parts specialist)
Tel. 01702 710211

REGULAR SHOWS FOR BEETLE ENTHUSIASTS

As telephone numbers and contacts change, the details are minimal, but a Google search should come up trumps.

February
DubFreeze – Bingley Hall, Stafford

April
Volksworld Show – Sandown Park, Esher, Surrey

May
Stanford Hall – Nr Lutterworth, Leicestershire
Big Bang – Santa Pod Raceway, Northants
All Types VW Show – Bodelwyddan Castle, Nr Rhyl

June
Stonor Park – Nr Henley-on-Thames, Oxforshire

July
British Volkswagen Festival – Three Counties
Showground, Malvern, Worcestershire
Bug Jam – Santa Pod Raceway, Wellingborough

August
Volkswagen Northwest – Tatton Park, Cheshire
VW Festival – Harewood House, Leeds

September
Beetle Drive – Crich Tramway Village, Derbyshire

INDEX